Praise for Leadership in Integrative STEM Education

"The authors of this text have done an excellent job highlighting practical advice and leadership practices that help promote Integrative STEM programming. This resource includes useful strategies for collaborative work, environmental design, community partnerships, and intentional professional development. Educational leaders who strive to develop STEM-literate citizens will benefit greatly from studying its contents." —Patrick Biggerstaff, EdD, director of career and technical & adult education, Area 31 Career Center, Ben Davis High School

"Educational leaders would definitely benefit from *Leadership in Integrative STEM Education.* The authors have shared step by step innovative ways for PK-12 leaders (district, school, and classroom) to create an integrative STEM environment based on collaboration and student-centered learning in all disciplines. It is a must read to prepare all students to be career/college ready." —Linda Curtis, EdD, former principal deputy director and associate director of academics, United States Department of Defense Education Activity

"School counselors play a significant role to help students open their eyes to a world of infinite possibilities. Our collective goal is to utilize inclusive practices to encourage every student to acquire inquiry, innovation, critical thinking, and problem-solving skills to realize their future dreams. The book authors persuasively communicate the critical importance of creating a climate and culture that motivates students to become engaged in activities and experiences." —Carol A. Dahir, PhD, professor and former chair of school counseling, New York Institute of Technology

"Integrative STEM education is the foundation for interdisciplinary science and will foster a sense of curiosity for those interested in learning, questioning, and creating—especially girls and other traditionally underrepresented populations. This book will help educational leaders cultivate inclusive and integrative science-based communities for everyone and promote opportunities in myriad scientific fields, including Public Health." —Andrea L. DeMaria, PhD, assistant professor of public health, Purdue University

"STEM education provides students with interdisciplinary opportunities to learn in authentic and relevant ways, but the critical role of PK-12 leadership in promoting STEM education has been mostly overlooked. This book provides a comprehensive review of key concepts, examples, and resources for educational leaders seeking to integrate STEM practice in their institutions, districts, schools, and classrooms." —David DeMatthews, PhD, associate professor of educational leadership and policy, University of Texas at Austin

"*Leadership in Integrative STEM Education* provides the tools necessary for educational leaders to make a change to our current system. To meet the needs of the future STEM career openings, we need to make a change now. The concepts, strategies, examples, and resources provided here are the first step to making this happen!" —Becky Moening, EdD, mathematics specialist, Wiley Publishing and adjunct faculty member, Ivy Tech Community College

"Integrative STEM education is brought full circle with the transparency given to school leaders' work in creating cultures of 21st-century STEM literate, skilled graduates. University faculty and PK-12 leaders can utilize this timely, comprehensive book in their courses and professional learning to shine light on the transformative role of leadership in guiding and assessing STEM." —Carol A. Mullen, PhD, professor of educational leadership, Virginia Tech

"Given the hugely influential effects of STEM in our daily lives, STEM education is a necessity. The issue, then, for school leaders is not whether to STEM but how to STEM. In response, this book offers an integrative and collaborative approach, includes a focus on equity issues, and involves all of the school's community." —Jim Scheurich, PhD, professor, Indiana University–Purdue University Indianapolis (IUPUI)

"Integrative STEM education is not just combining Science, Technology, Engineering, and Mathematics. It is a unique and critical subject to be taught from Pre-K to lifelong learning. This book can help educators understand how to teach, assess, and promote integrative STEM education from a viewpoint of educational leaders." —Hyuksoon Song, PhD, associate professor of education, Georgian Court University

"*Leadership in Integrative STEM Education* provides school leaders and educators a practical guide for adopting integrative STEM in all aspects of schooling. As the coordinator of STEM Leadership Institute and a school leader educator, I found this book very helpful to integrate STEM into all PK-12 classrooms through collaboration and community engagement." —Olcay Yavuz, PhD, associate professor of educational leadership & policy studies, Southern Connecticut State University

Leadership in Integrative STEM Education

Leadership in Integrative STEM Education

Collaborative Strategies for Facilitating an Experiential and Student-Centered Culture

Edited by
Rachel Louise Geesa
Mary Annette Rose
Krista Marie Stith

ROWMAN & LITTLEFIELD
Lanham • Boulder • New York • London

Published by Rowman & Littlefield
An imprint of The Rowman & Littlefield Publishing Group, Inc.
4501 Forbes Boulevard, Suite 200, Lanham, Maryland 20706
www.rowman.com

86-90 Paul Street, London EC2A 4NE, United Kingdom

British Library Cataloguing in Publication Information Available

Library of Congress Cataloging-in-Publication Data

Names: Geesa, Rachel Louise, 1982– editor. | Rose, Mary Annette, 1958– editor. | Stith, Krista Marie, 1984– editor.
Title: Leadership in integrative STEM education : collaborative strategies for facilitating an experiential and student-centered culture / edited by Rachel Louise Geesa, Mary Annette Rose, Krista Marie Stith.
Other titles: Leadership in integrative Science, Technology, Engineering, Mathematics education
Description: Lanham : Rowman & Littlefield, [2021] | Includes bibliographical references and index. | Summary: "Leadership in Integrative STEM Education provides a series of strategies for educational leaders to make informed decisions when building robust and inclusive integrative STEM programs at the organization-level"—Provided by publisher.
Identifiers: LCCN 2021021618 (print) | LCCN 2021021619 (ebook) | ISBN 9781475857351 (Cloth : acid-free paper) | ISBN 9781475857368 (Paperback : acid-free paper) | ISBN 9781475857375 (ePub)
Subjects: LCSH: Educational leadership—United States. | Science—Study and teaching—United States. | Technology—Study and teaching—United States. | Engineering—Study and teaching—United States. | Mathematics--Study and teaching—United States.
Classification: LCC LB2805 .L3443 2021 (print) | LCC LB2805 (ebook) | DDC 371.2/011—dc23
LC record available at https://lccn.loc.gov/2021021618
LC ebook record available at https://lccn.loc.gov/2021021619

∞™ The paper used in this publication meets the minimum requirements of American National Standard for Information Sciences—Permanence of Paper for Printed Library Materials, ANSI/NISO Z39.48-1992.

This book is dedicated to educational leaders who challenge preconceived notions about PK–12 schooling. Educational leaders who innovate drive the momentum to inspire and improve integrative science, technology, engineering, and mathematics (STEM) education, as well as promote inclusive excellence for *all* students.

Contents

List of Tables and Figures xv

Foreword by *Fenwick W. English* xix

Preface xxiii

Acknowledgments xxxi

1 Introduction: Educational Leadership and Integrative STEM Education 1

Krista Marie Stith, Rachel Louise Geesa, and Jim Egenrieder

STEM Literacy 2

STEM, Integrated STEM, and Integrative STEM 3

Championing Integrative STEM 7

Theoretical Grounding 10

Calls for STEM Improvements 10

Preparing Students in Knowledge and Skills 11

Navigating an Integrative STEM Ecosystem 16

Standards Alignment for Educational Leaders 21

Challenges with Integrative STEM Implementation 21

Conclusion 23

2 Leadership to Foster an Integrative STEM Mission and Culture 27

Rachel Louise Geesa with contribution by Toni Marie Mapuana Kaui

Collaboration for Integrative STEM Education 28

A Robust Integrative STEM Culture 31

Integrative STEM Opportunities for All 36

Conclusion 42

Nā Hunaahi: An Example of Mission and Culture in a Hawaiian Integrative STEAM Program 43

3 Equity, Diversity, and Inclusion within Integrative STEM Education 51

Rachel Louise Geesa, Mary Annette Rose, Krista Marie Stith, Kendra Lowery, and Joanne Caniglia

Equity, Diversity, and Inclusion Issues 52

Promising Strategies for Educational Leaders 54

Inclusive Practices 63

School Stakeholder Engagement in STEM 65

Conclusion 66

4 Considerations for Integrative STEM Infrastructure and Programming 71

Michael E. Grubbs and Krista Marie Stith

Context Considerations 72

Signature Learning and Pedagogies 73

Equipment and Materials 77

Exemplar of a Collaborative Integrative STEM Space 81

Further Considerations 83

Conclusion 89

5 Facilitating an Integrative STEM Curriculum 92
Mary Annette Rose and Krista Stith

Intended Learning Outcomes of Integrative STEM 93
Action Steps to Facilitate Integrative STEM Curriculum 98
Sharing Findings and Engaging the Community 105
Inspiring and Supporting Innovation 105
Facilitating the Development of Integrative STEM Curriculum 106
Conclusion 107

6 Collaboration in PK–12 Integrative STEM Instruction 112
Suparna Sinha, David J. Shernoff, and Cheryl Cuddihy

Integrative STEM Pedagogies and Characteristics 113
Importance of Collaboration in Integrative STEM 118
Challenges to Implementing Collaboration in Integrative STEM Practice 121
Evidence-Based Integrative STEM Curricular Models 123
Conclusion 126

7 Extended Learning Opportunities in Integrative STEM 131
Kate Shively with contribution by Carol Marcus Englander

Integrative STEM Extended Learning Opportunities 132
Evaluate School-Community Partnerships for Improvement 144
Conclusion 144
Rhode Island SMILE: An Example of Extended Learning in Integrative STEM 145

8 Promoting Professional Learning for Integrative STEM 156
Ginger Mink Teague, Krista Marie Stith, and Rachel Louise Geesa

A Praxis Shift for Educators through Professional Learning 157
Learning Impact for Educational Leaders 161
Learning Impact for Educators 162
Perceptions of Pioneering Educators 162
Additional Considerations for Professional Learning 164
Impactful Professional Learning 165
Conclusion 170

9 Assessment and Data-Informed Decision-Making in Integrative STEM 175
Mary Annette Rose, Krista Marie Stith, Rachel Louise Geesa, and Jim Egenrieder

Assessment Planning 176
Purpose of Assessments 179
Data Collection, Organization, and Analysis 188
Data-Informed Decision-Making 190
Conclusion 191

10 Evaluation of Integrative STEM Education 195
Rachel Louise Geesa, Mary Annette Rose, Krista Marie Stith, and Marilynn Marks Quick

Building Evidence-Based Evaluations 195
Evaluating Educators 203
Conclusion 211

Conclusion: Leading the Future Generation to Success through Integrative STEM Education 214
Krista Marie Stith, Rachel Louise Geesa, and Mary Annette Rose

Educational Leader Competencies in Integrative STEM 214
Focus on the Future 218

Index 220

About the Contributors 231

List of Tables and Figures

TABLES

1.1 Examples of Educational Leader and Teacher Roles in STEM Programming 4
1.2 Best Practices to Lead Integrative STEM Education 8
1.3 Knowledge and Skill Sets in STEM Educational Capacities 12
1.4 Examples of Knowledge and Skill Contributions from STEM Disciplines 13
1.5 Alignment of Professional Standards for Educational Leaders and Integrative STEM Leadership Competencies 22
2.1 Potential Members of an Integrative STEM Leadership Team 29
2.2 Exemplar District and School Mission and Vision Statements 33
2.3 School Vision of Katherine Johnson STEM Academy (2020) 35
2.4 Approaches for Leaders to Collaboratively Foster an Integrative STEM Culture 37
2.5 Exemplar Activities to Build and Sustain Stakeholder Engagement in an Integrative STEM Culture 41
3.1 Comparison of Racial Representation among Six United States STEM High Schools 57
4.1 Functions of Tools and Instruments in Integrative STEM 80
4.2 Exemplars of Integrative STEM Activities 83
5.1 National Goals and Intended Learning Outcomes for Integrative STEM 94

5.2 Sampling of Practices and Process Skills from National STEM Standards 97
5.3 Suggested Career and Technical Courses in STEM Pathways 101
6.1 Integrative STEM Pedagogies 114
6.2 Models of Co-teaching 119
7.1 Exemplar Organizations Supporting Integrative STEM Extended Learning Opportunities 136
8.1 Educator Perceptions of Benefits and Challenges after STEM Professional Learning Participation 163
8.2 Research-Based Characteristics of Impactful Professional Learning 166
9.1 Reflective Questions for Planning Process 177
9.2 Conceptual Understandings of an Alternative Fuels Experiment 178
9.3 Types and Purposes of Assessments in Integrative STEM 179
9.4 Examples of Performance Assessments 183
9.5 Twenty-First Century Student Work Rubric Dimensions and Indicators 186
9.6 Components and Elements of an Engineering Design Process Portfolio Scoring Rubric 187
10.1 Examples of Integrative STEM Evaluation Questions 196
10.2 Examples of State, Organization, and School Integrative STEM Goals 198
10.3 Domains and Elements of Indiana STEM School Certification Rubric 199
10.4 Examples of What is Seen and Heard in Effective Integrative STEM Classrooms 204

FIGURES

1.1 Career and college readiness through integrative STEM. 6
1.2 Elementary school students exploring the use of virtual reality goggles as part of an immersive learning activity. 15
1.3 Middle school students building a model bridge during an introduction to engineering. 16
1.4 Competencies of educational leadership in integrative STEM. 17

2.1 High school students video conferencing with fellow students for a group project. 38
2.2 Elementary school students collaborating together in class with manipulatives. 39
2.3 Students visiting a university laboratory to research their field data. 46
3.1 Socially responsible integrative STEM programs. 54
3.2 High school students conducting an experiment in the chemistry lab. 62
3.3 Elementary school students building circuits in the library. 62
4.1 Elementary students building and testing autonomous vehicles in a makerspace. 76
4.2 High school students using a drafting table and computer-aided drawing (CAD) program to develop a solution to an engineering design challenge. 77
4.3 Innovation Lab with adjustable, moveable furniture. 82
4.4 Signage to promote collaborative inquiry, experimentation, and engineering. 82
5.1 A nurse educator guiding high school students on venipuncture techniques. 95
5.2 Elementary school students tinkering with a computer motherboard in class. 95
6.1 Middle school students hypothesizing outcomes in an electronic demonstration with an electrical engineer. 115
6.2 Elementary school students testing a wind turbine they created with plastic bottles in class. 117
7.1 High school students working in a community garden. 135
7.2 Middle school students taking action in a service learning project at a public park. 135
7.3 SMILE students determining permeability of different soils. 149
8.1 Educators participating in professional learning about design plans in a makerspace. 158
8.2 Educators engaging in professional learning on 3D printer applications for their classes. 159
9.1 Microbiology teacher providing feedback to high school students as they interpret their observations. 184

9.2 Elementary school students presenting their model volcano and explaining how it works. 185
10.1 Middle school educators evaluating and revising curriculum maps. 202
10.2 An educational leader talking with elementary school students as they test their 3D models. 208

Foreword

There is a distinctive urgency by the authors of this book in presenting the case for integrative science, technology, engineering, and mathematics (STEM) programming as a long overdue change in education. From the first page they warn us about the fast-moving global shifts underway and the dangers involved if we ignore them. Their fears are not new but have new compelling urgency. What is no longer capable of being ignored is the dangerous, continuing, and expanding gap between our fast-moving social system and the response of the school to it.

More than a half-century ago, curriculum experts were trying to warn us about this moment that is now upon us:

> In societies experiencing little cultural change, the culture will be largely taken on unconsciously by the individual—although the school, where it exists, will emphasize certain elements of the culture by making them explicit through verbalization. On the other hand, in societies where fundamental associations are breaking down under the impact of social forces, fewer standards of conduct and elements of knowledge will be picked up informally, and these will tend to be inconsistent and conflicting. The problem of maintaining a stable, integrated culture in such a society will, therefore, be quite different from the problem in a static social system. *The demands made upon the school with regard to this problem will be correspondingly more taxing, and failure to meet them will be more fraught with social disaster* [emphasis added]. (Smith et al., 1950, p. 14)

These prescient professors also reminded their students then, and that would be well worth remembering now, that cultural change, unless it is superficial, must be viewed as an integral whole because "a culture not only consists of elements, but these elements are interrelated and so mutually adjusted that they form a configuration, or cultural pattern" (Smith et al., 1950, p. 15).

So it is that STEM is positioned as a new kind of complete cultural pattern (i.e., an integrative ecosystem). It not only involves matters of content knowledge, but also knowledge that is integrated and reconfigured beyond the traditional curricular silos that are typically found in many schools.

Those silos have been erected to embody and protect a vision that is an assembly-line factory-based model of teaching, learning, and noncollaborative division of our workforce. It has reinforced a kind of narrow focus and insularity that prevents an integrative and cohesive approach to problem-solving from being taught or, in some cases, even being imagined. It is a case where the old "cells and bells" model of schooling is the only one that fits this structure and where our work obliterates our capacity to think outside of it.

The adoption of integrative STEM extends into all aspects of schooling. As the chapters in the book spell out with great clarity, not only does an integrative STEM model create a new cultural responsiveness but also creates one that will begin to close the huge mismatch between a fast-moving social structure and the capability of it to be shaped in its social transformation. Schooling itself as a process is integrated into that transformation, thus enabling the school to remain coherent and aligned, a major antidote to closing the gap that exists today.

Perhaps nothing speaks to a new vision for schooling to be repurposed and integrated with STEM than the inclusion of the glaring need to deal with issues of equity, diversity, and inclusion in our society. These social issues have become one of the most compelling economic and political problems of our times. In too many cases and places, schools perpetuate them and make them worse. Solutions must begin with a new consciousness and awareness of how, if we are to survive as a democracy, the untenable distance between the haves and the have-nots must be reconciled.

What is at stake is the presence of a certain form of social capital. "Social capital is a broad concept that includes those factors that contribute to good governance in both the public and the private sectors" (Stiglitz, 2012, p. 153). The importance of social capital is that it "is the glue that holds societies together" (Stiglitz, 2012, p. 153). Extreme inequality erodes social capital and mutual trust.

The integrative STEM school depends on collaboration and community engagement. It aims to rebuild trust with community partnerships and stakeholder dialogue. The fact is that the conceptualization of STEM occurs on more than a national stage. Rather, it is a global stage that beckons STEM to serve more than the interests of one country to the detriment of others. As currently operational, the lack of equity in our current approach "promotes neither global efficiency nor equity; even more importantly, it puts our democracy in peril" (Stiglitz, 2012, p. 181).

So, STEM education is not about getting better test scores. It is about improving student learning and the desire to learn, not only for the present but also for life. The bottom line for the concept of integrative STEM is that it can and should be used to promote social responsibility. It is not fundamentally about making the status quo more profitable, more popular, or more unequal. It embraces the idea that integrative STEM rests on a shared interdependency between peoples anchored in the concept of equity and fairness for all.

This is a new kind of pattern, or an *ecosystem* that not only improves learning but also improves trust that is at the base of *social capital*. It is not only about schools. It is also about the society in which schools exist, and it reinforces its better angles in a shared future for all. This book is an initial blueprint for how to implement integrative STEM education and programs in schools. It not only includes the intellectual, conceptual, and material elements but also the idealism in which it remains as an inspiration and a penultimate aspiration.

Fenwick W. English
Professor and Department Chair of Educational Leadership
Teachers College
Ball State University

REFERENCES

Smith, B. O., Stanley, W. O., & Shores, J. H. (1950). *Fundamentals of curriculum development.* World Book Company.

Stiglitz, J. E. (2012). *The price of inequality: How today's divided society endangers our future.* W. W. Norton & Company.

Preface

Rachel Louise Geesa, Mary Annette Rose, and Krista Marie Stith

Integrative approaches to merging the study of science, technology, engineering, and mathematics (STEM) and other disciplines within PK–12 schools offer much promise in helping prepare creative problem-solvers for a scientifically and technologically driven society of the future. We refer to *integrative STEM* education as the intent to fuse the content and practices of two or more STEM subjects for the purpose of teaching and learning. Integrative STEM experiences provide students opportunities to integrate discipline-specific conceptual understandings, skills, and dispositions needed to explore and prepare for careers and higher education in STEM and non-STEM fields.

Several state, federal, and business organizations express the need for schools to adopt integrative STEM as a central component of their school mission and programming. Doing so has serious implications for school scheduling, infrastructure, curriculum development processes, educators' instructional and assessment practices, and students' learning experiences. Thus, the role of school leaders is critical to initiate, foster, and sustain STEM or STEAM (the "A" represents the arts) educational opportunities.

The purpose of this text is to describe and organize concepts, strategies, examples, and resources for current and future educational leaders seeking to navigate a shift to integrative STEM in their schools and school districts. We perceive *leaders* as educators and professional staff who have a vested interest in promoting integrative STEM education within public and private PK–12 schools or influencing decisions about school and educational programming. These leaders promote past STEM education work, are currently implementing STEM education practices, or want to innovate STEM education programs in their schools. Such leaders include:

a. *school and district administrators* (e.g., principals, assistant principals, deans, career and technical education directors, curriculum directors, superintendents, assistant superintendents);
b. *faculty members* (e.g., teachers, teacher leaders, curriculum specialists, academic coaches, department chairs, school improvement chairs, and other educators); and
c. *other professionals* (e.g., state-level STEM specialists, directors of STEM networks, scholars, teacher and educational leader educators, professional organization and association members and leaders, school counselors, and professional development and learning providers).

Leading a transition to integrative STEM requires a cultural shift (Myers & Berkowicz, 2015) from discrete school programming and schedules that separate disciplines to one that deliberatively supports collaborative curriculum development and integrated learning experiences. Such a shift emphasizes STEM pedagogies (e.g., project-based and design-based learning, inquiry, and experimentation) that challenge educators and their students to learn and apply interdisciplinary concepts and practices throughout the educational process (Geesa et al., 2020, 2021; Rose et al., 2019).

The approach to integrating different disciplines within lessons, schedules, and planning teams requires collaborative skills and takes time to plan, facilitate, and effectively execute. Furthermore, navigating the local and state frameworks, high-stakes testing, and community dynamics in the current educational climate can be challenging for new programming initiatives to take place and be sustainable. With support, educational leaders can be catalysts for preparing integrative STEM learning environments and curricular programming for PK–12 students.

As we reviewed materials and programs related to leadership and integrative STEM education, it became evident that there was no concise guide for educational leaders who want to develop, implement, and sustain inclusive *integrative* STEM programs in schools and districts. Programs across the United States have successfully implemented integrative STEM programming, and the authors of this book present exemplars in hopes that readers will identify meaningful ideas for their current schools and districts.

This book is a culmination of years of effort to identify key skills, knowledge, and competencies that successful educational leaders have operationalized when developing, implementing, and facilitating long-lasting integrative STEM programs for all students. We created a graduate-level course at Ball State University to provide educational leaders opportunities to examine foundational knowledge and skills used in integrative STEM education approaches. Additionally, our research includes visitations to award-winning STEM schools, interviews with school and state leaders, and piloting potential strategies with school leaders who are enrolled in the graduate-level course.

Our diverse educational backgrounds, research interests, and positions as STEM educators, school leaders, and teacher and leader educators complement our collaborative exploration of impactful actions educational leaders can take to enhance all students' learning outcomes through integrative STEM practices.

Our multiyear inquiry has revealed critical competencies of integrative STEM leaders (Geesa et al., 2020; Rose et al., 2019) within the following nine domains: (1) mission and culture; (2) equity, diversity, and inclusion; (3) infrastructure and programming; (4) curriculum; (5) instruction; (6) extended learning; (7) professional learning; (8) assessment; and (9) evaluation. Collaborative leadership within these competencies leads to coherent integrative STEM programming to prepare all students to be career and college ready and STEM literate.

Chapters in this book are dedicated to each of these nine competencies. Chapters highlight potential action steps, content, and skills that educational leaders have used to facilitate successful integrative STEM programs. The chapter authors are STEM leaders who serve as researchers, teacher and leader educators, school leaders, practitioners, and program directors throughout the United States.

In Chapter 1, Krista Marie Stith, Rachel Louise Geesa, and Jim Egenrieder introduce readers to integrative STEM education by defining the construct and offering examples of the principles, strategies, programs, and foci in schools. This chapter highlights the roles of leaders as decision-makers within an educational ecosystem—the environment and the interdependencies of leaders, educators, students, families, and the community. Additionally, the authors establish the critical need for leadership practices in this field.

In Chapter 2, Rachel Louise Geesa examines the mission and culture of schools in which integrative STEM programming is prioritized. The culture of these schools promotes innovation, inquiry, problem-solving, evidence-based decision-making, and collaboration among all school stakeholders, including a STEM leadership team. The chapter positions leaders as navigators to drive the school or district toward building an integrative mission and culture. Then, Toni Marie Mapuana Kaui shares specific examples within a school culture that embodies integrative STEAM education leading, teaching, and learning programs.

As a part of the mission and culture, educational leaders should strive to create and sustain equitable and inclusive opportunities for all students to participate in integrative STEM programming. In Chapter 3, Rachel Louise Geesa, Mary Annette Rose, Krista Marie Stith, Kendra Lowery, and Joanne Caniglia identify challenges to full participation in STEM programming and strategies for leaders to promote inclusive cultures through school, family, and community engagement.

In Chapter 4, Michael E. Grubbs and Krista Marie Stith discuss the conditions and qualities in school infrastructure and programming that provide all students access to integrative STEM learning spaces and appropriate and up-to-date materials, resources, and technology. The authors also share examples of scheduling, as well as developing and using laboratory and classroom spaces that enable inquiry, experimentation, and engineering for all students. Leaders make determinations on the modus operandi, the mode of operating, at the organization level and so considerations of infrastructure and programming are integral toward comprehensive STEM opportunities.

Educational leaders are instrumental to the development and implementation of a STEM-connected curriculum that enhances the readiness of all students for careers, college, and citizenship responsibilities. In Chapter 5, Mary Annette Rose and Krista Marie Stith describe intended learning outcomes and standards of STEM education, common and unique practices among STEM disciplines, and examples of STEM curricula within schools.

The authors discuss some of the benefits of a locally developed curriculum versus a turn-key curriculum and then offer recommendations to facilitate collaborative development of locally relevant STEM curriculum.

Students from preschool to high school should experience integrative STEM content and practices while engaged in learning experiences that reflect authentic STEM problems and practices. In Chapter 6, Suparna Sinha, David J. Shernoff, and Cheryl Cuddihy discuss STEM pedagogies, collaborative activities, and instructional strategies that facilitate and support integrative STEM education. The authors share evidence of STEM and STEAM learning outcomes fostered by educational leaders who have strong integrative pedagogical content knowledge.

To expand integrative STEM education outside of the regular school day, educational leaders need to be familiar with extended learning opportunities in STEM and STEAM. Kate Shively describes the need for and examples of extended learning opportunities at PK–12 levels in Chapter 7. Central to extended learning, the author discusses leadership strategies to promote and enhance school and community partnerships that support integrative STEM education experiences. Then, Carol Marcus Englander shares a statewide program that provides extended learning opportunities for all students in integrative disciplinary approaches.

In a culture of lifelong learning, school and district leaders need to promote professional learning for integrative STEM. In Chapter 8, Ginger Mink Teague, Krista Marie Stith, and Rachel Louise Geesa discuss the importance of assessing the professional development needs of school and district leaders and educators as well as the extended time required for meaningful professional learning. The authors also share examples of professional learning strategies that enhance educators' teaching practices and methods for educational leaders to provide actionable feedback to educators to enhance integrative STEM instruction.

Educational leaders need to be familiar with the broad range of assessment methods required to assess integrative STEM learning progress and student achievement to support integrative curricular and instructional methods. In Chapter 9, Mary Annette Rose, Krista Marie Stith, Rachel Louise Geesa, and Jim Egenrieder explore student assessment, especially the use of performance tasks and assessments, which are complementary for design-, project-, and problem-based learning, and the use of data to inform decisions for integrative STEM programming.

In concert with continuous improvement goals, current and aspiring educational leaders should evaluate the performance and qualities of their integrative STEM programs, curricula, educators, staff, and fellow leaders. In Chapter 10, Rachel Louise Geesa, Mary Annette Rose, Krista Marie Stith, and Marilynn Marks Quick describe evaluative criteria and processes by which to evaluate educator, student services personnel, staff, leader, program, and school performance in implementing integrative curricula and programs and making strides toward continuous improvement.

In the Conclusion, Krista Marie Stith, Rachel Louise Geesa, and Mary Annette Rose discuss future directions for educational leaders to take to develop, facilitate, and maintain long-lasting integrative STEM schools and programs for PK–12 students to be career and college ready and STEM-literate citizens. The authors summarize key integrative STEM leader competencies and program needs within the nine domains discussed throughout the book.

We believe educational leaders are instrumental to catalyzing and sustaining the cultural shift required to implement integrative STEM programming in PK–12 schools. The systems-level perspective of school leaders is required to coordinate the many facets of the school culture that contribute to a coherent integrative STEM program. However, the skill sets required for transformational change are not likely embodied by one school leader but rather distributed and shared among members of the school community.

Above all else, effectual leaders establish the collaborative processes that empower diverse stakeholders—educators, school counselors, community leaders, parents, caregivers, and students—to establish and implement a shared vision for preparing students to navigate an increasingly complex world. It is our hope that this book serves as a resource for current and future educational leaders in PK–12 schools when considering the range of needs and strategies to infuse integrative STEM in their educational setting.

REFERENCES

Geesa, R. L., Stith, K. M., & Rose, M. A. (2020). Preparing school and district leaders for success in developing and facilitating integrative STEM in higher education. *Journal of Research on Leadership Education,* 1–21. https://doi.org/10.1177/1942775120962148

Geesa, R. L., Stith, K. M., & Teague, G. M. (2021). Integrative STEM education and leadership for student success. In F. English (Ed.), *The Palgrave Handbook of Educational Leadership and Management Discourse* (pp. 1–20). Palgrave Macmillan. https://doi.org/10.1007/978-3-030-39666-4_36-1

Myers, A. P., & Berkowicz, J. (2015). *The STEM shift: A guide for school leaders*. Corwin.

Rose, M. A., Geesa, R. L., & Stith, K. (2019). STEM leader excellence: A modified Delphi study of critical skills, competencies, and qualities. *Journal of Technology Education, 31*(1), 42–62. https://doi.org/10.21061/jte.v31i1.a.3

Acknowledgments

We are thankful and appreciative to the many people who have contributed to this book. These individuals shared their extensive knowledge and insights in integrative STEM education and educational leadership in a powerful way to enhance educational programs for all PK–12 students to experience success. The dedication of all people involved in the book to write and share information while also teaching and working in various educational sectors during the global pandemic was a testimony to their commitment in preparing students in integrative STEM settings for more inclusive opportunities.

We are fortunate to work with educational leaders and STEM experts across the United States who participated in our research and education for several years. Their experiences and firsthand accounts of the joys and challenges of developing STEM literacy in students and equitable and inclusive educational programs are invaluable.

We are grateful to the leadership team and faculty of Ball State University Teachers College for opportunities to collaborate in such authentic and significant ways. With differing expertise in educational leadership, gifted education, integrative STEM education, and technology education, this collaboration created a fertile medium to investigate integrative STEM ecosystems. Our research informed the development and implementation of a graduate-level course about integrative STEM principles and pedagogy for educational leaders, and state, national, and international scholarly, peer-reviewed publications and presentations..

We acknowledge our contributors for sharing their expertise and authentic experiences in integrative STEM. These contributors include: Joanne Caniglia, Cheryl Cuddihy, Jim Egenrieder, Carol Marcus Englander, Fenwick W. English, Michael E. Grubbs, Toni Marie Mapuana Kaui, Kendra Lowery, Marilynn Marks Quick, David J. Shernoff, Kate Shively, Suparna Sinha, and Ginger Mink Teague.

We thank Fenwick W. English, professor and chairperson of the Department of Educational Leadership at Ball State University, for his insights into the book development process. In addition, the editorial assistance from our managing editor, Carlie Wall, and editorial director, Tom Koerner, at Rowman & Littlefield, was invaluable. We have gained much understanding about book publishing through their patience and knowledge.

Several educational programs are highlighted in this book, and we would like to recognize these programs and contributions as case studies. We are grateful for our years of incredible experiences with PK–12, undergraduate, and graduate students. In addition to our higher-education teaching experiences, we have taught in PK–12 schools. The students, teachers, school counselors, staff, educational leaders, and family and community stakeholders from these experiences are the inspiration and motivation of our work.

We are appreciative of our professional colleagues, family members, and friends who provided their personal support and encouragement as we navigated the development of this book. Thank you for your kindness, encouragement, and guidance.

1

Introduction: Educational Leadership and Integrative STEM Education

Krista Marie Stith, Rachel Louise Geesa, and Jim Egenrieder

Relate the school to life, and all studies are of necessity correlated.

–John Dewey, *The School and Society* (1899)

There is a crucial need to prepare PK–12 students for a world that is continuously evolving with emergent anthropological, environmental, political, technological, medical, and ethical challenges. These global challenges will need innovative "trans-institutional" and "trans-national" solutions that will be catalyzed by the collective actions of citizens (The Millennium Project, 2017, para. 2).

However, there are rising concerns among government and business leaders that educational systems, such as schools and districts, are (a) not preparing the future citizenry with aptitudes to engage in global interconnectedness, and (b) not providing quality STEM education experiences to meet global challenges (Mansilla & Chua, 2017; United Nations Educational, Scientific and Cultural Organization, 2015).

STEM capableness is critical in the twenty-first century economy, and government and business leaders across multiple sectors call for innovations in teaching and learning. As a possible keystone in the building of a STEM citizenry, the intentional integration of multiple disciplines in a supportive educational environment is showing evidence of students forming identities as STEM professionals (National Academy of Engineering & National Research Council, 2014; Toma & Greca, 2018). This approach, we refer to as *integrative STEM education*, envelopes integrated content and pedagogy for inquiry and authentic problem-solving.

To support integrative STEM knowledge, skills, and equitable opportunities for diverse student populations, pioneering educational leaders have guided their schools and districts to reshape student engagement with STEM and non-STEM disciplines (Mohr-Schroeder et al., 2020).

A compilation of the strategies used by these pioneering educational leaders, and programs at large, can help other PK–12 leaders consider integrative STEM education practices within their own programs.

Integrative STEM education refers to teaching and learning experiences that connect the concepts, principles, and practices of multiple STEM and non-STEM disciplines. A coherent integrative STEM curriculum stretches seamlessly across disciplines and grade levels, engaging students in authentic, experiential learning that promotes STEM literacy.

With STEM literacy as a goal for schools and districts, the purpose of this chapter is to shape a framework that begins to answer the following question: *In what areas of school programming and leadership can an educational leader support the development of STEM literacy through integrative STEM education?*

STEM LITERACY

STEM literacy is a broad and sometimes ambiguous term, but most definitions in the literature refer to "skills, abilities, factual knowledge, procedures, concepts, and metacognitive capacities" for societal, economic, and personal well-being through interdisciplinary areas of study (Zollman, 2012, p. 3).

Characteristics of a STEM-literate individual (e.g., managing, analyzing, and synthesizing from multiple streams of information; respectfully collaborating in complex environments; solving ill-defined problems) are now considered a critical skill set. A STEM-literate individual can thrive in a world where STEM fields are expected to be increasingly significant to the local, national, and global social and economic landscapes.

Within these landscapes lie the specialized educational ecosystems of schools and districts. These ecosystems, similar to a sensitive biological ecosystem like the rainforest, are filled with interdependencies of people in different roles (e.g., leader, teacher, student, family member). The success of one role directly impacts the abilities of others to thrive. STEM literacy is more easily cultured when the ecosystem of the school and district, and the interdependencies of those in the ecosystem, exist in harmony.

In *Charting a Course for Success: America's Strategy for STEM Education*, the Committee on STEM Education of the National Science and Technology Council (2018) states:

> Now more than ever the innovation capacity of the United States—and its prosperity and security—depends on an effective and inclusive STEM education ecosystem. Individual success in the 21st century economy is also increasingly dependent on STEM literacy; simply to function as an informed consumer and citizen in a world of increasingly sophisticated technology requires the ability to use digital devices and STEM skills such as evidence-based reasoning. (p. v)

Educational leaders must impart an urgent need to provide the programming and the faculty to support collaborative ecosystems for students that are meaningful, relevant, and with utility to prepare students for society.

STEM, INTEGRATED STEM, AND INTEGRATIVE STEM

Increasingly, most definitions of STEM education address the integration of science, technology, engineering, and mathematics; but the intensity and the rigor of planning for intentional integration is often understated. Three hypothetical examples in Table 1.1 show alignments of the roles of the teacher and educational leader in STEM programming.

Table 1.1. Examples of Educational Leader and Teacher Roles in STEM Programming

Role	*School A*	*School B*	*School C*
Educational Leader	The principal encourages rigorous learning experiences.	The principal encourages cross-disciplinary connections.	The principal provides time for teachers to co-plan, supports the budget for equipment and supplies, leads teachers in a data walk, and celebrates and shares projects with the community.
Teacher	An elementary school teacher increases the number of mathematics worksheets.	A middle school biology teacher incorporates physics terminology and visualizations to describe how joints move in the body.	An algebra teacher, a career and technical education teacher, a chemistry teacher, and an Advanced Placement Biology teacher co-plan a collaborative project where students devise and test strategies to improve soil health on campus.

Note: A data walk is a process for leaders and other stakeholders to view large amounts of data and engage in dialogue related to data analysis and results. Data may be presented similarly to a museum or gallery exhibition.

In these scenarios, the roles and experiences for students, teachers, and leaders vary. Yet, all three scenarios would be considered STEM experiences under definitions provided by many governments, businesses, educational entities, and organizations. School C incorporates potent and purposeful connections of multiple disciplines, experiential learning pedagogies, and collaborative planning and learning to solve a problem that more closely aligns with an integrative STEM educational experience for students.

In the School C example, the problem of poor soil health is authentic, environmentally relevant, and actionable to solve. Soil health is essential to food production and, thus, relevant to students' nourishment and future career paths (e.g., agriculture and human health). Soil is locally accessible and inexpensive, so students can investigate it from multiple perspectives at the local level. The problem of soil health offers extensive opportunities for students to learn about the physical, biological, and chemical components of soil health, as well as to devise and test strategies that could alter soil conditions (e.g., contaminants, soil fertility and nutrients, soil absorbency, and rainwater runoff).

Integrative STEM pedagogy and praxis engage students in thinking and performing as scientists, technologists, engineers, artists, and mathematicians to solve real-world problems in collaborative environments. Much like STEM professionals, students move through these fields of disciplines fluidly and use the combination of knowledge, skills, and attitudes to solve problems (e.g., scientific inquiry, experimentation, engineering design).

In School C, students would be using the mathematical knowledge of a landscaper, the inquiry and experimentation skills of a soil scientist (agronomist), the prototyping and testing skills of an engineer, and the writing and communication skills of a policy maker and environmental advocate. Each student collaborates with peers to strategize how to improve soil conditions and communicate their potential solutions. Instead of learning one discipline in isolation, they experience interdisciplinarity in action. Additionally, schools can partner with community organizations and industries or other schools to further collaborate and compare soil projects.

From this hypothetical example of Schools A, B, and C, there is a continuum of integrativeness in preparing students for career and college readiness. A visualization of STEM education, integrated STEM, and integrative STEM set along this spectrum within the context of curricular design is shared in Figure 1.1.

The curricular design with the least intent of integrativeness is *intra*disciplinary. In intradisciplinary teaching and learning, curricular design has minimal connections across different disciplines. As connections between the disciplines are intentionally made, Drake and Burns (2004) provide definitions for multi-, inter-, and transdisciplinary.

*Multi*disciplinary curriculum is a moderate integration with "standards of the disciplines organized around a theme" (Drake & Burns, 2004, p. 17). The disciplines are distinctly separate, but are introduced together as part of a lesson or unit.

*Inter*disciplinary curriculum is a moderate to intense integration with "interdisciplinary skills and concepts embedded in disciplinary standards" (Drake & Burns, 2004, p. 17). Thus, the boundaries among disciplines are less distinct compared to intra- and multidisciplinary approaches.

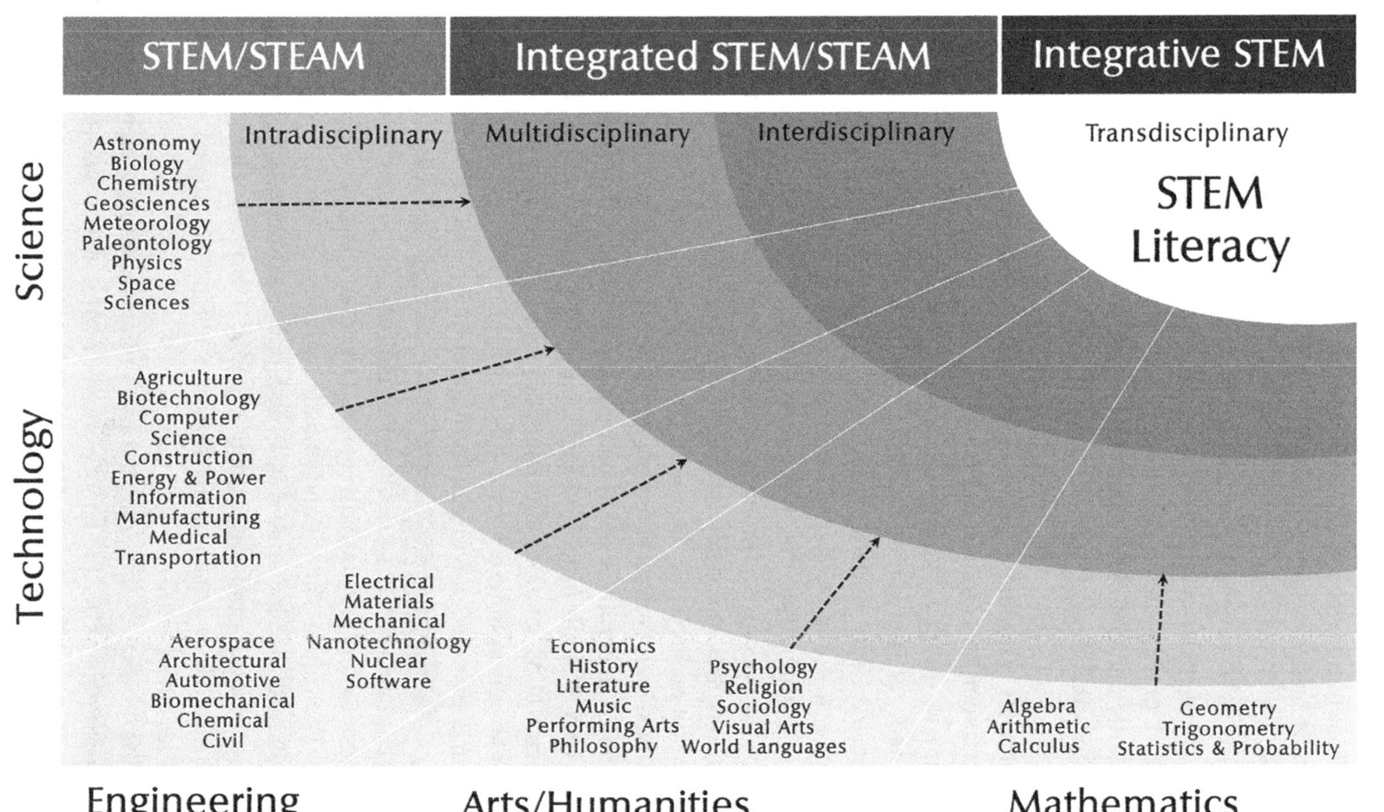

Figure 1.1. Career and college readiness through integrative STEM.

*Trans*disciplinary curriculum is an intense integration where "all knowledge [is] interconnected and interdependent" (Drake & Burns, 2004, p. 17). Disciplines are embedded within a lesson or unit in real-world contexts, and students develop their STEM literacy.

There are many interpretations of STEM education, integrated STEM, and integrative STEM among schools and districts. In this section, definitions of intra-, inter-, multi-, and transdisciplinary curricula were provided to describe minimal to intense integrativeness of curricula across a spectrum. In the next section, the actions of educational leaders toward achieving integrative STEM at the organizational level are addressed.

CHAMPIONING INTEGRATIVE STEM

Educational leaders play important roles in implementing integrative STEM projects, establishing a schedule that supports collaboration, provisioning resources, and garnering support from school stakeholders and community partners. Leaders with school- or district-wide administrative responsibilities are well-positioned to envision and evaluate potential experiential learning activities and experiences from a holistic perspective. Educational leaders also can champion integrative STEM through modeling of best practices.

Though educational leaders may understand the logistics of and be able to champion the introduction of integrative STEM, it is critical for the actual *design and implementation* of integrative STEM programs at the school or district level to be collaborative. For systemic change to support an integrative STEM learning culture, ideations, and decisions must incorporate the *entire* ecosystem and all stakeholders within it.

The implementation and coordination of projects similar to School C would significantly rely on teachers' co-planning and co-teaching efforts. Educational leaders, however, are similarly well-positioned to envision the logistics necessary to support the coordinated efforts required to encourage transdisciplinary connections among STEM and non-STEM areas and community partnerships. Coordinating systemic change may require modifications to the schedule, professional learning program, and budgets for supplies and materials.

Educational leaders are also well-positioned to identify school and community partners who possess expertise or resources to contribute to integrative STEM learning experiences. Leaders communicate to others—board members, parents, business leaders, and other community members—about the value of integrative STEM experiences and how they may be interwoven into school programming.

Educational leaders can establish the constructs of integrative STEM education in a school or district through STEM leadership best practices noted in Table 1.2.

Table 1.2. Best Practices to Lead Integrative STEM Education

Best Practices	*Actions for Educational Leaders*
STEM program goals and desired outcomes	• Promote the well-being and academic success of students while also attending to accountability measures of current educational policies • Support a culture of innovation, inquiry, problem-solving, and evidence-based decision-making • Promote a paradigm of learning as a lifelong process
Program evaluation planning	• Evaluate grade-level vertical alignments and authentic, performance-based assessments of standards
Teacher and staff professional learning communities	• Coordinate the master schedule, so teachers have time to prepare authentic and transdisciplinary learning through co-planning and co-teaching • Provision time and access to STEM-related professional development for educators to enhance their teaching practices, mentoring, or peer-to-peer coaching • Challenge teachers to explore and refine ideas
Planning learning activities and experiences	• Support the development of executive function and interpersonal skills (e.g., critical thinking, creativity, problem-solving, collaboration, communication, self-direction, adaptability, college and career readiness) for all students to become STEM-capable citizens • Support a student-centric pedagogical approach • Promote student engagement in designing, engineering, making, testing, reflecting, and documenting by using strategies the foster students' reasoning, problem-solving, creativity, and critical thinking skills • Engage students in creative thinking assignments, which also include complex and challenging content • Encourage the exploration of uncertainties and construction of knowledge from experiences

Table 1.2. *(Continued)*

Best Practices	*Actions for Educational Leaders*
Programs for equitable opportunities and addressing achievement gaps	• Encourage participation of students underrepresented in STEM education, including students with dis/abilities, students of color, under-resourced (lower socioeconomic level) students, and, in some disciplines, female students • Promote equitable access to STEM educational programming (e.g., participation in STEM academies, projects, competitive teams, and community-based learning experiences) • Require that learning spaces be accessible to all students; be equipped with technologies that enable inquiry, experimentation, and engineering; and promote collaboration and project work
Engaging the community and reporting and sharing outcomes	• Support classroom involvement in solving real-world problems and projects through an integrated approach • Provide opportunities for students to pursue solutions to problems, challenges, or needs within the local community • Develop local school and business partnerships to provide internships, mentorships, teacher fellowships, field trips, and collaborative school-community projects • Support afterschool programs and student organizations with teacher stipends or by engaging community members to serve as coaches, mentors, and sponsors • Provide actionable feedback to teachers and students through a variety of methods and sources

The direct involvement of the leader to model best practices to develop and sustain an integrative STEM culture is essential. Educational leaders can use this list of best practices to create goals, benchmarks, pilot projects, timelines, or even rubrics for program implementation or evaluation.

In *The STEM Schools Project* (The Meeder Consulting Group, 2012), the development of a STEM culture of nine United States intermediate, middle, and high schools was studied. The results of the study revealed that educational leaders are central to the direction and support of the transition to a STEM-focused culture. The educational leaders of the nine schools experienced their own journeys, but each school followed similar best practices by creating definitions of STEM education and STEM literacy, and developing their vision for STEM learning.

Leaders can share examples, elicit and solicit ideas, and provide feedback on solutions within their school ecosystem to design and implement integrative STEM experiences. Additionally, leaders can communicate refined proposals to board members and governing bodies. Educational leaders can then facilitate successful implementation of their initiatives by demonstrating the best practices of school leadership from the selected models.

THEORETICAL GROUNDING

Students learn "by building personal interpretations of the world based on their experiences and interactions with the environment" and a co-construction of knowledge from experiences that are "socially situated" (Thibaut et al., 2018, p. 3). Therefore, the collaborative nature of integrative STEM is grounded in the tenets of cognitive science, particularly social constructivism. Social constructivism is the co-construction of new knowledge and learner's active participation within a contextual learning process (Vygotsky, 1978). Though not addressed in-depth in this text, additional information may be found in other sources (e.g., Geesa et al., 2021; Sanders, 2009; Thibaut et al., 2018).

CALLS FOR STEM IMPROVEMENTS

Arguably, the best practices of integrative STEM education have always been relevant to preparing students for society. However, beginning with the years of the "Space Race" in the 1960s and accelerating in recent years, there has been a large shift in state policies and funding that supports the preparation of students for a scientific and technological society. A number of challenges faced the United States educational system in the 1980s, including the deterioration of science, mathematics, and engineering education and an aggressive drive for high-test scores and standardized testing methods (National Science Board, 1986; Timar & Guthrie, 1980; Wood, 1988).

The National Commission on Excellence in Education (1983) released *A Nation at Risk: The Imperative for Educational Reform* in response to the rising awareness of global competitiveness and petitioned more rigorous curriculum of disciplines. The American Association for the Advancement of Science (1990) released *Science for All Americans* arguing that through the connection of natural and social sciences, mathematics, and technology, students would be better prepared in a culture increasingly influenced by these areas.

Rising Above the Gathering Storm, a report of the National Academy of Sciences, National Academy of Engineering, and Institute of Medicine (2007), emphasized that the focus on science and mathematics was declining in the United States while increasing in other countries, thus weakening the nation's global competitiveness.

In 2010, the President's Council of Advisors on Science and Technology's executive report, *Prepare and Inspire: K–12 Education in Science, Technology, Engineering, and Math (STEM) for America's Future*, stated "too many American students conclude early in their education that STEM subjects are boring, too difficult, or unwelcoming, leaving them ill-prepared to meet the challenges that will face their generation, their country, and the world" (President's Council of Advisors on Science and Technology, 2010, p. 6).

Based on these national reports and reviews of international data, government and business leaders tasked school systems for better preparations to expand the number of students who pursue careers in STEM fields, broaden participation of underrepresented groups, and increase STEM literacy for all students.

PREPARING STUDENTS IN KNOWLEDGE AND SKILLS

There are two major curricular thrusts to prepare STEM-literate students. The first approach is academic—preparing students scholastically for college readiness. The second approach is career and technical—equipping students with the workplace-ready skill sets for jobs and providing experiences that guide students in identifying career paths and education and training plans required to pursue them. Integrative STEM education interconnects the knowledge and skill capacities between these curricular thrusts, leading to the following capacities for all students in Table 1.3.

Table 1.3. Knowledge and Skill Sets in STEM Educational Capacities

Knowledge and Skills	*Description*
Analysis and evaluation	Determining correlations, causation, root causes, cost-benefit and risk-benefit comparisons, and the effects of confounding variables
Calculated risks and recovering from mistakes	Trying ideas that may not be successful, and recognizing the resulting understandings could reveal a more promising solution
Collaboration	Coordinating the planning and implementation of teamwork that may require a variety of roles, strategies, communications, reporting, and evaluations as a team
Creative or innovative solutions	Having the confidence and ability to identify, design, develop, and implement a solution in a new or novel way
Critical thinking	Demonstrating the ability to discern or distinguish reliable facts, recognize obfuscation, and validate assumptions and assertions
Design	Comprehending the attributes of design, creative strategies, and purposeful methods and processes that result in practical solutions, useful products, and systems that can be explained and understood by others
Predictive analysis	Applying knowledge, data models, and simulations to predict an experimental outcome or results of an anticipated event
Problem-solving	Troubleshooting smaller challenges and gaining confidence in approaches to big problems
Real-world applications	Demonstrating the ability to identify and apply new skills or understandings to real challenges, problems, or opportunities where they can be impactful
Reflection	Reviewing activities, discoveries, successes, disappointments, and errors to describe new understandings and inform future endeavors
Using data	Identifying, aggregating, and analyzing data in exploring topics in a wide variety of subject areas

Habits of Mind

STEM-literate students and workers are increasingly recruited for management, technical sales, design, and technical writing roles. Many employers, school leaders, and curriculum developers have recognized the importance of the "habits of mind" often demonstrated by graduates of engineering and technical training programs, where workplace readiness and project leadership are central tenets.

The National Academy of Engineering lists six habits of mind of an engineering practitioner: (a) systems thinking, (b) creativity, (c) optimism, (d) collaboration, (e) communication, and (f) ethical considerations (Katehi et al., 2009). Not only should students encompass these dispositions, but it is also important for educational leaders and educators to model these habits of mind as well. A shared paradigm that fosters habits of mind is critical for sustainable integrative STEM pedagogies and practices.

Unique Contributions of Individual STEM Disciplines

In addition to general educational capacities listed in Table 1.3, each STEM discipline contributes unique bodies of knowledge and skill sets (see Table 1.4) to an integrative STEM curriculum. A comprehensive integrative STEM program should also offer students opportunities to develop deep understandings and skill sets within a single STEM pathway, thus enhancing college and career readiness.

Table 1.4. Examples of Knowledge and Skill Contributions from STEM Disciplines

Discipline	*Science*	*Technology/ Engineering*	*Mathematics*
Knowledge	• Learning and understanding through observation and experimentation • Recognizing and explaining relationships based on evidence and logic	• Understanding the characteristics and scope of technology and design in our lives • Understanding the societal and economic impacts of technology and design	• Making predictions or estimates of the outcomes of a study • Considering equations that represent the factors of a problem or challenge
Skills	• Using a scientific inquiry process that includes a research question and a hypothesis • Conducting investigations using skills and tools common to professional scientists	• Using technology and design in exploring and understanding other fields of study • Applying innovative solutions within the core concepts of technology (e.g., systems, resources, processes, ethics)	• Graphing the results of product testing or other experimental outcomes • Creating accurate diagrams or scaled models of possible solutions

Science education supports students in understanding our natural world and encompasses the skill sets to explore and investigate scientific phenomena. Through observation, experimentation, and scientific inquiry, students reveal the world as is and the effects of a variable on a specific outcome, from which inferences can be made. Science may also represent the body of knowledge derived from those processes.

The Next Generation Science Standards (NGSS; National Research Council, 2013) support students in developing the body of knowledge regarding scientific processes and the skills necessary to explore scientific phenomena. The NGSS provide purposeful connections with other disciplines that align with integrative STEM paradigms and practices.

Technology can be described as any purposeful modification of the natural world. Nonliving things that surround people in homes, schools, and workplaces can be considered a technology, and every new technology can change the way we interact with the world. Examples include communication, transportation, and production.

Engineering is the process of solving problems or challenges through the use of design. Engineering is often recognized as an integration of science, mathematics, and technology, and the design processes used by engineers is an important part of assessing integrative STEM education. The Standards for Technological and Engineering Literacy by the International Technology and Engineering Educators Association (2020) provides detailed descriptions of integrated technology and engineering core standards, processes, and contexts connected with integrative STEM.

Mathematics is the study of relationships between things, real or imaginary, based on logic. These relationships are often quantified numerically. Although numeracy is an important or critical part of elementary mathematics, middle and high school students also benefit from exploring the logical relationships between things, modeling these relationships, and predicting the probability of future events based on past measurements. In this context, a student might recognize the relevance of mathematics to everyday life.

Non-STEM Disciplines

Though STEM education receives a great deal of attention, it is critical to recognize non-STEM disciplines as integral to a holistic integrative STEM experience. STEM professionals are expected to be strong writers, understand important historical events, have opinions on philosophical and ethical arguments, communicate their ideas artistically and perhaps internationally, and be mindful of how political landscapes impact their professional and personal lives. Students should experience interdisciplinarity with the purposeful integration of non-STEM disciplines so that their educational experience correlates with the real world (e.g., see Figures 1.2 and 1.3).

An integrative STEM program's goals at the classroom, school, or district level will vary based on the school's current learning ecosystem and the collective actions of stakeholders (e.g., educators, families, communities). However, schools and districts should not take an either-or stance on addressing academic or career and technical education. Instead, a hybrid approach through integrative STEM can holistically expose students to real world, postsecondary experiences. Support for the purposeful

Figure 1.2. Elementary school students exploring the use of virtual reality goggles as part of an immersive learning activity. iStockphoto LP.

Figure 1.3. Middle school students building a model bridge during an introduction to engineering. iStockphoto LP.

integration of knowledge and skills from multiple STEM and non-STEM disciplines, as well as fostering the habits of mind, can serve educational leaders well in guiding sustainable, integrative STEM programming.

NAVIGATING AN INTEGRATIVE STEM LEARNING ECOSYSTEM

Strengthening integrative STEM programming within a school likely requires systemic change. Leaders must navigate, to the best of their abilities, the challenges of change. Educational leaders can support others in understanding *why* introducing or sustaining these initiatives is important, and *how* integrative STEM education should be designed, coordinated, and implemented within the school or district educational ecosystem at large.

Educational leaders serve educators, families, and communities by making informed and data-driven decisions that will fully support the designers and implementers of an integrative STEM program through mission and culture; equity, diversity, and inclusion focus; infrastructure

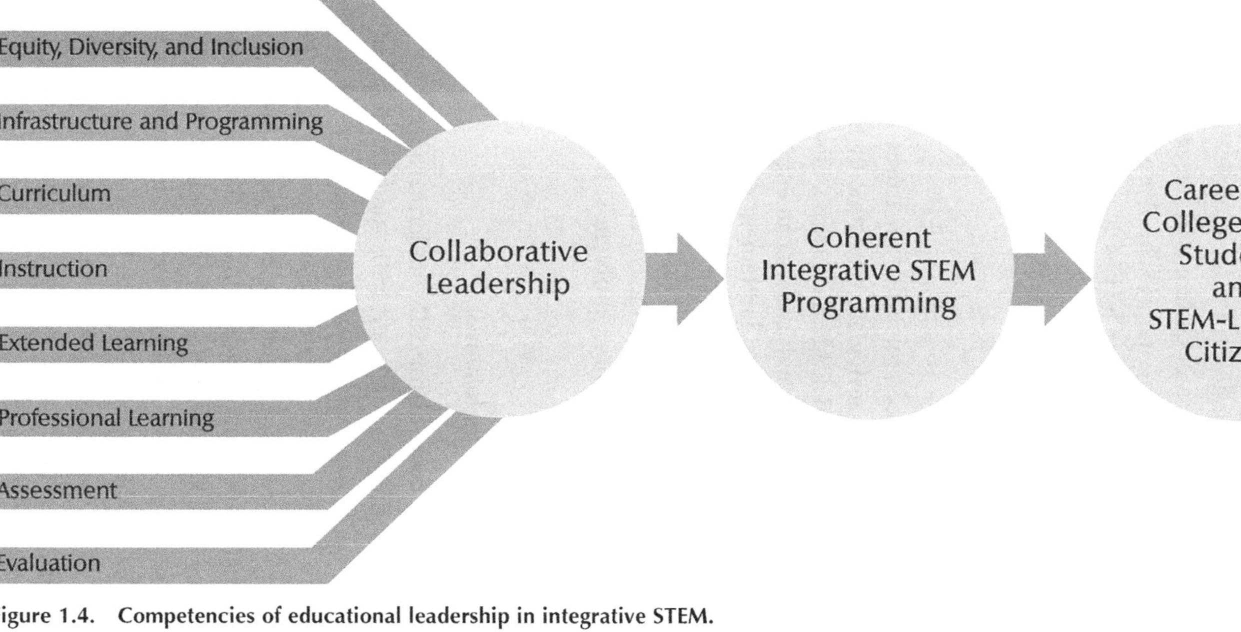

Figure 1.4. Competencies of educational leadership in integrative STEM.

and programming; curriculum; instruction; extended learning opportunities; professional learning experiences; student assessment; and program and educator evaluation (Geesa et al., 2020; Rose et al., 2019).

Ultimately, the collaboration of educational leaders and stakeholders within the school or district ecosystem will interweave integrative STEM education within multiple domains of school programming. The following nine competencies of integrative STEM leadership in schools should be considered in supporting career and college readiness and STEM literacy for all students, equitably (see Figure 1.4).

Mission and Culture

Leaders must attend to accountability measures related to current educational policies, yet also articulate the value of integrative education to promote the well-being and academic success of students. For stakeholder buy-in and support, educational leaders can empower a STEM leadership team to guide the development, implementation, and evaluation of integrative STEM goals, expectations, programs, and initiatives.

Though each school's integrative STEM vision and mission will relate to the school's learning ecosystem, educational leaders can promote a culture of innovation, inquiry, problem-solving, and evidence-based decision-making.

Equity, Diversity, and Inclusion

Groups that have been historically underrecruited and poorly retained (e.g., women, ethnically and culturally underrepresented populations), and prospective first-generation college attendees are a rich resource of STEM talent. Additionally, social and environmental systems at large can be enhanced with equity, diversity, and inclusive practices.

Educational leaders use data to ensure that all students have access to integrative STEM curriculum and instruction; participation in STEM academies, projects, and competitive teams; and community-based learning experiences. Educational leaders focus on increasing participation of students from underrepresented populations in STEM by supporting inclusive practices (e.g., accessibility for special needs, connecting to language learning, encouraging gender responsiveness), and striving for socially just learning environments.

Infrastructure and Programming

Educational leaders support the accessibility for all students to STEM learning spaces, which promotes collaboration and project work. Whether students are in large collaborative areas (e.g., makerspaces) or a dedicated station in a classroom, the space is equipped with technologies that enable inquiry, experimentation, and engineering.

Educational leaders support curriculum-appropriate and up-to-date materials, resources, and technologies that facilitate interdisciplinary and transdisciplinary approaches to learning. They ensure students have access to digital devices and connectivity. Educational leaders implement a schedule that allows time for integrative STEM experiences for students and planning time for educators.

Curriculum

Educational leaders support the integration of STEM curriculum (e.g., concepts, principles, and practices), both horizontally at each grade level and vertically through all grade levels. Well-articulated series of courses and learning experiences create pathways to STEM and non-STEM careers. The STEM curriculum should align with the school vision, mission, and goals and be open to the integration of community partnerships (e.g., business organizations and other academic institutions) to enrich the curriculum.

Instruction

Leaders support the experiential instructional approaches (e.g., design-, inquiry-, project-, and problem-based learning) educators use to engage students in researching, predicting, experimenting, designing, engineering, making, testing, analyzing, reflecting, and documenting. These approaches require students to identify and solve real-world problems or challenges, while also learning the necessary content as identified by the state's educational body.

Educational leaders are supportive of open-ended assignments and alternative assessments that require students to use knowledge and skills from multiple disciplines and are inclusive in nature.

Extended Learning

Educational leaders build school-business partnerships to provide internships, mentorships, sponsorships, and collaborative projects. They support afterschool programs and student organizations by engaging community members to serve as coaches, mentors, and sponsors. They see the value of extended learning as opportunities to further enrich STEM experiences for students. Leaders also consider logistics to ensure that all students from within the school may participate in such activities based on schedules, supervision, transportation, and cost.

Professional Learning

Educational leaders provide time and STEM-related professional learning for educators to enhance their curriculum development skills, teaching practices, and assessment strategies. They provide mentoring or peer-to-peer coaching among educators. Educational leaders provide professional learning that targets effective models in the instructional use of inquiry, experimentation, design, and engineering pedagogies.

Educational leaders also encourage educators to experiment with design-, inquiry-, problem-, and project-based instructional approaches. Additionally, they encourage, support, and challenge educators to revise and explore their ideas for new integrative STEM approaches.

Assessment

Educational leaders support a variety of methods to measure students' understanding of and ability to implement thinking modes (e.g., scientific inquiry, experimentation, design thinking, computational thinking, engineering design processes). Leaders consider assessments as one data set, among many, to be informed of how integrative STEM curriculum, pedagogies, and practices impact students.

Evaluation

With observation protocols, educational leaders provide actionable feedback to educators that enhances curriculum and instruction. Leaders systematically gather data sets from multiple ecosystem sources to inform the evaluation of integrative STEM programming. They consider their state's accountability measures while also considering the school's integrative STEM mission. Leaders effectively evaluate the vertical alignment of integrative STEM curriculum and ensure alignment exists with grade-level state standards and integrative STEM learning goals.

STANDARDS ALIGNMENT FOR EDUCATIONAL LEADERS

These competencies of integrative STEM leaders are described in greater detail throughout the book with strategies used by pioneering educational leaders. Additionally, there is close alignment between the 10 Professional Standards for Educational Leaders from the National Policy Board for Educational Administration (2015) and the identified nine competencies for educational leaders in integrative STEM (see Table 1.5). Not every strategy will work for every school educational ecosystem; however, interweaving integrative STEM content, principles, and practices within all competencies can lead to a stronger integrative STEM foundation.

CHALLENGES WITH INTEGRATIVE STEM IMPLEMENTATION

Pioneering PK–12 educational leaders who have implemented integrative STEM pedagogies have identified challenges that may limit or inhibit programming change. The following are identified challenges of integrative STEM implementation:

- acceptance of risk to innovate instruction while also achieving accountability goals;
- complexities with developing integrative STEM schedules, resources, and funding;
- design of the school mission, values, and goals that address both student and community needs in integrative STEM;
- identification and sustainability of community partnerships (e.g., institutions of higher education, businesses, industry groups);
- lack of buy-in from other educational leaders and stakeholders;

Table 1.5. Alignment of Professional Standards for Educational Leaders and Integrative STEM Leadership Competencies

Standards	*Integrative STEM Leadership Critical Competencies*								
	Mission and Culture	*Equity, Diversity, and Inclusion*	*Infrastructure and Programming*	*Curriculum*	*Instruction*	*Extended Learning*	*Professional Learning*	*Assessment*	*Evaluation*
1. Mission, Vision, and Core Values	X	X	X						X
2. Ethics and Professional Norms		X	X		X				
3. Equity and Cultural Responsiveness	X	X	X	X	X	X	X	X	X
4. Curriculum, Instruction, and Assessment	X	X	X	X	X		X	X	X
5. Community of Care and Support for Students	X	X	X			X			
6. Professional Capacity of School Personnel		X		X	X		X		X
7. Professional Community for Teachers and Staff	X	X		X	X		X	X	X
8. Meaningful Engagement of Families and Community		X	X			X	X		X
9. Operations and Management	X	X	X	X	X	X	X	X	X
10. School Improvement	X	X	X	X	X	X	X	X	X

Note: Column 1 identifies National Policy Board for Educational Administration (NPBEA; 2015) standards. Table adapted from "Preparing School and District Leaders for Success in Developing and Facilitating Integrative STEM in Higher Education," by R. L. Geesa, K. M. Stith, and M. A. Rose, 2020, *Journal of Research on Leadership Education*, p. 17 (https://doi.org/10.1177/1942775120962148). Copyright 2020 by The University Council for Educational Administration.

- provision of equitable learning experiences for diverse groups of student populations;
- provision of sufficient planning and instructional time for educators and students to engage in integrative STEM activities;
- provision of professional learning that targets integrative STEM pedagogy and praxis;
- unfamiliarity with alternative assessments and evaluation instruments;
- unfamiliarity with integrative curriculum development; and
- unfamiliarity with preferred instructional approaches (e.g., project-based learning and co-teaching).

With these identified challenges, strategies to navigate programming change are available to educational leaders throughout this book.

CONCLUSION

Government and business leaders are tasking educational systems to pursue robust STEM experiences that will prepare STEM-literate students with knowledge and skills across multiple disciplines. Integrative STEM education is a pedagogical approach that will prepare students for a society where they will make informed decisions and solve problems related to themselves, their families, and their communities.

The mission of integrative STEM is to prepare students for career and college readiness so that students are well-positioned to pursue postsecondary pathways of their choosing that will lead to personal and professional fulfillment. These students are resilient problem-solvers who appreciate global interconnectedness as critical for overcoming challenges (e.g., environmental ,sustainability, democratic fairness, stewardship, and responsible citizenship). Additionally, these students view STEM literacy as a lifelong process that evolves alongside changes in their personal and professional lives.

Educational leaders can support integrative STEM through multiple domains of school programming: mission and culture; equity, diversity, and inclusion; infrastructure and programming; curriculum; instruction; extended learning; professional learning; assessment; and evaluation (Geesa et al., 2020; Rose et al., 2019). Within each domain, pioneering educational leaders have identified challenges and implemented solutions to guide their schools and districts toward integrative STEM experiences.

With educational leaders dedicated to an integrative STEM framework that is designed to implement skills and content, students can achieve a level of STEM literacy that prepares them to enter a society impacted by global challenges that require collaborative solutions.

REFERENCES

American Association for the Advancement of Science. (1990). *Science for all Americans*. http://www.project2061.org/publications/sfaa/online/sfaatoc.htm

Committee on STEM Education of the National Science & Technology Council. (2018). *Charting a course for success: America's strategy for STEM education.* https://www.energy.gov/sites/default/files/2019/05/f62/STEM-Education-Strategic-Plan-2018.pdf

Dewey, J. (1899). *The school and society: Being three lectures*. University of Chicago Press.

Drake, S. M., & Burns, R. C. (2004). *Meeting standards through integrated curriculum*. ASCD.

Geesa, R. L., Stith, K. M., & Rose, M. A. (2020). Preparing school and district leaders for success in developing and facilitating integrative STEM in higher education. *Journal of Research on Leadership Education,* 1–21. https://doi.org/10.1177/1942775120962148

Geesa, R. L., Stith, K. M., & Teague, G. M. (2021). Integrative STEM education and leadership for student success. In F. English (Ed.), *The Palgrave Handbook of Educational Leadership and Management Discourse* (pp. 1–20). Palgrave Macmillan. https://doi.org/10.1007/978-3-030-39666-4_36-1

International Technology and Engineering Educators Association. (2020). *Standards for technological and engineering literacy: Defining the role of technology and engineering in STEM education.* https://www.iteea.org/stel.aspx

Katehi, L., Pearson, G., & Feder, M. (2009). The status and nature of K–12 engineering education in the United States. *The Bridge*, *39*(3), 5–10. https://www.nae.edu/File.aspx?id=16147

Mansilla, V. B., & Chua, F. S. (2017). Signature pedagogies in global competence education: Understanding quality teaching practice. In S. Choo, D. Sawch, A. Villanueva, & R. Vinz (Eds.), *Educating for the 21st Century* (pp. 93–115). Springer.

Mohr-Schroeder, M. J., Bush, S. B., Maiorca, C., & Nickels, M. (2020). Moving toward an equity-based approach for STEM-literacy. In C. C. Johnson, M. J. Mohr-Schroeder, T. J. Moore, & L. D. English (Eds.), *Handbook of Research on STEM Education* (1st ed., pp. 29–38). Routledge. https://doi.org/10.4324/9780429021381-4

National Academy of Engineering & National Research Council. (2014). *STEM integration in K–12 education: Status, prospects, and an agenda for research.* The National Academies Press. https://doi.org/10.17226/18612

National Academy of Sciences, National Academy of Engineering, & Institute of Medicine. (2007). *Rising above the gathering storm: Energizing and employing America for a brighter economic future.* The National Academies Press. https://www.nap.edu/catalog/11463/rising-above-the-gathering-storm-energizing-and-employing-america-for

National Commission on Excellence in Education. (1983). A nation at risk: The imperative for educational reform. *The Elementary School Journal, 84*(2), 113–130. https://doi.org/10.1086/461348?mobileUi=0&

National Policy Board for Educational Administration. (2015). *Professional standards for educational leaders.* https://www.npbea.org/wp-content/uploads/2017/06/Professional-Standards-for-Educational-Leaders_2015.pdf

National Research Council. (2013). *Next Generation Science Standards: For states, by states.* The National Academies Press.

National Science Board. (1986). *Undergraduate science, mathematics and engineering education: Role for the National Science Foundation and recommendations for action by other sectors to strengthen collegiate education and pursue excellence in the next generation of U.S. leadership in science and technology.* https://www.nsf.gov/nsb/publications/1986/nsb0386.pdf

President's Council of Advisors on Science and Technology. (2010). *Prepare and inspire: K–12 education in science, technology, engineering, and math (STEM) for America's Future: Executive Report.* Executive Office of the President, President's Council of Advisors on Science and Technology. https://nsf.gov/attachments/117803/public/2a--Prepare_and_Inspire--PCAST.pdf

Rose, M. A., Geesa, R. L., & Stith, K. (2019). STEM leader excellence: A modified Delphi study of critical skills, competencies, and qualities. *Journal of Technology Education, 31*(1), 42–62. https://doi.org/10.21061/jte.v31il.a.3.

Sanders, M. (2009). Integrative STEM education: Primer. *The Technology Teacher, 68*(4), 20–26.

The Meeder Consulting Group. (2012). *The STEM schools project: How schools create a STEM culture.* https://www.worthington.k12.oh.us/cms/lib/OH01001900/Centricity/Domain/229/STEM%20SCHOOLS%20OVERVIEW%20MAY%202012.pdf

The Millennium Project. (2017). *15 global challenges*. http://www.millennium-project.org/projects/challenges/

Thibaut, L., Ceuppens, S., De Loof, H., De Meester, J., Goovaerts, L., Struyf, A., Boeve-de Pauw, J., Dehaene, W., Deprez, J., De Cock, M., Hellinckx, L., Knipprath, H., Langie, G., Struyven, K., Van de Velde, D., Van Petegem, P., & Depaepe, F. (2018). Integrated STEM education: A systematic review of instructional practices in secondary education. *European Journal of STEM Education, 3*(1), 1–12. https://doi.org/10.20897/ejsteme/85525

Timar, T. B., & Guthrie, J. W. (1980). Public values and public school policy in the 1980s. *Educational Leadership, 38*(2), 112–115. http://www1.ascd.org/ASCD/pdf/journals/ed_lead/el_198011_timar.pdf

Toma, R. B., & Greca, I. M. (2018). The effect of integrative STEM instruction on elementary students' attitudes toward science. *Eurasia Journal of Mathematics, Science and Technology Education, 14*(4), 1383–1395. https://doi.org/10.29333/ejmste/83676

United Nations Educational, Scientific and Cultural Organization. (2015). *Education for all 2000–2015: Achievements and challenges*. https://en.unesco.org/gem-report/report/2015/education-all-2000-2015-achievements-and-challenges

Vygotsky, L. S. (1978). *Mind in society: The development of higher psychological processes*. Harvard University Press.

Wood, T. (1988). State–mandated accountability as a constraint on teaching and learning science. *Journal of Research in Science Teaching, 25*(8), 631–641. https://doi.org/10.1002/tea.3660250803

Zollman, A. (2012). Learning for STEM literacy: STEM literacy for learning. *School Science and Mathematics, 112*(1), 12–19. https://doi.org/10.1111/j.1949-8594.2012.00101.x

2

Leadership to Foster an Integrative STEM Mission and Culture

Rachel Louise Geesa

The overarching role of educational leaders is to lead schools to meet all students' social, emotional, academic, and career and college readiness needs. Students' needs differ in various contexts (e.g., geographic, cultural, linguistic, socioeconomic). As such, educational leaders must foster a school mission and culture that sustains strong family-school-community partnerships to prepare students for careers and future education (National Center on Safe Supportive Learning Environments, 2020).

School culture focuses on the educational practices, beliefs, and expectations within a school (Fullan, 2007). The mission helps school stakeholders describe the school's purpose or "what they do and why they do it," while the vision explains "what they hope to achieve if they successfully fulfill their organizational purpose or mission" (Great Schools Partnership, 2015, para. 1).

In an integrative STEM school culture, characteristics of design-thinking, problem-solving, inquiry, and evidence-based decision-making are included to increase students' achievement, motivation, and preparation for jobs and higher education upon completion of their PK–12 education program. Leaders of integrative STEM educational programs strive to develop STEM-literate students who can thrive within a society driven by scientific and technological innovation.

Integrative STEM culture in a school or district supports and energizes innovation and collaborative problem-solving by educators and students. To guide educational leaders toward fostering an integrative STEM culture, the purpose of this chapter is to (a) discuss the need for the school leadership team and school stakeholders to collaborate for integrative STEM education; (b) share ways to develop and sustain integrative STEM mission, vision, and goals; and (c) explore shared leadership and community engagement practices for an integrative STEM culture.

COLLABORATION FOR INTEGRATIVE STEM EDUCATION

Collaboration is crucial in defining and following the school's mission, vision, and goals for educational leaders and other school stakeholders (e.g., educators, staff, students, business and community leaders, government officials) to address student, family, and community needs. The purpose and goals are clearly stated in the mission and vision. The mission and goals also show respect for the value systems of the community. Within collaborative partnerships, school stakeholders can work together toward a shared mission and vision of a positive educational culture for students as they prepare for careers and further education in STEM and non-STEM academic disciplines and vocations.

LaForce et al. (2016) identified eight culturally-essential elements of inclusive STEM high schools. The objective of these schools is to provide STEM education to all students, regardless of their achievement, demographic, and socioeconomic backgrounds. The elements of the schools include personalization of learning; problem-based learning; rigorous learning; career, technology, and life skills; school community and belonging; essential community; staff foundations; and essential factors (LaForce et al., 2016). Similar to other forms of school improvement, the development of an integrative STEM culture that focuses on innovation and provides sequenced curricula to guide students is an ongoing and collaborative process.

Educational leaders need to routinely measure the effectiveness of the current integrative STEM learning environment and goals for their efficacy toward achieving the school's mission and vision. Leaders should not only track students' STEM achievements, but also track opportunities to be innovative, take risks, and learn through inquiry- and design-based experiences. Through real-world learning opportunities and collaboration with school stakeholders, leaders can provide experiences for students to identify connections between their current learning and potential careers.

Using a Leadership Team

A team dedicated to integrative STEM leadership is needed for a school to foster an integrative STEM culture. The team should be dedicated to democratic ideals of education—equity, fairness, respect, and participative decision-making—and improved educational learning experiences for students as the team works to establish and foster a STEM culture. Team members need to participate in regularly scheduled meetings where past agendas, results, and new ideas are discussed to strengthen STEM education access and advancement in schools.

A diverse STEM leadership team should include participants from STEM and non-STEM fields (see Table 2.1). According to Smith et al. (2017), "reaching out to engage families and communities also strengthens the school's ability to network within the community to find new supports and resources to partner to meet the needs of students" (para. 4). Team members may represent a variety of areas of expertise in STEM disciplines, years of experience in STEM education and workforce, and connections to the school and community.

Table 2.1. Potential Members of an Integrative STEM Leadership Team

Member	*Position*
Business or industry partner	Business owner, industry employee, or similar role
Caregiver	Parent, family member, or similar role
Community partner	Government employee, school board member, school donor, or other stakeholder
District leader	Superintendent, assistant superintendent, curriculum director, career and technical education director, or similar position
Graduate student or academic leader	Graduate student or academic leader in a STEM field or related discipline
Non-STEM teacher	Teacher in non-STEM fields (e.g., fine arts, gifted education, language arts, social studies, special education, and world languages)
School leader	Principal, assistant principal, dean, or similar position
School staff	Educational technologist, information technology specialist, custodian, librarian, or other staff position
STEM teacher	Teacher of science, technology, engineering, mathematics, or integrative STEM
Student	Student representative of current school program
Student support specialist	School counselor, social worker, school psychologist, or similar position

Educational leaders need to work with stakeholders to determine the appropriate number and roles of team members. "Strong leadership teams create a safe, nurturing learning environment for students. . . . Leadership teams creating these environments help develop student agency" (Smith et al., 2017, para. 5). Student agency refers to students' ownership in their learning of content and experiences in relevant and meaningful activities.

Engaging All Stakeholders and Guiding with Data

Educational leaders should be well-versed on the national, state, and local initiatives related to STEM education (e.g., economic status of the community, business, and employment trends associated with future needs). Educational leaders, in collaboration with school stakeholders, should identify, discuss, and record assets and deficits of the current STEM program and trends in integrative STEM education.

Achievement data in STEM disciplines, examples of existing STEM curricula and pedagogies, and current STEM extended learning opportunities for students and professional learning for educators should be discussed, as well. With this information, educational leaders can guide stakeholders and members of the leadership team to set goals for funding, research, and initiatives; identify information gaps; and suggest strategies for improving awareness of the status of integrative STEM education in the school and district.

Members of an integrative STEM leadership team need to work together to build trusting, positive relationships with one another and the greater community by sharing resources, communicating with one another, and working toward common goals. Their responsibilities on the leadership team may vary, but team members should be involved in making decisions and sharing their insights. This rapport helps team members consider local business needs and visions for the community to develop authentic integrative STEM learning experiences for students.

School stakeholders from varied backgrounds, beyond the leadership team members, should be involved in collaborative discussions to share integrative STEM ideas. By including diverse stakeholders from traditionally underrepresented or underserved populations, equitable and inclusive opportunities in STEM education can be more attainable and relevant to the participants. Educational leaders can invite stakeholders to attend school town hall meetings, visit schools, and participate in conversations related to a focus on integrative STEM to increase their engagement.

Understanding the Current Culture

Educational leaders need to collaborate with school stakeholders to accurately characterize and analyze the current school mission, vision, and goals concerning integrative STEM. For instance, the Indiana Department of Education (IDOE; 2021) has a STEM certification process for schools in the state to work toward, which requires self-audits of school culture with input from stakeholders. The IDOE uses a rubric to determine each school's capacities to integrate STEM practices within the larger program (Table 10.3).

The STEM leadership committee should review school-wide and disaggregated achievement data, student demographic data (e.g., gender, race, ethnicity, language, socioeconomic status), and data from surveys, interviews, and focus groups with students, educators, families, and community and business leaders. These data can be used as a foundation in planning a path forward and making informed decisions.

Additionally, leader and stakeholder reflections, interviews, and school audits inform discussions about the desirable and complementary community goals or assets relative to integrative STEM education. Needs assessments and regular reviews of integrative STEM initiatives with family-school-community partners are important, as well. Through these actions, educational leaders and school stakeholders can collaboratively inform the mission, vision, goals, and local plan to establish and support an integrative STEM culture.

A ROBUST INTEGRATIVE STEM CULTURE

After assessing the existing status of integrative STEM education and culture, educational leaders and school stakeholders should ask, "What *integrative STEM principles and values* should inform our mission and vision?" and "Where should we be in terms of *integrative STEM education*?" The STEM-related needs of students (e.g., higher education preparation, career pathways) and the community (e.g., future jobs, professional roles) should be considered as the culture develops and evolves. Schools should be safe, equitable, and collaborative learning environments where students can drive their education, experiment, and expand their knowledge and skills in various STEM fields.

Including an Integrative STEM Focus

To achieve STEM-literacy, students need experiences and interactions in integrative, cooperative, and engaging STEM learning approaches. The school mission, vision, and goals should be inclusive of integrative STEM habits of mind (e.g., systems thinking, creativity, optimism, collaboration, communication, and ethical considerations; Katehi et al., 2009) to prepare students for future achievements in STEM-related paths. Whole school design challenges, co-taught courses, and student-driven learning experiences may be effective pathways for continuous improvement.

It is also critical to focus on integrating STEM content with content in non-STEM subjects, as careers require students to think in collective and creative ways. Although STEM-friendly learning environments are created and supported, state and national standards must also be considered in STEM teaching pedagogies, curricula, and programming throughout schools.

Developing the Mission and Vision

School mission and goals are collaboratively defined with school stakeholder buy-in and support. Integrative STEM experiences in design-thinking, problem-solving, and data-driven decision-making are essential elements of the school mission and goals within a STEM culture (e.g., see Table 2.2). According to Great Schools Partnership (2015), "well-articulated mission and vision statements":

- assist a school community to reflect on its educational values, operational objectives, purposes as an institution, and anticipated student outcomes;
- provide a way to develop support for the school community educational values and improvement plan, or encourage school and community stakeholders to work in diverse ways toward new goals; and

Table 2.2. Exemplar District and School Mission and Vision Statements

District or School	*Mission Statement*	*Vision Statement*
Boulder Valley School District (2020) Boulder, Colorado	The mission of the Boulder Valley School District is to create challenging, meaningful and engaging learning opportunities so that all children thrive and are prepared for successful, civically engaged lives.	We develop our children's greatest abilities and make possible the discovery and pursuit of their dreams which, when fulfilled, will benefit us all. We provide a comprehensive and innovative approach to education and graduate successful, curious, lifelong learners who confidently confront the great challenges of their time.
El Paso Independent School District (2020) El Paso, Texas	The El Paso Independent School District graduates every student prepared for higher learning and careers to empower them as knowledgeable and engaged citizens, innovators, and drivers of a robust, bicultural economy.	The El Paso Independent School District will be a premier educational institution, source of pride and innovation, and the cornerstone of emerging economic opportunities producing a twenty-first century workforce.
Frost Elementary School (2020) Cumberland, Maryland	Frost Elementary School's staff, parents, and community are dedicated to the intellectual, personal, social, and physical growth of students. Our highly qualified staff recognizes the value of professional development in order to rigorously challenge students. Our teaching practices are both reflective and responsive to the needs of our students. Through diversified experiences, our students discover their potential, achieve readiness for college and careers, and succeed in a safe and caring environment.	The vision at Frost Elementary School is to prepare and motivate our students for a rapidly changing world by instilling in them critical thinking skills, a global perspective, and a respect for core values of honesty, loyalty, perseverance, and compassion. Students will have success for today and be prepared for tomorrow.
R. B. Hudson STEAM Academy (2020) Selma, Alabama	The mission of R. B. Hudson STEAM Academy is to produce world changers by providing innovative learning opportunities to include parental and community partnerships through Science, Technology, Engineering, Arts, and Math in a safe, nurturing environment.	The vision of R. B. Hudson STEAM Academy is to develop scholars' critical thinking skills through rigorous and relevant content in order to maximize their potential in a global society.

Note: Quoted from *Mission, Vision, Values and Goals*, by Boulder Valley School District, 2020 (https://www.bvsd.org/about/mission-and-vision); Vision/Mission, by El Paso Independent School District, 2020 (https://www.episd.org/site/Default.aspx?PageID=886); *Frost Elementary School: Vision and Mission statements*, by Frost Elementary School, Allegany County Public Schools, 2020 (https://www.acpsmd.org/Page/1520); and *Selma City Schools: R. B. Hudson STEAM Academy*, by R. B. Hudson STEAM Academy, 2020 (https://www.selmacityschools.org/rbhudsonmiddleschool_home.aspx).

- turn attention to collective academic programs and shared learning goals for all students to experience success. (para. 4)

Table 2.2 includes exemplar mission and vision statements related to integrative STEM attitudes and practices.

Leaders of integrative STEM programs and schools can operationalize practices to develop and foster a mission and vision in the following four steps:

1. *Seek input*: Leaders solicit input and feedback about integrative STEM values and beliefs from school and community stakeholders and collaboratively review the current school mission and vision.
2. *Develop statements:* Leaders work with integrative STEM leadership team members to analyze stakeholder input and create draft mission and vision statements or revise current statements.
3. *Refine statements:* Leaders share draft statements with all stakeholders and seek input to modify and enhance the statements to better reflect STEM-related student and community needs and aspirations.
4. *Finalize and publicize:* Leaders confirm the statements with the leadership team and ensure the collectively agreed-on integrative STEM mission and vision statements are shared with family-school-community partners to guide the school and district.

Although academic skills and outcomes are often included in mission and vision statements, educational leaders should consider incorporating a focus on student self-actualization, social and emotional development, and pursuit of happiness in statements as well.

Determining Goals of Integrative STEM

"Key ideas, values, and beliefs are the beginning of powerful visions" (Gabriel & Farmer, 2009, p. 53). The development of an integrative STEM mission and vision should be shared with students and school stakeholders because they indicate what they and their community need and want. This process takes time. Goals and steps to achieve the mission and vision need to be set. Leaders need to make the school goals, along with the mission and vision statements, commonly known throughout the school.

Leadership team members can refer to the mission, vision, and goals of other schools and districts to consider what should be a part of their school's goals and values. Katherine Johnson STEM Academy within Los Angeles Unified Schools District shares a vision that focuses on students' social, emotional, and academic needs to prepare students for success in their futures (see Table 2.3).

For instance, Katherine Johnson STEM Academy (2020) is committed to five values: commitment to excellence, deep ownership, growth mindset, selfless teamwork, and all in. "All in" refers the preparation and commitment of educators and leaders to be accessible and ready to support students and families each day (Katherine Johnson STEM Academy, 2020, para. 7). These values guide decisions made within the school and support the mission, vision, and goals.

Table 2.3. School Vision of Katherine Johnson STEM Academy (2020)

Vision: *We believe in a world where all children can become 21st-century problem solvers with great hearts and great minds.*

21st-century problem solvers:	Students with great hearts:	Students with great minds:
• are critical thinkers • are communicators • are collaborative • are creative • identify problems • look for solutions • use different approaches to solve a problems • are innovative and resourceful • take risks • embrace others' ideas • demonstrate perseverance and resilience • reflect on their processes • understand equality, equity, and justice	• demonstrate kindness • reflect on and understands their emotions and actions • get to know people to demonstrate personal respect • build and aim to keep trust • accept differences and uplift others • love both the journey and including others in it • create safe spaces for self and others to learn and grow • look for solutions that are best for all, not only self • serve others • practice empathy • act selflessly	• have wonder • apply learning to life • ask questions • are persistent • persevere to reach goals • are open to new ideas • can adapt to new situations • look forward to achieving the next goal • show their best efforts and encourage others to do likewise • consult multiple sources • questions their own thinking • consider others' perspectives • enjoy learning

Note: Quoted from *Our Vision, Mission, and Value*, by Katherine Johnson STEM Academy, 2020, Los Angeles Unified School District, Board of Education (https://kjstemacademy.org/vision).

Since each school and district functions in a unique environment, the mission, vision, and goals should be responsive to the present conditions. Chapter 7 includes a specific example of an educational program's environment shaping practices and integrative STEM culture. However, educational leaders can facilitate discussions to ensure the overarching focus in implementing integrative STEM education with students is to support social and emotional wellness, promote academic success and workforce development, and develop contributing members of a global society.

INTEGRATIVE STEM OPPORTUNITIES FOR ALL

As student advocates, educational leaders ensure students receive access to learning experiences that are appropriate, rigorous, and socially just. Although some perspectives of STEM education include focusing on STEM subjects as separate entities, integrative STEM education provides a holistic, collaborative approach to teaching and leading for authentic learning. Educational leaders guide this shift in instructional practices to include a mission to provide integrative STEM opportunities for *all* PK–12 students and a vision for students to become productive and healthy global citizens.

Leading in an Integrative STEM Culture

Considerations for educational leaders to foster and sustain an integrative STEM culture differ from considerations for traditional educational programs. A pedagogical shift to collaborative, student-driven teaching, learning, and leading practices and integrative curricula through planning, coordinating, and formative evaluation needs to occur. Leaders should facilitate opportunities with school stakeholders for research, discussion, collaboration, and professional learning to better understand the integration of content areas and project what knowledge and skills students should gain to be career and college ready in various integrative STEM fields (e.g., see Table 2.4).

Integrative STEM leaders guide schools to address the student and community needs with goals that focus on the acquisition and sharing of STEM-related knowledge, skills, and competencies. The knowledge and skills students obtain add value to the school and community, and students

Table 2.4. Approaches for Leaders to Collaboratively Foster an Integrative STEM Culture

Approach	*Description*
1. Be collaborative	Leaders develop strong family-school-community partnerships to build connections among the school, homes, and communities in which the leaders serve. Leaders foster safe, accessible, and collaborative environments for educators, school counselors, students, and other stakeholders to make decisions and share integrative STEM ideas.
2. Be reflective	Leaders model the collaborative and reflective practices they would like to see within their educators and students. Leaders use STEM-related data and involve others in shared decision-making strategies to improve accessibility to STEM education in the school and community to enhance the integrative STEM culture.
3. Be intentional	Leaders hire educators, staff, and fellow leaders who share integrative STEM-related expectations and beliefs about innovative pedagogy, curricula, collaborative learning, and addressing community needs. Leaders encourage educators to mentor one another and take risks to increase learning outcomes in STEM disciplines.
4. Be innovative	Leaders provide educators professional learning opportunities related to design-, problem-, project-, and inquiry-based teaching and learning practices. Leaders model these practices in an integrative STEM culture with school stakeholders, businesses, and community partners to solve real-world problems through interdisciplinary ways within the school and community.
5. Be communicative	Leaders reflect upon and emphasize integrative STEM goals, pedagogies, and curricula in formal communication. Leaders share positive outcomes, future highlights, and a collective mission and vision to build a sense of belonging and STEM understanding for all stakeholders. Signs, posters, and announcements highlight expectations and STEM foci.
6. Be authentic	Leaders build trust with stakeholders and regularly share and make efforts to strengthen the mission and vision within the school and community (e.g., unique motto, graphics, special events, learning environment). Leaders collaborate with students, families, and community partners of diverse populations to recognize STEM achievements and reinforce shared goals for STEM-capable citizenry.
7. Be committed	Leaders commit to envisioning, supporting, monitoring, and celebrating an integrative STEM culture. Leaders provide all students safe, positive, and inspiring learning environments to excel in integrative STEM disciplines. Leaders express value in innovation and regularly connect with school stakeholders to share the mission, vision, and principles of STEM learning.

become assets and contributing members of the local, national, and global society through positive partnerships and leadership initiatives.

Ebony Bridwell-Mitchell (as cited in Shafer, 2018a, 2018b), an Associate Professor of Education at the Harvard Graduate School of Education, outlined five interrelated elements to develop and sustain a school culture. These elements include: fundamental beliefs and assumptions, shared values, norms, patterns and behaviors, and tangible evidence. Through a focus on these elements, leaders can take steps to collaboratively foster an integrative STEM culture in schools (see Table 2.4).

Providing Integrative STEM Curricula and Instruction

Although STEM education emphasizes science, technology, engineering, and mathematics disciplines, *integrative* STEM education highlights the connections between STEM and non-STEM content for interdisciplinary, multidisciplinary, and transdisciplinary learning experiences. This integrative educational approach allows students and educators to participate and collaborate in inquiry-driven, student-centered lessons with opportunities to apply integrative STEM concepts to problems relevant to their environment (e.g., see Figures 2.1 and 2.2).

Figure 2.1. High school students video conferencing with fellow students for a group project. iStockphoto LP.

Figure 2.2. Elementary school students collaborating together in class with manipulatives. iStockphoto LP.

Integrative STEM-related teaching pedagogies rely on the interconnections between disciplines. Educational leaders need knowledge, skills, and competencies to guide coherent systems of curricula and instruction to encourage integrative STEM within the school culture (Geesa et al., 2020, 2021; Rose et al., 2019). Guidance and training for educators and leaders to improve their practices and facilitate collaborative STEM initiatives with stakeholders may require additional time, resources, and funding, but are needed to support the school vision, mission, and goals.

Rose et al. (2019) identified critical characteristics for educational leaders to achieve integrative STEM learning outcomes. According to their findings, student-centric pedagogical approaches, integrative curricula, and a commitment to lifelong learning are important. Leaders also need to support student experiences to design, engineer, make, test, reflect upon, and document their work to answer questions and prepare for higher education and the workforce. Leaders need to encourage educators to focus their curricula on solving real-world problems and think creatively and collaboratively through complex content and experiences to address students' needs in integrative STEM.

Sharing Integrative STEM Knowledge

Educational leaders can develop ways to communicate, share ideas, and collectively work toward a shared mission, vision, and goals. According to DuFour (2004), "educators who are building a professional learning community recognize that they must work together to achieve their collective purpose of learning for all" (p. 9). Leaders can encourage the development and sustainability of these learning communities by supporting stakeholders' time, resources, and professional learning needs.

Educators are the trained experts in specific disciplines. It is important for them to have opportunities to meet with fellow educators, business partners, and community members to build relationships, plan collaborative initiatives, and consider new ways to educate students in integrative STEM. However, initiating and sustaining learning communities can be challenging as educational "staff must focus on learning rather than teaching, work collaboratively on matters related to learning, and hold itself accountable for the kind of results that fuel continual improvement" (DuFour, 2007, p. 7).

Building and Sustaining Community Support

Although educators, students, and families may have more direct and daily interactions and involvement within the school environment, educational leaders must identify ways to connect and partner with members of the community, businesses, and organizations to strengthen the school culture (see Table 2.5). According to Bridwell-Mitchell, "in a strong culture, there are many, overlapping, and cohesive interactions, so that knowledge about the organization's distinctive character—and what it takes to thrive in it—is widely spread" (Shafer, 2018b, para. 4).

To fulfill their role to foster a positive school culture, educational leaders and stakeholders may need additional training, ongoing support, and ways to engage with the community in an integrative STEM culture. The continuous school improvement plan should include opportunities for school and community stakeholders to participate in integrative STEM professional learning and extended learning opportunities related to:

Table 2.5. Exemplar Activities to Build and Sustain Stakeholder Engagement in an Integrative STEM Culture

Activity	*Integrative STEM Examples*
Awards ceremonies and testimonials	• Integrative STEM business, community, or career guest speakers share experiences, training, and activities with students and school stakeholders. • School and community award ceremonies and local events recognize student growth, achievement, and leadership in STEM.
Community partner celebrations	• Community and business partners and families participate in recognition events for STEM programs and sponsor integrative STEM school events. • Schools receive STEM equipment and supply donations, and community and business partners fund integrative STEM professional learning opportunities.

Cultural community celebrations	• Schools, businesses, and community partners celebrate and recognize people in STEM, such as:
	  • Black and African-American people in STEM during Black History Month (also known as African-American History Month) (February),
	  • Women in STEM during Women's History Month (March), and
	  • Hispanic and Latinx American people in STEM during Hispanic Heritage Month (September 15–October 15).

Press releases	• Educational leaders and community partners publicize local, state, and national STEM-related student, educator, program, and school awards. • Local community organizations, businesses, and other stakeholders announce student achievement, scholarships, and competitions in integrative STEM.
Quarterly forums	• Leadership teams discuss STEM-related district and state standards with school stakeholders to provide diverse STEM curricular options to students. • Student formative and summative assessment instruments and STEM school achievement data are shared with family-school-community partners.
School newsletter	• School stakeholders share and receive school news highlighting student successes and family-school-community partnerships in integrative STEM. • Community, business, and school publications and social media postings include community partner updates and STEM leadership team information.
Standard school-site publication	• Leadership teams involve community, business, and school stakeholders in the school handbook and school improvement plan revisions for STEM education. • Community members access information about integrative STEM in schools through a school-community resource guide and school website.
Volunteer recognition events	• Community, business, and school STEM volunteers participate in school and district recruitment orientations and volunteer development programs. • School STEM volunteers participate in school and district award and appreciation events and interact with school stakeholders.

Note: Column 1 includes activity options from "Improving Achievement in Low-Performing Schools: Key Results for School Leaders," by R. E. Ward and M. A. Burke, 2004 (https://us.corwin.com/en-us/nam/improving-achievement-in-low-performing-schools/book226440).

- equitable and inclusive learning strategies,
- evaluation and assessment methods,
- integrative STEM curricula and instructional practices, and
- programs outside of the school day in which students may participate in.

By reviewing successful integrative STEM programs and initiatives and talking with key stakeholders in other schools and districts that have a robust STEM education program, educational leaders can be better informed as they build family-school-community partnerships to ensure that proper integrative STEM programs and curricula are in place for students to experience. Leaders should deliberatively plan and implement a variety of regular activities to engage a diverse group of stakeholders and gain their commitment to an integrative STEM culture (see Table 2.5).

Leaders must recognize that a positive integrative STEM culture is driven by the expectations, beliefs, and vision of students, school stakeholders, and leaders. Collaborative family-school-community partnerships need to be formed and sustained to advance a powerful culture for integrative STEM. These partnerships involve support for student learning and engagement activities, recognition and collaboration with school stakeholders committed to STEM learning, and opportunities for students to apply their knowledge and skills in and beyond school.

CONCLUSION

In integrative STEM schools and programs, educational leaders are responsible for building and sustaining an integrative STEM culture that meets the needs of the students and community. In this chapter, the need for collaboration among a leadership team and school stakeholders to advance integrative STEM education was discussed. Perceived benefits of integrating STEM education into a school and district should be collaboratively identified and assessed.

Effective ways to develop and sustain integrative STEM mission, vision, and goals were shared. Through a clear and specific mission and vision, educational leaders can guide family-school-community partnerships and build collaborative relationships to use data to make decisions, facilitate professional learning experiences, and continuously improve equitable integrative STEM opportunities.

The school improvement process is ongoing, and educational leaders should foster the development, implementation, and evaluation of integrative STEM goals, expectations, programs, and initiatives. Through shared decision-making practices, educational leaders and school stakeholders can make collective decisions about stakeholder and community engagement in the mission and vision and aspire to continuous school improvement in learning outcomes for students within an integrative STEM culture.

Nā Hunaahi: An Example of Mission and Culture in a Hawaiian Integrative STEAM Program

Toni Marie Mapuana Kaui

Endemic to the island of Hawai`i, `iliahi, better known to the world as Hawaiian sandalwood (*Santalum paniculatum*), thrives when the plants around it also thrive. As a symbiotic plant, the health of the `iliahi depends greatly on the health of the plants around it. Like the symbiotic needs of the `iliahi, a community and its school share this kind of reciprocal relationship—the community flourishes when its school does and vice versa.

Nā Hunaahi is a newly established, cultural-focused high school located on the east side of Hawai`i island. Its programming is dedicated toward sustaining the native Hawaiian language, culture, and design through integrative STEAM. As an independent school, its stakeholders collaborated to craft a school mission exemplifying its vision, describing its purpose and goals, and articulating its pedagogy and practice.

There were three immediate educational needs the community requested Nā Hunaahi to address. First, Hawaiian-immersion students wanted greater career exploration opportunities. Second, parents and caregivers requested rigorous academic content promoting critical thinking and problem-solving. Third, the founder desired research-supported programming to close an identified achievement gap.

The school addresses this first need through its integrative, culturally relevant STEAM curriculum. Integrative STEAM education refers to the purposeful incorporation of arts and humanities in STEM disciplines. Students collaborate with their teachers to design a curriculum allowing them to investigate possible career interests and industries. This curriculum aligns with the mission to provide students with personalized learning. In adhering to its commitment to perpetuating the native Hawaiian language and culture, student-led curriculum is developed around a cultural practice allowing students to learn while giving back to their community.

Parents brought forth the second request of designing, developing, and delivering rigorous academic content challenging their children to think critically and problem-solve. At the school, students tackle real-world design challenges by employing the engineering design process. These design challenges promote design thinking, expose students to a process for solving problems, encourage students to work collaboratively and cooperatively, and instruct students of the benefits of iterative design (Sanders, 2012).

The final issue arose due to the founder's strong support of educational reform supporting curriculum, instruction, and assessment that research demonstrated to close the achievement gap. As an underrepresented and underserved student population, native Hawaiian young adults continue to lag behind their dominant majority peers in mathematics and English language arts (Hawaii State Department of Education, n.d.).

These three community issues and its associated responses launched the Nā Hunaahi (2020) mission statement:

> Nā Hunaahi prepares students for their futures, whether it be to pursue further education or training, to assume adult roles in their families, careers, and/or communities, and/or to cultivate personal well-being. In achieving this purpose, it nurtures a culture of learning and inclusivity so every student and adult feels safe and supported in taking risks to learn new things; it personalizes learning so students learn the skills to own their education and become lifelong learners; it responds to students by meeting them where they are with timely and differentiated supports; and it advances students based on demonstrated mastery. (para. 1)

An Integrative, Culturally Relevant STEAM Program

Nā Hunaahi implements a competency-based educational model "by advancing upon demonstrated mastery rather than on seat time, students are more engaged and motivated, and educators can direct their efforts to where students need the most help" (Sturgis & Casey, 2018, p. 7). In addition, this competency-based model employs collaborative curriculum planning that promotes student agency—taking responsibility for one's education; holding oneself, peers, and teachers/mentors accountable for their learning; and expecting parental and caregiver involvement throughout their high school journey.

An integrative, culturally relevant STEAM program is a rigorous and applicable program developed using students' cultural knowledge and prior experiences. Within this program, faculty design personalized, multidisciplinary curricula consisting of real-world projects student solve by implementing and applying an engineering design process. These projects support the perpetuation of native or indigenous cultural practices through improvement or advancement of the practice (Kaui, 2016) (e.g., see Figure 2.3).

To develop personalized student curricula (PSC), the teacher meets individually with each student to discuss long-term, mid-term, and short-term goals, ambitions, and dreams. A second meeting includes parents who also share their hopes and dreams for their children and agree on an initial action plan for the school year together. Information from these meetings inform the development of a PSC framework. Then, the teacher meets with the student to review and revise the intial framework. An integral and important aspect of an integrative, culturally relevant STEAM program involves continual communication among the student, parents, and educators.

Parallel to these meetings, the educational leaders meet with community representatives. Most recently, Nā Hunaahi partnered with Hui Ho`oleimaluō (2020), an organization working to revitalize a community fishpond. Initially, partners discussed the needs of the community and how the school might contribute to fulfilling those needs. Educational leaders shared the different careers students chose to pursue for

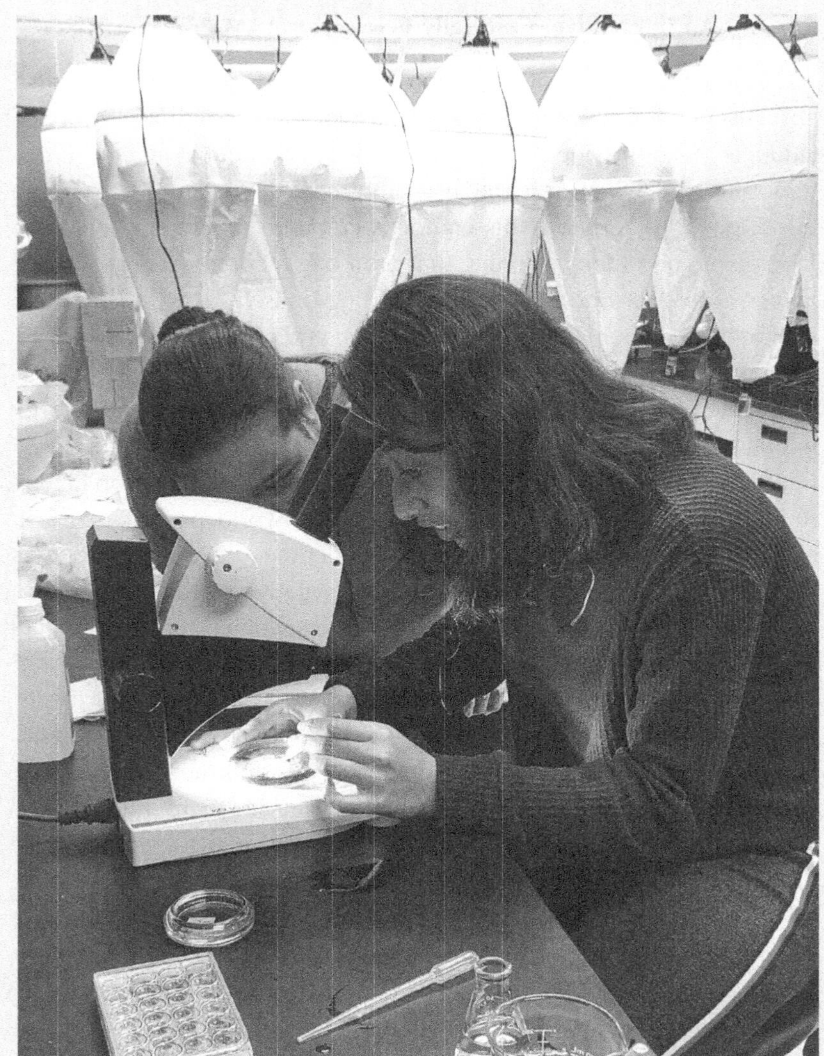

Figure 2.3. Students visiting a university laboratory to research their field data.
Toni Marie Mapuana Kaui

the current school year, while Ho`oleimaluō articulated its research needs. With intentional and purposeful planning, PSCs evolved to contribute to the needs of community.

The student becomes the owner of the PSC document and learns to responsibly monitor their plan and request meetings to review and revise it as needed. Parents continue to be an integral part of their child's educational experience. Parent meetings take place at the conclusion of each six-week grading period, where they receive updated student transcripts. In students' freshman year, they learn how to conduct progress meetings, so that by the last two grading periods the students administer their own progress meetings with the teachers and their parents.

With support from their teachers and parents, students at Nā Hunaahi develop the knowledge, skills, and experience necessary for them to demonstrate student agency during their time at the school, and eventually become accountable for their learning and achievement. Doing so supports their ability to advocate for themselves in any future endeavors they choose to pursue.

Summary

Nā Hunaahi believes learning happens everywhere with educators, peers, parents, family, and the community. The extent of one's learning and achievement depends greatly on student agency, relevance of content, level of challenge and engagement, and the depth of care of an educator or mentor. The mission and philosophy of Nā Hunaahi expresses each of these dependents within its culture.

Nā Hunaahi is responsive to the needs and aspirations of students, families, and the community. Through the integrative STEAM curriculum that gives students and the community a voice, there is a commitment to increasing and improving the well-being of all parties involved; carving out a permanent place for the school within the community for years to come. Nā Hunaahi looks forward to providing more students with an integrative, culturally relevant STEAM education built from the goals, aspirations, and dreams of its students, families, and community with opportunities to explore, create, investigate, imagine, and achieve.

REFERENCES

Boulder Valley School District. (2020). *Mission, vision, values and goals.* https://www.bvsd.org/about/mission-and-vision

DuFour, R. (2004). What is a "professional learning community"? *Educational Leadership, 61*(8), 6–11.

DuFour, R. (2007). Professional learning communities: A bandwagon, an idea worth considering, or our best hope for high levels of learning? *Middle School Journal, 39*(1), 4–8. https://doi.org/10.1080/00940771.2007.11461607

El Paso Independent School District. (2020). *Vision/mission.* https://www.episd.org/site/Default.aspx?PageID=886

Frost Elementary School, Allegany County Public Schools. (2020). *Frost Elementary School: Vision and mission statements.* https://www.acpsmd.org/Page/1520

Fullan, M. (2007). *The new meaning of educational change* (4th ed.). Teachers College Press.

Gabriel, J. G., & Farmer, P. C. (2009). *How to help your school thrive without breaking the bank.* Association for Supervision and Curriculum Development. http://www.ascd.org/publications/books/107042/chapters/developing-a-vision-and-a-mission.aspx

Geesa, R. L., Stith, K. M., & Rose, M. A. (2020). Preparing school and district leaders for success in developing and facilitating integrative STEM in higher education. *Journal of Research on Leadership Education*, 1–21. https://doi.org/10.1177/1942775120962148

Geesa, R. L., Stith, K. M., & Teague, G. M. (2021). Integrative STEM education and leadership for student success. In F. English (Ed.), *The Palgrave Handbook of Educational Leadership and Management Discourse* (pp. 1–20). Palgrave Macmillan. https://doi.org/10.1007/978-3-030-39666-4_36-1

Great Schools Partnership. (2015). *The glossary of education reform for journalists, parents, and community members: Mission and vision.* https://www.edglossary.org/mission-and-vision/

Hawaii State Department of Education. (n.d.). *Zones of school innovation.* http://www.hawaiipublicschools.org/VisionForSuccess/AdvancingEducation/milestones/RaceToTheTop/Pages/ZSI.aspx

Hui Hoʻoleimaluō. (2020). *Hui Hoʻoleimaluō.* https://www.huihooleimaluo.com/

Indiana Department of Education. (2021). *Indiana STEM education: Science, technology, engineering, and mathematics.* https://www.in.gov/doe/students/stem-school-certification/

Katehi, L., Pearson, G., & Feder, M. (2009). The status and nature of K–12 engineering education in the United States. *The Bridge, 39*(3), 5–10. https://www.nae.edu/File.aspx?id=16147

Katherine Johnson STEM Academy. (2020). *Our vision, mission, and values.* Los Angeles Unified School District, Board of Education. https://kjstemacademy.org/vision

Kaui, T. M. (2016). *Developing cultural competence and promoting culturally responsive teaching in STEAM educators of Native Hawaiian students.* [Doctoral dissertation]. Virginia Tech. http://hdl.handle.net/10919/79845

LaForce, M., Nobel, E., King, H., Century, J., Blackwell, C., Holt, S., Ibrahim, A., & Loo, S. (2016). The eight essential elements of inclusive STEM high schools. *International Journal of STEM Education, 3*(21), 1–11. https://doi.org/10.1186/s40594-016-0054-z

Nā Hunaahi. (2020). *About: Mission.* http://nahunaahi.org/about.html

National Center on Safe Supportive Learning Environments. (2020). *Family-school-community partnerships.* American Institutes for Research. https://safesupportivelearning.ed.gov/training-technical-assistance/education-level/early-learning/family-school-community-partnerships

R. B. Hudson STEAM Academy. (2020). *Selma City Schools: R. B. Hudson STEAM Academy.* https://www.selmacityschools.org/rbhudsonmiddleschool_home.aspx

Rose, M. A., Geesa, R. L., & Stith, K. (2019). STEM leader excellence: A modified Delphi study of critical skills, competencies, and qualities. *Journal of Technology Education, 31*(1), 42–62. https://doi.org/10.21061/jte.v31i1.a.3

Sanders, M. E. (2012). Integrative STEAM education as “best practice.” In H. Middleton (Ed.), *Explorations of Best Practice in Technology, Design, & Engineering Education* (Vol. 2, pp. 103–117). Griffith Institute for Educational Research.

Shafer, L. (2018a). *Building a strong school culture.* Harvard Graduate School of Education. https://www.gse.harvard.edu/news/uk/18/09/building-strong-school-culture

Shafer, L. (2018b). *What makes a good school culture?* Harvard Graduate School of Education. https://www.gse.harvard.edu/news/uk/18/07/what-makes-good-school-culture

Smith, F., Mihalakis, V., & Slamp, A. (2017). *4 ways that leadership teams create conditions for success in schools.* Bill & Melinda Gates Foundation. http://k12education.gatesfoundation.org/blog/school-leadership-teams-create-conditions-success-in-schools/

Sturgis, C., & Casey, K. (2018). *Quality principles for competency-based education.* https://aurora-institute.org/wp-content/uploads/Quality-Principles-Book.pdf

Ward, R. E., & Burke, M. A. (2004). *Improving achievement in low-performing schools: Key results for school leaders.* Corwin. https://us.corwin.com/en-us/nam/improving-achievement-in-low-performing-schools/book226440

3

Equity, Diversity, and Inclusion within Integrative STEM Education

Rachel Louise Geesa, Mary Annette Rose, Krista Marie Stith, Kendra Lowery, and Joanne Caniglia

The rationale for integrative STEM in PK–12 education is typically framed in terms of an economic necessity, such as "education in the STEM subjects is vital not only to sustaining the innovation capacity of the United States but also as a foundation for successful employment, including but not limited to work in the STEM fields" (Honey et al., 2014, p. vii).

Yet, in the age of a global pandemic (i.e., coronavirus disease 2019 [COVID-19]), climate change, and conflicts that arise among an increasingly heterogenous population, the rationale should also include the potential of integrative STEM to enhance social responsibility. Socially responsible practices promote respect, self-determination, and the affirmation of human agency for themselves and others in a diverse society (Bell, 2016). Bell (2016) characterized social justice as a goal and a process, resulting in equitable fulfillment of the needs of all social identity groups.

Education for social responsibility raises awareness about the interdependencies between innovation and unequal distribution of burdens and rewards that are placed on people, workers, natural resources, and ecosystems. Educators promote the building of inquiry and analytical skills that enable students to recognize social inequities and environmental degradation, as well as develop the communication and participation skills required to contribute to the welfare of their community and the conservation of resources that sustain them.

Researchers, however, have documented many instances where gaps exist in access to quality STEM education and representation in STEM occupations when analyzed by various identity categories, such as race, gender, and socioeconomic status (SES) (Baye & Monseur, 2016; Canning et al., 2019; Ireland et al., 2018; Martinez & Gayfield, 2019). In addition, the practices and structure of schools may contribute to greater social inequities. For instance, stratifying students based on mathematics and science achievement may perpetuate social and academic marginalization within schools.

This chapter addresses two areas of integrative STEM in PK–12 education. It sheds light on issues related to equity, diversity, and inclusion and offers implementation strategies for educational leaders to enhance accessibility paths for *all* students to explore and experience integrative STEM education.

EQUITY, DIVERSITY, AND INCLUSION ISSUES

Social and economic disparities influence equitable access to and retention in integrative STEM programming offered by schools. These inequities have resulted in achievement gaps. The *Science and Engineering Indicators* (National Science Board, 2019) show achievement disparities among a national cohort by demographic indices, including ethnicity, gender, race, and SES. These gaps are evident throughout the PK–12 experience. Specific results from the National Science Board (2019) include:

- A 9-point mathematics gap between low- and high-SES elementary students at the beginning of kindergarten; a 13-point mathematics gap by the end of their 5th grade year; and a 29-point mathematics gap by the end of their 8th grade year;
- Asian students tend to outperform students of other races (e.g., White/Caucasian, Black/African American, Hispanic) in all grades; and
- Black/African Americans and underserved students do not enter college at the same rate as their White/Caucasian counterparts, which, reduces the diversity of the STEM labor force. (pp. 7–8)

Martinez and Gayfield (2019) used an intersectional framework to analyze the combined interaction of sex, race, and ethnicity within the STEM workforce. An intersectional lens takes into account the intersections or interactions of a person's multiple identities, instead of exploring individual identities. This is important because when groups of multiple identities are aggregated within the results of one identity, they are rendered invisible.

As Ireland et al. (2018) explained regarding Black women and girls in STEM fields, "when the unique experiences of Black women and girls are hidden in aggregate results, their intersectional experiences are largely ignored" (p. 228). Martinez and Gayfield (2019) found five combinations that were underrepresented in STEM occupations relative to their general population, including White women, Hispanic women, Black women, Hispanic men, and Black men. Furthermore, these findings indicated that regardless of race and ethnicity, "men had higher median earnings than their female counterparts" (p. 17).

Barriers faced by those attempting to enter STEM employment differ for people of different genders, races, and ethnicities. For example, a Pew Research Center (Funk & Parker, 2018) survey indicated that the "lack of encouragement for girls and Blacks and Hispanics to pursue STEM from an early age" was a major reason for underrepresentation in some STEM areas (para. 38). In another study demonstrating the role that faculty play in outcomes for students, Canning et al. (2019) found that STEM university faculty who believed that ability is fixed (not malleable) had larger racial achievement gaps compared to growth mindset faculty.

Educational leaders and STEM educators should take these barriers and unequal outcomes into account as they design and implement curriculum and instruction (Geesa et al., 2020, 2021; Rose et al., 2019). Integrative STEM education programs can support social responsibility while operationalizing the principles of equity and inclusiveness throughout the school culture (see Figure 3.1).

Educational leaders should inspire and direct these efforts. Therefore, they must understand how characteristics of the school culture (e.g., power relationships, curriculum, materials, patterns of classroom interactions) and beliefs and attitudes of school personnel may influence pedagogical practices that can support or inhibit the academic success of all students. Educational leaders must strive to create equitable and inclusive

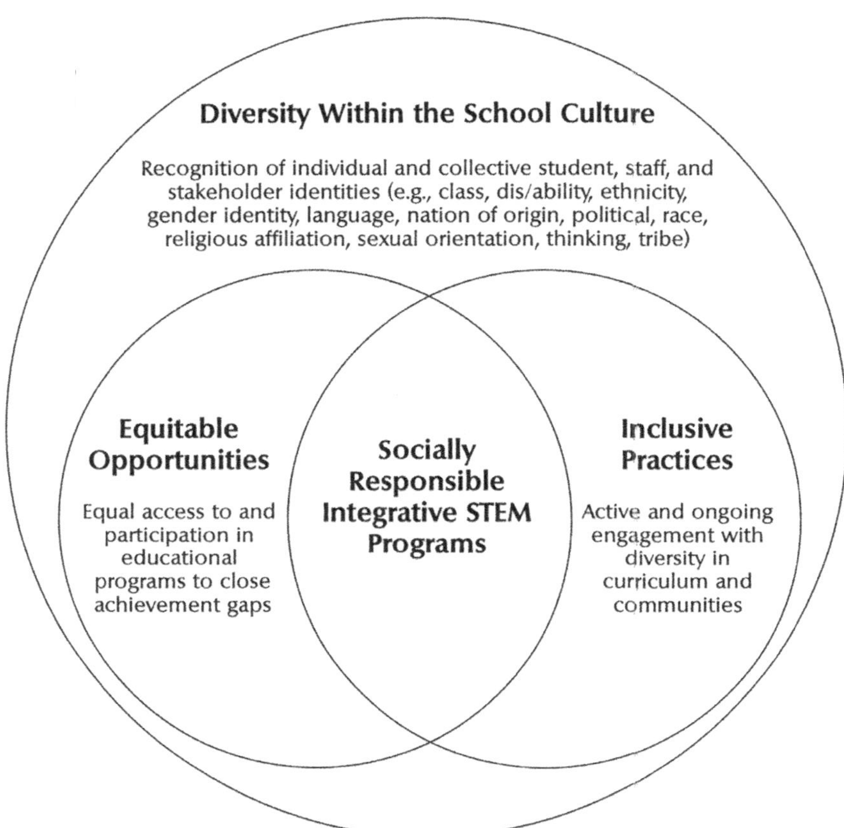

Figure 3.1. Socially responsible integrative STEM programs.

integrative STEM programs. Otherwise, programs will likely perpetuate existing patterns of discrimination, low expectations, cultural bias, and disparities in achievement and access to educational and occupational opportunities.

PROMISING STRATEGIES FOR EDUCATIONAL LEADERS

Through *inclusive practices*, educational leaders can attempt to address these systemic problems by working collaboratively with the entire school population—educators, school counselors, community partners, and other staff—to analyze the culture and develop more equitable paths to success for diverse populations of learners. The goal of inclusive practices is to communicate the belief that all students "belong and are able to thrive" (Johnson, 2019, p. 208) within the school and community, while decreasing school-based patterns that perpetuate divides between groups based on demographics. The following strategies show promise for contributing to a culture of inclusion relative to integrative STEM.

Examining Disparities

An examination of disparities is often understood through a critical theoretical lens that orients one toward analyzing the effects of power and privilege within and between different social groups, individuals, and institutions (Ireland et al., 2018). Intersectional data analysis is essential for equity-oriented educational leaders to present an accurate portrait of the experiences of members of "intersecting marginalized groups" in their school or district and monitor progress toward disrupting inequitable practices (Ireland et al., 2018, p. 229).

Data sources to be analyzed include demographics, perceptions of the school by stakeholders (e.g., students, educators), school activities and processes of the district or school, and achievement test results. Data tools available to educational leaders may be predetermined by the district, but additional data tools are available to further investigate equity and inclusion from local, district, state, and publicly available databases.

The Data Equity Walk, developed by The Education Trust (2015, 2020), is an example of intersectional analysis. This exercise provides an opportunity for educational leaders, educators, students, community members, and other stakeholders to better understand and discuss educational data and equity issues within 45 to 60 minutes. Participants conducting a Data Equity Walk discuss, review, and analyze data related to achievement and opportunity gaps, in addition to educational outcomes and school climate.

Guiding questions for participants during a Data Equity Walk include:

1. What are your general reactions to the data? What questions do these data raise for you?
2. What's the story behind the data? Does this relate to any personal experiences you've had?
3. What further information would be helpful?

4. What solutions can you think of to address the issues raised by these data? (The Education Trust, 2015, slide 1)

These guiding questions are applicable in multiple educational contexts; however, educational leaders could use them to consider equity, diversity, and inclusion issues in integrative STEM education and their academic programs.

For example, an equity audit (Skrla et al., 2004) of student subgroups by single and intersectional identity categories of participation in STEM courses would yield information related to the equity dimension of the framework in Figure 3.1. Results of the equity walk could be the focal point for reflecting on potential barriers to equitable access to STEM courses and prompt solution-finding to remove identified barriers.

Inclusive STEM Schools

Traditionally, the academically highest performing students are accepted to STEM-focused magnet schools or academies that include an application process where priority may be placed on grade-point averages and state standardized assessment scores. Inclusive STEM schools, however, recruit and enroll based on student interest and motivations. Table 3.1 shows students' racial representation of three schools identified within the 2020 Best High School Rankings (U.S. News & World Report, 2020) and three schools identified as inclusive STEM schools by Lynch et al. (2018).

From the percentages of students' racial representation in these schools, one may infer how selection of students in the identified "best" STEM high schools, based on prior academic performance, can continue to perpetuate the achievement gap in STEM. However, high-quality STEM does not need to be relegated to the schools identified as best in the nation by U.S. News & World Report.

Inclusive STEM schools provide high-quality STEM programming and have been suggested as a possible solution for "equity and social mobility gaps in STEM" (LaForce et al., 2016; Lynch et al., 2018, p. 713). Means et al. (2017) found that students from inclusive STEM schools were more likely to report they received rigorous instruction and engaged in project-based work than students who attended comparison (neighborhood)

Table 3.1. Comparison of Racial Representation Among Six United States STEM High Schools

School	*American Indian/ Alaskan Native*	*Asian*	*Black*	*Hawaiian Native/ Pacific Islander*	*Hispanic/ Latino*	*Two or more races*	*White*
Rated Best STEM High Schools (U.S. News & World Report, 2020)							
The Early College at Guilford, Greensboro, North Carolina	0.0%	43.0%	9.0%	0.0%	3.0%	5.0%	41.0%
Basis Chandler, Chandler, Arizona	0.4%	77.0%	4.0%	0.1%	2.0%	2.0%	15.0%
Monta Vista High School, Cupertino, California	0.1%	80.0%	4.0%	0.1%	0.2%	3.0%	13.0%
Inclusive STEM Schools (Lynch et al., 2018)							
Chicago High School for Agricultural Science, Chicago, Illinois	<1%	<1%	38.9%	<1%	24.1%	4.2%	31.7%
Wayne School of Engineering, Goldsboro, North Carolina	N/A	0.6%	30.8%	N/A	6.8%	14.5%	47.4%
Gary and Jerri-Ann Jacob High Tech High, San Diego, California	1.0%	7.4%	10.6%	6.4%	41.3%	0.2%	33.0%

Note: These schools were randomly selected from "Best STEM High Schools," by U.S. News & World Report, 2020 (https://www.usnews.com/education/best-high-schools/national-rankings/stem); and "Understanding Inclusive STEM High Schools as Opportunity Structures for Underrepresented Students: Critical Components," by S. J. Lynch, E. P. Burton, T. Behrend, A. House, M. Ford, N. Spillane, S. Matray, E. Han, and B. Means, 2018, *Journal of Research in Science Teaching*, 55(5), pp. 712–748 (https://doi.org/10.1002/tea.21437).

schools. Inclusive schools are also diverse in student demographics, such as the schools studied by Lynch et al. (2018) in Table 3.1.

Peters-Burton et al. (2014) explained that two crucial components of inclusive schools are (a) to support students to pursue STEM careers through "bridge programs, tutoring programs, extended school day, extended school year, or looping" (p. 67); and (b) to design a STEM mission with stated goals to prepare all students for success in STEM and recruit students who are underserved. Educational leaders may find transferrable strategies by studying current inclusive STEM schools and observing how curricula, structures, and enacted visions to increase underrepresented student groups' entries into STEM pipelines can be implemented.

In 2009, the National Inventors Hall of Fame STEM (NIHF-STEM) Middle School in Akron, Ohio opened (Akron Public Schools, 2020b). NIHF-STEM High School opened three years later (Akron Public Schools, 2020a). This open admissions high school enrolls about 100 ninth-grade students each year in its STEM-focused curriculum (Akron Public Schools, 2020b). By studying both the middle and high school, educational leaders may gain insights of ways to make schools inclusive and STEM-focused.

The NIHF-STEM Middle School vision includes a focus on STEM education to provide students opportunities to invent and think creatively, while the mission is "to nurture a community of empowered learners who will succeed in a global society" (Akron Public Schools, 2020b, Mission section). Community partnerships are critical, and the high school established working relationships with companies and academic institutions within Akron (e.g., Invent Now, City of Akron, University of Akron) for all students to have job-related experiences (Akron Public Schools, 2020b).

NIHF-STEM High School and Middle School opens its learning facilities to students, families, and other community members by providing spaces and educational programming for individuals and groups. These include inclusive, afterschool enrichment programs for students, such as Cyberpatriot Challenge Team, Kidwind Challenge, and Soap Box Derby Club (Akron Public Schools, 2020b, 2020c).

Understanding Students' Funds of Knowledge

Educational leaders and educators should be familiar with cultural and social aspects of their students' lives in order to enhance their educational outcomes. Students' *funds of knowledge* include their academic and personal background and experiences, skills, and cultural interactions in social settings and global perspectives (Hogg, 2011; Llopart & Esteban-Guitart, 2018; Vélez-Ibáñez & Greenberg, 1992).

Moll (2014) identified three elements crucial for understanding students' funds of knowledge that include (a) research through home visits to build relationships and identify cultural family resources; (b) classroom integration of student interests, activities, and skills that take place outside of school; and (c) study group meetings for educators, leaders, and researchers to review and analyze findings from household and classroom practices.

Educational leaders can encourage educators to integrate students' funds of knowledge into their classroom practices. Students should be encouraged to make learning relevant based on their interests and backgrounds (Johnson & Johnson, 2016). For instance, science educators may include personal and community goals for students within the scientific inquiry process because personal interest is key to generating interest and engagement in learning science. Furthermore, criticisms of science curriculum that does not adequately present and discuss the contributions of diverse scientists to the field should be rectified to include those underrepresented voices and contributions (National Research Council, 2012).

Educational leaders need to strengthen school, family, and community relationships. For example, leaders may share invitations for school and community events that enrich the knowledge, skills, and interests of students and their families regarding STEM initiatives. Research on the various funds of knowledge among families reveals possibilities for ways to integrate this knowledge into content and assessments. For example, children who grow up in agricultural communities may have a more sophisticated understanding of nature than their urban and suburban peers (National Research Council, 2012).

Developing Growth and Asset-Based Mindsets about STEM Learning

Equity and inclusion in STEM education may also be enhanced by educational leaders who model and promote reflection about their mindset regarding student capabilities in integrative STEM education. Mindset refers to one's beliefs about whether human traits, like talent and intelligence, are fixed or can be changed or grown (Canning et al., 2019; Dweck, 2008).

Educators and leaders who adopt fixed mindsets believe that intelligence and ability are innate qualities that may not be further developed (Canning et al., 2019). Valencia (2010) explained that this deficit thinking model posits "that the student who fails in school does so because of his/her internal deficits or deficiencies" (pp. 6–7) that manifest as low academic achievement, low motivation, and misbehaviors. However, educational leaders and educators "who espouse growth mindset beliefs endorse the idea that ability is malleable and can be developed through persistence, good strategies, and quality mentoring" (Canning et al., 2019, p. 1).

Dismantling deficit thinking should occur in tandem with the development and operationalization of a growth mindset. Educational leaders should encourage educators to shift from a deficit-based model to an asset-based model of thinking that focuses on strengths and competencies (e.g., what educators/students can do) and aligns with a growth mindset (Renkly & Bertolini, 2018; Rose, 2006).

Asset-based thinking and deficit-based thinking should not be confused as "positive" perceptions and "negative" perceptions of student capacities; instead, these thinking systems centralize on opposing needs and foci of students.

Asset-based thinking characteristics include being:

- Driven by student strengths,
- Focused on student opportunities, and
- Attentive in asking, "In what ways can we build upon this student's present assets and talents?"

Deficit-based thinking characteristics include being:

- Driven by student needs,
- Focused on student problems and challenges, and

- Attentive in asking, "What is missing, and must be found, for this student to be successful?"

One way to facilitate such a shift to asset-based thinking is through professional learning opportunities. Although asset-based thinking should to be weaved throughout educators' practices, one concrete place to start is through professional learning on topics of equity, diversity, and inclusion (e.g., culturally relevant pedagogy, explicit and implicit bias, social justice). Additionally, professional learning can be optimized when constructed among groups rather than individual faculty members.

Scanlan and Theoharis (2015) asserted, "the sociocultural learning theory of communities of practice (COPs) holds that much of what we learn occurs through purposeful interactions with others" (p. 5). With schoolwide goals, educational leaders can guide others to embrace diversity within their classrooms and share meaningful integrative STEM curricula and programs with all students (e.g., see Figures 3.2. and 3.3), and engage in data-based assessment of their progress towards equity and inclusion, emanating from asset-based frameworks (Skrla et al., 2004).

Educational leaders should include the following elements in the creation of professional development:

- encourage educators to recognize their biases and consider ways to address these biases for more equitable learning opportunities in schools,
- emphasize that mistakes and failures pinpoint opportunities for learning as part of a learning cycle,
- make curriculum challenging and relevant for all students, and
- provide opportunities for educators to discuss the diverse needs of their students and devise integrative STEM learning experiences to address these needs.

To demonstrate possibilities for how raising awareness and unpacking deficit thinking might manifest itself within schools, educational leaders could share fictitious examples of an educator's deficit-based perspective and asset-based perspective of the same student, such as:

Figure 3.2. High school students conducting an experiment in the chemistry lab. iStockphoto LP.

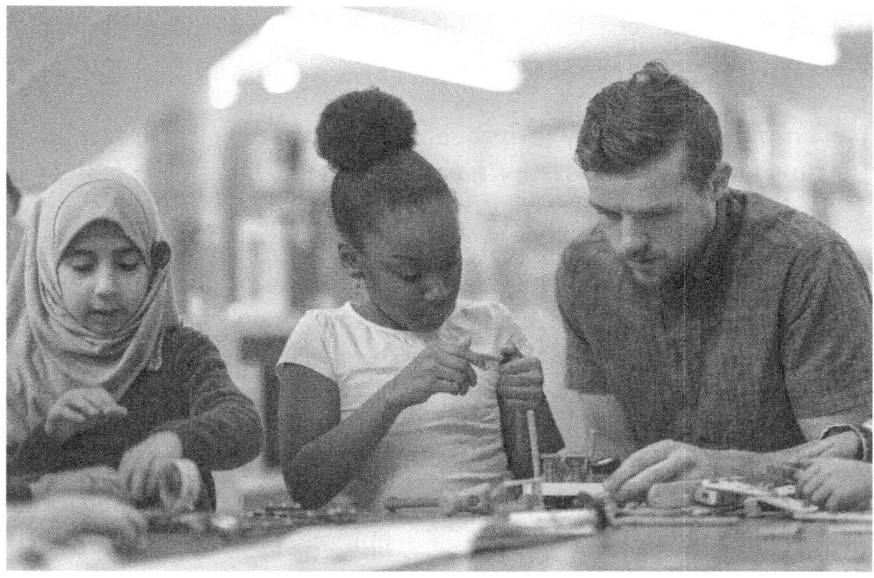

Figure 3.3. Elementary school students building circuits in the library. iStockphoto LP.

- *Deficit perspective:* Monique will be a great asset to your engineering team. She can prepare the oral and video presentation of your team's solution to the design challenge. You boys can assemble the robot and troubleshoot the computer code.
- *Asset perspective:* Let's take a moment to list the skills you individually bring to this engineering challenge. Make sure you consider such skills as being organized, detail-oriented, and having fine-motor skills. Monique, these skills are especially useful when assembling the small parts of the robot.

Educators could be asked to (a) discuss the underlying biases made about Monique in both perspectives, (b) identify how the educator in the second example mitigated possible bias when discussing roles, and (c) brainstorm how the educator in the first example could acknowledge and address the mistake of assuming the role for the female student.

INCLUSIVE PRACTICES

There are multiple pathways to provide equitable opportunities for students to experience integrative STEM education and programs (Means et al., 2017). Inclusive practices in integrative STEM should include curriculum, instruction, and assessments that ensure students with various language fluencies, abilities, learning backgrounds, and personal experiences have equitable pathways in their education.

Universal Design for Learning: Special Needs and Language Learners

Students with special needs and English language learners may require specialized programs or individualized learning plans that augment the general education program (e.g., special education, gifted education). Educational leaders need to guide educators and stakeholders to accommodate students at various intellectual, developmental, and physical abilities and provide all students quality integrative STEM experiences that nurture their full potential.

Educational leaders may work within curriculum frameworks and carry out the curriculum design process to integrate STEM disciplines.

One framework that supports accessibility for all students is Universal Design for Learning (UDL; Meyer et al., 2014). UDL provides learning options for students at all ability levels and includes three principles for educational leaders and educators to use to address the needs of students: "1) provide multiple means of engagement; 2) provide multiple means of representation; and 3) provide multiple means of action and expression" (Meyer et al., 2014, p. 4).

Educational leaders can refer to UDL principles and implement this framework in their schools and districts. Educators may find new or different resources, assistive technologies, and professional learning opportunities they may use to put UDL into practice in their schools and programs. With support from educators, staff, and stakeholders, educational leaders can provide engaging integrative STEM learning environments for as many students as possible.

It should also be noted that students who are emerging English language learning or with the specialized language of STEM disciplines may need additional or differentiated forms of support to develop more confidence and understanding of STEM concepts. Inclusivity in STEM classrooms requires the support of educators to engage all students in collaborative learning activities using various forms of communication (e.g., verbal, written, demonstration) in STEM practices (Powell et al., 2018).

Encouraging Gender-Responsive STEM Education

Educational leaders should identify and address gender inequities in their schools. In 2017, the United Nations Educational, Scientific, and Cultural Organization (UNESCO; 2017) commissioned an international study of gender inequality. The study examined the trends of women and girls in STEM occupations and learning, factors influencing their STEM participation and achievement, and potential interventions at the individual, family, school, and societal levels in STEM education.

These findings raised considerations for educational leaders to facilitate integrative STEM to increase girls' and women's interest in and engagement with STEM education. UNESCO (2017) recommended several school-level interventions:

- recruiting male and female teachers,
- removing gender bias from learning materials,
- facilitating access to gender responsive career counseling (e.g., girls' access to counselors to increase their interest and support in STEM),
- linking girls to mentorship opportunities, and
- expanding access to scholarships and fellowships. (p. 64–69)

SCHOOL STAKEHOLDER ENGAGEMENT IN STEM

Educational programs outside regular school hours are becoming available to students (National Research Council, 2015), and educational leaders can also involve families and community members in integrative STEM education opportunities. According to STEM Next (2020), "families play a vital role in raising youth awareness of the value of STEM and in brokering youth participation in activities that build STEM interest and skills" (para. 4).

Although hosting family STEM nights or events at schools is important, it is also important to listen to stakeholders to understand their needs and thoughts related to STEM learning. To engage caregivers, families, and others in students' STEM education, the New York Hall of Science (NYSCI) and the Oregon Museum of Science and Industry (OMSI) develop programs with families by "customizing programs that build capacity in communities" (Kekelis & Sammet, 2017, p. 2).

These organizations also identified strategies for educators to promote stakeholder involvement in STEM learning, including creating multigenerational- and multicaretaker-oriented programs, helping families make connections between STEM learning and STEM careers, facilitating exposure to diverse role models, and starting STEM learning early.

From these intentional approaches to include families and community members in STEM education throughout students' educational programs, Kekelis and Sammet (2017) found that "families expressed interest in programs for the entire family, opportunities to interact with people in their native language, and an environment where they feel comfortable and not out of their depth" (p. 3). Educational leaders can use similar approaches to create inclusive environments for all stakeholders and join STEM learning in school and home environments.

National research programs and service organizations facilitate programs and services in collaboration with families to bring STEM into their homes. Educational leaders can share many of these resources:

- Afterschool Alliance (2020): Supports working families by providing afterschool programs to guide and enhance students' learning and provide a safe place for students to be;
- Global Family Research Project (2019): Promotes strategies and provides resources for students to experience success in various environments through global exchange; and
- National Association of Family, School, and Community Services (2020): Promotes child development and student achievement through "high impact family and community engagement" (para. 2).

Educational leaders must be mindful that students may need additional financial support to access resources and participate in STEM programs. Families may struggle with transportation, childcare, work conflicts, and registration fees that serve as barriers for STEM-focused opportunities, as well.

CONCLUSION

Inclusive integrative STEM practices support all students to learn content and become engaged in STEM learning. Educators are essential in supporting and facilitating student motivation and engagement. Educational leaders can set a tone of and value for social responsibility that embraces inclusion and a change of mindsets that have the potential to shape the development of equitable STEM learning.

Educational leaders can provide opportunities by creating equitable and inclusive schools, incorporating project-based learning, strengthening professional learning programs, reaching out to families and communities, and bringing out-of-school programs to the schools. Underlying all these efforts is the necessity to examine intersectional data of diverse student subgroups to make informed decisions based on existing research and experience working with educators, students, and families to create an environment of equity that welcomes all students in learning STEM content.

REFERENCES

Afterschool Alliance. (2020). *Afterschool Alliance.* http://www.afterschoolalliance.org/

Akron Public Schools. (2020a). *National Inventors Hall of Fame STEM High School (NIHF-STEM).* https://stemhigh.akronschools.com/

Akron Public Schools. (2020b). *National Inventors Hall of Fame STEM Middle School (NIHF-STEM).* https://stemmiddle.akronschools.com/

Akron Public Schools. (2020c). *National Inventors Hall of Fame STEM Middle School (NIHF-STEM): Extended learning opportunities.* https://stemmiddle.akronschools.com/programs/extended_learning_opportunities

Baye, A., & Monseur, C. (2016). Gender differences in variability and extreme scores in an international context. *Large-scale Assessments in Education, 4*(1), 1–16. https://doi.org/10.1186/s40536-015-0015-x

Bell, L. A. (2016). Theoretical foundations for social justice education. In M. Adams, L. Bell, D. J. Goodman, & K. Y. Joshi (Eds.), *Teaching for diversity and social justice* (3rd ed., pp. 3–26). Routledge.

Canning, E. A., Muenks, K., Green, D. J., & Murphy, M. C. (2019). STEM faculty who believe ability is fixed have larger racial achievement gaps and inspire less student motivation in their classes. *Science Advances, 5*(2). 1–7. https://doi.org/10.1126/sciadv.aau4734

Dweck, C. S. (2008). *Mindset: The new psychology of success*. Random House Digital, Inc.

Funk, C., & Parker, K. (2018, January 9). *Women and men in STEM often at odds over workplace equity.* Pew Research Center. https://www.pewsocialtrends.org/2018/01/09/women-and-men-in-stem-often-at-odds-over-workplace-equity/

Geesa, R. L., Stith, K. M., & Rose, M. A. (2020). Preparing school and district leaders for success in developing and facilitating integrative STEM in higher education. *Journal of Research on Leadership Education*, 1–21. https://doi.org/10.1177/1942775120962148

Geesa, R. L., Stith, K. M., & Teague, G. M. (2021). Integrative STEM education and leadership for student success. In F. English (Ed.), *The Palgrave Handbook of Educational Leadership and Management Discourse* (pp. 1–20). Palgrave Macmillan. https://doi.org/10.1007/978-3-030-39666-4_36-1

Global Family Research Project. (2019). *Global Family Research Project.* https://globalfrp.org/

Hogg, L. (2011). Funds of knowledge: An investigation of coherence within the literature. *Teaching and Teacher Education, 27*(3), 666–677. https://doi.org/10.1016/j.tate.2010.11.005

Honey, M., Pearson, G., & Schweingruber, H. (Eds). (2014). *STEM integration in K–12 education: Status, prospects, and an agenda for research*. The National Academies Press.

Ireland, D. T., Freeman, K. E., Winston-Proctor, C. E., DeLaine, K. D., Lowe, S. M., & Woodson, K. M. (2018). (Un)hidden figures: A synthesis of research examining the intersectional experience of Black women and girls in STEM education. *Review of Research in Education, 42*(1), 226–254. https://doi.org/10.3102/0091732X18759072

Johnson, E. J., & Johnson, A. B. (2016). Enhancing academic investment through home-school connections and building on ELL students' scholastic funds of knowledge. *Journal of Language & Literacy Education, 12*(1), 104–121. https://files.eric.ed.gov/fulltext/EJ1100968.pdf

Johnson, K. M. S. (2019). Implementing inclusive practices in an active learning STEM classroom. *Advances in Physiology Education*, *43*(2), 207–210. https://doi.org/10.1152/advan.00045.2019

Kekelis, L. & Sammet, K. (2017). *STEM careers + families: Learning from centers and museums.* STEM Next Opportunity Fund. https://stemnext.org/wp-content/uploads/2017/12/Case-Study_FinalV2.pdf

LaForce, M., Noble, E., King, H., Century, J., Blackwell, C., Holt, S., Ibrahim, A., & Loo S. (2016). The eight essential elements of inclusive STEM high schools. *International Journal of STEM Education, 3*(21), 1–11. https://doi.org/10.1186/s40594-016-0054-z

Llopart, M., & Esteban-Guitart, M. (2018). Funds of knowledge in 21st century societies: inclusive educational practices for under-represented students. A literature review. *Journal of Curriculum Studies, 50*(2), 145–161. https://doi.org/10.1080/00220272.2016.1247913

Lynch, S. J., Burton, E. P., Behrend, T., House, A., Ford, M., Spillane, N., Matray, S., Han, E., & Means, B. (2018). Understanding inclusive STEM high schools as opportunity structures for underrepresented students: Critical components. *Journal of Research in Science Teaching, 55*(5), 712–748. https://doi.org/10.1002/tea.21437

Martinez, A. & Gayfield, A. (2019). *The intersectionality of sex, race, and Hispanic origin in the STEM workforce.* Social, Economic, and Housing Statistics Division, United States Census Bureau. https://www.census.gov/library/working-papers/2019/demo/SEHSD-WP2018-27.html

Means, B., Wang, H., Wei, X., Lynch, S., Peters, V., Young, V., & Allen, C. (2018). Expanding STEM opportunities through inclusive STEM-focused high schools. *Science Education, 101*(5), 681–715. https://doi.org/10.1002/sce.21281

Meyer, A., Rose, D. H., & Gordon, D. (2014). *Universal design for learning: Theory and practice.* CAST Professional Publishing. http://castpublishing.org/books-media/udl-theory-and-practice/

Moll, L. C. (2014). *L. S. Vygotsky and education.* Routledge.

National Association for Family, School, and Community Engagement. (2020). *Family engagement defined.* https://nafsce.org/page/definition

National Research Council. (2012). *A framework for K–12 science education: Practices, crosscutting concepts, and core ideas.* The National Academies Press. https://doi.org/10.17226/13165

National Research Council. (2015). *Identifying and supporting productive STEM programs in out-of-school settings.* The National Academies Press. https://doi.org/10.17226/21740

National Science Board. (2019). Elementary and secondary mathematics and science education. *Science and Engineering Indicators 2020.* NSB-2019-6. https://ncses.nsf.gov/pubs/nsb20196/

Peters-Burton, E. E., Lynch, S. J., Behrend, T. S., & Means, B. B. (2014). Inclusive STEM high school design: 10 critical components. *Theory Into Practice, 53*(1), 64–71. https://doi.org/10.1080/00405841.2014.862125

Powell, A., Nielsen, N., Butler, M., Buxton, C., Johnson, O., Ketterlin-Geller, L., & McCulloch, C. (2018). *Creating inclusive preK-12 STEM learning environments.* Education Development Center. http://cadrek12.org/sites/default/files/Creating_Inclusive_PreK12_STEM_Learning_Environments.pdf

Renkly, S., & Bertolini, K. (2018). Shifting the paradigm from deficit oriented schools to asset based models: Why leaders need to promote an asset orientation in our schools. *Empowering Research for Education, 2*(1), 23–27. https://openprairie.sdstate.edu/ere/vol2/iss1/4

Rose, H. A. (2006). Asset-based development for child and youth care. *Reclaiming Children and Youth, 14*(4), 236-240. http://www.iicrd.org/sites/default/files/resources/Asset-based_Development_for_child_and_youthcare_0.pdf

Rose, M. A., Geesa, R. L., & Stith, K. (2019). STEM leader excellence: A modified Delphi study of critical skills, competencies, and qualities. *Journal of Technology Education, 31*(1), 42–62. https://doi.org/10.21061/jte.v31i1.a.3

Scanlan, M., & Theoharis, G. (2015). Introduction: Intersectionality and educational leadership. In G. Theoharis & M. Scanlan, (Eds.) *Leadership for Increasingly Diverse Schools*, (pp. 1–11). Routledge.

Skrla, L., Scheurich, J. J., Garcia, J., & Nolly, G. (2004). Equity audits: A practical leadership tool for developing equitable and excellent schools. *Educational Administration Quarterly, 40*(1), 133–161. https://doi.org/10.1177/0013161X03259148

STEM Next. (2020). *The family engagement project.* STEM Next Opportunity Fund. https://stemnext.org/engaging-families/

The Education Trust. (2015, March). *Guiding questions* [PowerPoint Slides]. https://west.edtrust.org/wp-content/uploads/2015/11/Example-2-UC-Berkeley.pdf

The Education Trust. (2020). *Data Equity Walk Toolkit.* https://west.edtrust.org/wp-content/uploads/2015/11/Example-2-UC-Berkeley.pdf

United Nations Educational, Scientific, and Cultural Organization. (2017). *Cracking the code: girls' and women's education in science, technology, engineering and mathematics (STEM).* United Nations Educational, Scientific, and Cultural Organization. https://unesdoc.unesco.org/ark:/48223/pf0000253479

U.S. News & World Report. (2020). *Best STEM high schools.* https://www.usnews.com/education/best-high-schools/national-rankings/stem

Valencia, R. R. (2010). *Dismantling contemporary deficit thinking: Educational thought and practice.* Routledge.

Vélez-Ibáñez, C. G., & Greenberg, J. B. (1992). Formation and transformation of funds of knowledge among U.S.–Mexican households. *Anthropology & Education Quarterly*, *23*(4), 313–335. https://www.jstor.org/stable/3195869

4

Considerations for Integrative STEM Infrastructure and Programming

Michael E. Grubbs and Krista Marie Stith

In responding to STEM education teaching and learning practices, there have been calls to refine curriculum, pedagogy, and knowledge expectations for all students. As Brusic et al. (2019) report, STEM educational reform has resulted in considerable research efforts from the educational sector (e.g., Brown, 2012; Mizell & Brown, 2016) and the federal government (National Science & Technology Council, Committee on STEM Education, 2018).

Research on STEM education has largely investigated what is being taught, how educators are prepared, and measures of assessment for how students should and do learn. However, there have been fewer considerations at the school and district level to support integrative STEM infrastructure and programming. Integrative STEM values and practices (e.g., problem-/design-based learning, collaboration, creativity, innovation, experimentation, risk-taking, investigation, making) can be infused and supported by well-planned integrative STEM spaces.

This chapter presents considerations for creating school infrastructure and programming (i.e., the physical environment, scheduling, educational technology, and guidance) that supports integrative STEM education. An exemplar of developing and using collaborative laboratory spaces, equipped with technologies that enable inquiry, experimentation, and engineering will be shared. Lastly, recommendations of appropriate materials, resources, and technologies that facilitate integrative approaches to teaching and learning will be discussed.

CONTEXT CONSIDERATIONS

Each community serves a distinct population, economy, and region that varies in goals and resources. Consideration of the community and context can shape the facility, learning environment, practices, and student-level outcomes for a specific school. Therefore, educational leaders should review integrative STEM education infrastructure plans by collaboratively mapping their community resources against their school and classroom space needs. For example, a district closely associated with a car manufacturing plant may have a different infrastructure vision than a district closely associated with a national park.

Institutions of higher education, libraries, businesses and industries, governmental offices, military groups, organizations, agencies, and outreach centers can be community partners that support a school's integrative STEM infrastructure. Examples of community resources are donations or assistance to attain equipment and funding, providing expertise for infrastructure design, and invitations for educators to receive on-site professional learning experiences in STEM fields. These opportunities can provide a contextual direction for infrastructure transformation.

Type of School

As Kostourou (2014) makes reference to a 1944 speaking event when "Winston Churchill said during the rebuilding of the House of Commons, 'We shape our dwellings, and afterwards our dwellings shape us,' reflecting the relationship between the design of the built environment and our behavior both as individuals and a society" (p. 131). As educators begin to consider impacts of their learning space, it is important to point out existing models of STEM school infrastructure:

- elite or selective STEM-focused schools,
- inclusive STEM-focused schools,
- STEM-focused career and technical education schools or programs, and
- STEM programs in comprehensive schools that are not STEM-focused.

Whether designing or modifying an existing space to support an integrative STEM educational program, a natural starting point is to consider which of the four categories are envisioned. For example, an elective or selective school may be designed to emphasize Advanced Placement or college-bound routes, thus dictating a more academic-based approach. A regional career and technical center, however, may be designed with equipment that has been more thoroughly vetted through local partnerships, businesses, advisory councils, and needs documented in articulated credits with local community colleges.

SIGNATURE LEARNING AND PEDAGOGIES

Educational leaders have additional considerations they need to contemplate when planning for integrative STEM education in PK–12 schools (Geesa et al., 2020, 2021; Rose et al., 2019). One consideration is the signature pedagogies of multiple STEM content areas, and the impact it will have on the design of spaces and the selection of equipment, materials, and technology. Shulman (2005) defines signature pedagogies as "types of teaching that organize the fundamental ways in which future practitioners are educated for their new professions" (p. 52).

Consider the different approaches to training professionals within the following fields: medicine, culinary arts, and engineering. The signature pedagogy for educating medical doctors may take place in a health laboratory, using a scientific inquiry pedagogy with tissue-processing equipment. The signature pedagogy for educating chefs may take place in a culinary laboratory, using an experimental pedagogy with food processing equipment. The signature pedagogy for educating engineers could be in an engineering laboratory, using a design-based pedagogy, with material processing equipment. These signature pedagogies, though distinctly unique, can be integrated for PK–12 students so that they can experience the diverse action-oriented activities of developing STEM professionals.

Thinking about the signature pedagogies of scientists, technologists, engineers, and mathematicians is an excellent starting point for educational leaders to consider designing the physical space for fostering innovation and creative thinking, as well. For example, scientists must be proficient at science, but also be proficient in the interconnections of other disciplines (e.g., in technology to disseminate findings, engineering solutions to scientific problems, and mathematics to make sense of scientific phenomena).

Kelley and Knowles (2016) presented a model for considering how STEM content areas interrelate to situate STEM learning. Using a block-and-tackle metaphor of an integrated system, they propose that STEM educators develop a *community of practice* that applies the driving force that links scientific inquiry, engineering design, technological literacy, and mathematical thinking. As a community of practice is a group of individuals with shared passions and progress in creating new knowledge together, integrative STEM infrastructure should support students moving collaboratively with tools and instruments of multiple disciplines.

Dual-utility of the space(s) should consider (a) physical space and tools to support inquiry, design, and mathematical analyses; and (b) physical space for making, producing, experimenting, and testing. Both environments foster critical and creative thinking for students. Once the school's infrastructure goals, signature pedagogies, and utility of the space are identified, the infrastructure plan allows leaders to collaborate with stakeholders to assess and design the physical space.

Information Technology

The design and scientific inquiry process through the intentional application of integrative STEM content is at the core of integrative STEM. Therefore, a variety of opportunities for students to practice inquiry (e.g., reviewing the literature, accessing data sets and modeling tools, fostering critical thinking for problem- or project-based learning experiences) should be provided.

Technology infrastructure provides digital tools for schools and districts to connect educators and students to quality resources and content. Integrative STEM teaching and learning, in particular, requires robust information technology systems, management personnel, and privacy safeguards. The National Educational Technology Plan provides educational leaders information related to the construction and implementation of a comprehensive district educational plan (United States Department of Education, Office of Educational Technology, 2017a).

The plan begins with establishing a development team, setting school or district technology goals, and evaluating the current network infrastructure and available devices. Examples of a robust technology infrastructure include high-speed Internet access throughout the school; disseminating technological devices to students; and a management plan for responsible material use, student privacy, and school policies (United States Department of Education, Office of Educational Technology, 2017b).

High-speed Internet access that is reliable and scalable is needed to enable educators to leverage digital simulations, streaming video services, and virtual laboratories. Learning and assessments within distributed learning contexts should be equitable for all students to participate in activities in school and their home learning environment. Therefore, this network should extend high-speed connectivity to every handheld device in every instructional space, and possibly into the surrounding community.

A high-performance computer network and information technology staff are critical components to operationalizing principles of integrative STEM programs (e.g., innovation, collaboration, computational thinking, design). Information technology staff also provide cybersecurity measures to keep students and educators in a responsible digital learning space and help to maintain the technological infrastructure and student devices.

Thus, high-quality integrative STEM experiences encompass Internet-enabled collaborative tools, computer-aided design software, and digital library resources as essential components of integrative STEM inquiry. As these components are considered, careful selection of resources to represent multiple student groups should be undertaken. Students should have a variety of media to brainstorm, model, and communicate their inquiry and problem-solving journeys.

Learning Environment Furnishings

Leaders should ensure learning environments (e.g., classrooms, labs, makerspaces) are created with ample manipulative space and furniture. For example, fixed wall structures limit the autonomy of educators to rearrange the space for student-, group-, or educator-led activities. Rather, the spaces should allow for flexible learning areas (e.g., sliding dry erase boards, post-it paper charts, technology that allows for touch screen/sharing of calculations).

A multimedia lab with lighting and noise controls to support digital video and audio production by educators and students is especially useful for supporting teaching and informational materials. Flexibility in the design of learning environments is essential. Opportunities to use multipurpose furniture (e.g., tables with storage areas and dry erase tops) can facilitate collaboration and better use space throughout the classroom.

Making, Experimenting, and Testing in Learning Environments

Active learning environments where designing, making, experimenting, refining ideas, and testing solutions occurs should be considered as part of physical space in integrative STEM education (e.g., see Figures 4.1 and 4.2). Educational leaders need to consider areas that foster open-ended, collaborative design, and problem-solving endeavors for students to learn and apply more advanced discipline-centric practices.

Makerspaces, spaces for students to make and tinker with materials, are gaining interest in formal and informal learning spaces. However, leaders should be cognizant of challenges for a fluid integration of makerspace

Figure 4.1. Elementary students building and testing autonomous vehicles in a makerspace. iStockphoto LP.

Figure 4.2. High school students using a drafting table and computer-aided drawing (CAD) program to develop a solution to an engineering design challenge. iStockphoto LP.

teaching and learning culture within the large school culture (Shively et al., 2021). Decisions will include makerspace accessibility for students and educators, equipment and technologies, storage space, times and schedules to use the space, and maintenance and investment in equipment and inventory. An exemplar is provided later in the chapter of how educational leaders of a school collaborated with stakeholders to design a makerspace and current logistics within their programming.

EQUIPMENT AND MATERIALS

Equipment for planning and use within active learning spaces should cover a breadth and depth of needs for solving STEM problems through an integrative approach. Educational leaders should plan production area equipment based on basic and advanced needs and consider how space will evolve in response to industry and higher education changes.

Basic Equipment

There is a wide range of equipment that educational leaders should consider for integrative STEM education learning spaces. A list of educational specifications should be reviewed or created and disseminated to check for consistency across schools and programs. Equipment should first be provided that allows for basic processing of materials (e.g., scissors, hammers, glue guns, hand tools).

Traditional equipment for industrial arts/technology and engineering education settings should be provided (e.g., tabletop drill presses, band saws, scroll saws, planers, jigsaws, portable screwdrivers). This foundational equipment allows educators to capture an array of interests and skill sets of students and provides a starting point for educators transitioning from other content areas.

Students should be able to authentically think and work like STEM professionals, thus, equipment should be procured that address the practices in which those STEM professionals engage. Students are then positioned to authentically immerse in laboratory settings of multiple STEM fields using observation and data-gathering equipment (e.g., thermometers, microscopes) and analytical equipment (e.g., basic and advanced calculators).

Ideally, large collaborative settings are provided to all students. However, if a large space is not available, mobile carts can serve as an alternative to share equipment and materials among educators. Educators can be supported to design a section of their classrooms to use for integrative STEM activities, as well. A designated classroom table or workbench, for example, can be used for action-oriented processes. If possible, outdoor spaces can also serve as a location for collaborative problem-solving.

Advanced Equipment

Once educational leaders consider basic level equipment, they should expand upon the equipment list for alignment to advanced opportunities that connect to postsecondary education and workforce development. For example, advanced 3D printing, computer numerical control machines, laser engravers, or plasma cutters allow for authentic engineering design applications as students navigate the integrative STEM education experiences they are provided.

Additional equipment and educational technologies that enable authentic scientific investigations, data analysis, mathematical modeling, and communicating results should also be procured. Virtual modeling software, data-logging systems, centrifuge equipment, and advanced microscopes will extend learning opportunities and create a more authentic learning environment.

Materials

Upon selection of basic and advanced equipment, the materials available to educators and students should be the next step in the infrastructure plan. Educators should have ready access to materials for experimentation and modeling that are benign and easily processed (i.e., low-tech materials) or take a greater level of expertise and advanced equipment to manipulate (i.e., high-tech materials).

Educational leaders can designate an individual (e.g., STEM lab coordinator) to ensure labs and classrooms are well-stocked in advance of the school year, and a steady stream of provisions can be provided at various checkpoints (e.g., end of the quarter or grading period, halfway through the year, and as course enrollment increases). When additional items are needed, educators should have a form to request such materials.

Low-Tech Materials

Examples of low-tech materials that should be provided for fundamental integrative STEM education include balsa wood, adhesives, cardboard, dowel rods, plastic containers, string, fasteners, and simple machines.

High-Tech Materials

Opportunities for more advanced materials should be provided based on the experience level of the student, educator expertise, and specific learning environment for implementation. Educational leaders need to consider and monitor the degree to which high-tech materials are provided to ensure they are used appropriately and supporting the most applicable learning. High-tech materials can provide students with challenging and meaningful learning experiences by mastering advanced equipment needed for the materials. Examples of high-tech materials are metals, polymers, ceramics, and composites. A comprehensive list of examples of tools and instruments is included in Table 4.1.

Table 4.1. Functions of Tools and Instruments in Integrative STEM

Function	*Tool and Instrument Examples*
Coding	Arduinos, Bloxels, Littlebits, Makey Makey, Raspberry Pi starter kits, Spheros, Squishy Circuits
Combining	Clamps, drills, hot glue guns, wrenches
Forming	Dremel tools, Files, Rasps, Soldering irons
Material processing	Hot press, laser cutter, sewing machines, screen printer, 3D printer
Materials for student use (consumables)	Aluminum foil, balloons, cardboard, cardstock, ceramics, composites, copper tape with conductive adhesive, cotton balls, metals, newspaper, paint, paperclips, plaster, polymers, rubber bands, sand and soil, scrap paper, straws, string, tape (e.g., duct tape, moving tape), toothpicks, wood
Materials for student use (nonconsumables)	K'Nex, LED Lights, Legos, marbles, modeling clay, Play-Doh, writing utensils (e.g., pencils, pens, markers)
Measuring, analyzing, and testing	Analog and digital platform scales, indicator strips, micrometers, pipettes, rulers, tape measures, thermometers, Vernier probes, weight sets
Observing	Audio and visual equipment, binoculars, microscopes, 3D models
Safety	Aprons, ear plugs, first aid kits, gloves (chemical/liquid resistant/ insulating protection), headphones, safety glasses
Separating	Pliers, scissors, utility knives

Lastly, the space to support integrative STEM activities may need additional considerations if used for PK–12 grades. High schools are often unique in the course objectives that may require specific equipment whereas elementary and middle schools are often more general in their curricular frameworks and may not rely on specific equipment. The ability for educators to shift equipment and supply usage within a wide range of grade levels should be discussed collaboratively.

EXEMPLAR OF A COLLABORATIVE INTEGRATIVE STEM SPACE

Burris Laboratory School is a K–12 school in Muncie, Indiana, that opened a collaborative integrative STEM space in Fall 2018, referred to as the *Innovation Lab*. Prior to the initial designing of the Innovation Lab, the school's educational leaders and several educators visited multiple makerspaces and laboratory settings of other K–12 programs to gather ideas that could be transferrable to their own environment. A grant was awarded to pay for refurbishing the Innovation Lab from a former computer lab and classroom.

To prepare to use the space, the educators participated in extensive professional learning opportunities regarding creative thinking, design thinking, and Project Lead The Way's activity-, project-, and problem-based approach to instruction. During this time, the educators also provided a "wish list" of equipment and supplies needed for integrative STEM activities (e.g., construction tools, consumables, educational technologies, safety equipment).

With this information, several important decisions were made regarding the Innovation Lab by educational leaders to build the infrastructure and programming of a collaborative space for integrative STEM:

- The lab is outfitted with adjustable, movable furniture (e.g., work benches, seating, storage) that can be raised and lowered to accommodate K–12 students and those with special needs (see Figure 4.3).
- The lab is designed with signage to promote collaborative inquiry in integrative STEM (see Figure 4.4).
- The lab is equipped with a variety of educational technologies (e.g., computers, 3D printers, portable microphones, a speaker system) for both educator and student use.
- High-tech tools (e.g., laser cutter, hot press), low-tech tools (e.g., drills, hammers, wrenches), and educational kits (e.g., Makey Makey) support students as they design, make, and test models.
- Safety procedures are clearly displayed, and safety equipment is installed and accessible (e.g., HEPA/VOC filters, safety glasses, first aid kit).
- One educator serves as the lab manager, communicating with educational leaders regarding inventory and troubleshooting potential challenges.

Figure 4.3. Innovation Lab with adjustable, moveable furniture. Burris Laboratory School.

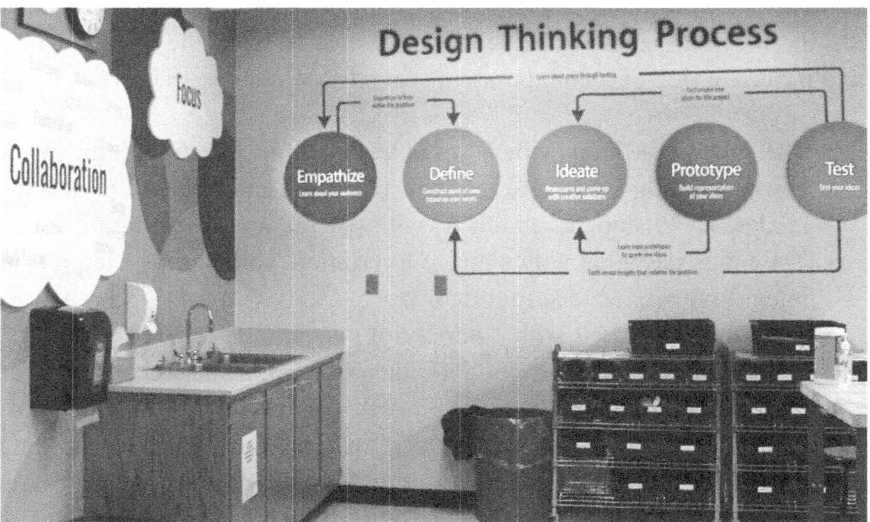

Figure 4.4. Signage to promote collaborative inquiry, experimentation, and engineering. Burris Laboratory School.

- Educators are scheduled for blocks of guaranteed times in the Innovation Lab with the flexibility to schedule additional time as needed using an online shared calendar.
- The lab provides a home base for elementary and middle school afterschool robotics teams and other clubs.

The infrastructure and programming should serve as a vehicle for students to move through the STEM disciplines fluidly. Table 4.2 provides three examples of integrative STEM activities that incorporate multiple disciplines and equipment within a project.

Table 4.2. Exemplars of Integrative STEM Activities

Researchers	*Grade Level*	*Project Objective*	*Example Equipment*
Cook and Bush (2017)	Elementary School	Developed a prosthetic limb for a kindergartener	Models of skeletal anatomy of arm; TinkerCAD design software to 3D print a physical prototype
Grubbs and Deck (2015)	Middle School	Developed a water turbine to be an alternative energy source for a home	Raw materials (e.g., cardboard, zip ties, dowel rods, and spoons); water source and water collection bin or sink; equipment or device to hold turbine, multimeter, and rubber band pulley system
Stith and Geesa (2020)	High School	Developed microbial fuel cells as an alternative energy source for a home	Raw materials (e.g., carbon cloth, wire, and plastic containers); bacterial samples and nutrient agar; multimeters, beakers, and graduated cylinders; Excel spreadsheets for data collection and analysis of electricity generation

Note: Information collected from "Design Thinking in Integrated STEAM Learning: Surveying the Landscape and Exploring Exemplars in Elementary Grades," by K. L. Cook and S. B. Bush, 2018, *School Science and Mathematics, 118*(3–4), pp. 93–103 (https://doi.org/10.1111/ssm.12268); "The Water Turbine: An Integrative STEM Education Context," by M. E. Grubbs and A. Deck, (2015), *Technology and Engineering Teacher*, 75(2), p. 26–30; and "Artistic Biotechnology: A Design Thinking Platform for STEAM Praxis" by K. M. Stith and R. L. Geesa, 2020, In K. Thomas and D. Huffman (Eds.), *Challenges and Opportunities for Transforming From STEM to STEAM Education*, pp. 51–74, IGI Global (https://www.igi-global.com/chapter/artistic-biotechnology).

FURTHER CONSIDERATIONS

Additional considerations (e.g., up-to-date resources, scheduling, funding, spaces for educator collaboration, safe learning environments, diversity and inclusion of students) affect how educational leaders implement integrative STEM education to support teaching and learning. Therefore, educational leaders have several variables to consider and plan for as they facilitate integrative STEM education. As learning environments are designed, these considerations will confirm that the goals and vision of integrative STEM education are achieved and sustained. Recommendations for the sustainability of integrative STEM infrastructures are provided.

Up-to-Date Resources

Educational leaders need to routinely check and provide appropriate and up-to-date materials, resources, and technology that facilitate integrative approaches to learning or disseminate these responsibilities to a STEM coordinator. This can be done through a variety of systems and measures. The establishment of a program advisory council can aid in ensuring labs are aligned to the needs of students, educators, higher education institutions, and local industries.

The council could rotate the location of their meetings (e.g., school, industry, or higher education buildings) to review and offer feedback of lab spaces. These opportunities also promote conversation regarding access and use of equipment that schools and districts may not be able to fund or allow in a school setting due to constraints (e.g., space and servicing). Action steps for leaders to sustain the infrastructure include:

- provide ample opportunities for professional learning across school sites, allowing educators time to see other instructors' labs and spaces, use of equipment, safety signage, and instructional approaches; and
- follow professional associations that provide developments and innovation in technologies (e.g., International Technology and Engineering Educators Association and Association for Educational Communications and Technology).

Schedules for Collaboration

Educational leaders should devise a staffing plan and master schedule that dedicates time and spaces for collaborative planning, assessment data review, community leader involvement, and project-/problem-based learning experience implementation. Collaborative planning is essential to vertically and horizontally align STEM content and learning experiences. Planning allows for the development of transdisciplinary learning through problem- and project-based activities.

Professional learning opportunities should be provided for planning transdisciplinary projects and aligning curriculum in a meaningful way. Several strategies show potential for carving out more collaborative planning time among educators and leaders. One strategy especially appropriate for elementary and middle school is to co-teach STEM and non-STEM subjects during a double-class period.

This aligns planning time with enhancing the depth of understanding regarding the interconnections of the content and learning goals, as well as student needs and identities. Flexibility in staffing should also include other school personnel. "Coteaching with a special education teacher can address diverse learning needs in an inclusive classroom" (Grillo, et al., 2016, p. 48), as could engaging language and social studies educators in integrative STEM education programs when the school serves students with multiple languages and cultures.

At the high school, banking time (e.g., reducing individual planning time per day to increase collaborative planning time on another day) or specifying an enrichment period on a biweekly or monthly basis should be considered (Rosenberg et al., 2018). Both strategies can be useful to support multidisciplinary planning teams, especially when an integrative STEM coach or assessment specialist facilitates the teams' alignment, assessment review, and project planning.

Parallel schedules, afterschool and early dismissal times, educator externships, and in-service days can be purposefully used for educators to plan and assess progress toward implementing integrative STEM education. Regardless of the school system or structure of the schedule, educational leaders need to be thoughtful about the planning time that is required for integrative STEM education. Ongoing feedback between school- and district-based leadership and educators will allow for adjustments to be made throughout the school year to meet the needs of instructors.

Concurrently, scheduling issues will need to be considered to ensure effective use of collaborative spaces. For elementary, middle, and high school educators, a variety of scheduling plans for integrative STEM activities to be purposefully integrated into the curricula exist, such as:

- *summer workshops:* provide an opportunity for educators to focus on collaboratively developing integrative STEM activities as their schedules are not as impeded by class schedules when school is not in session;
- *planning blocks:* provide time for developing and maintaining integrative STEM activities for daily or block instruction; and
- *professional learning communities:* provide a guaranteed time (e.g., daily, weekly, and monthly) for educators to work collaboratively to develop integrative STEM activities or coordinate ongoing projects.

Action steps for leaders to take to sustain the schedule and programming include:

- develop a staffing plan and master schedule with opportunity for educator feedback; and
- support educators with the necessary planning time to work collaboratively together, or with community partners, to develop integrative STEM curricula.

Funding

Educational leaders need to purposefully and strategically allocate money to support integrative STEM education programs. Leaders' understanding of the costs associated with integrative STEM education is central to a sustainable program. Funding should be distributed to educators or schools via a site-based management model to allow for equal and equitable support. This can be based on a per-pupil ratio, with adjustments made dependent on needs of educators and schools. Through this measure, funding is largely consistent due to the cost of materials as a result of projections for anticipated curricular needs.

Alternatively, funding can supplement or enhance the replacement of consumable materials throughout the school year. The purchase of all materials at once may be the most realistic option to initiate a program as built-in grant budgets are secured. Educational leaders who are beginning new integrative STEM education programs, or hope to expand a program and have current limited funding, may turn to competitive grant options.

Through this model, success can be evaluated and scaled up with appropriate funding secured.

Action steps for leaders to take to sustain the funding for programs, materials, and learning environments include:

- work with an integrative STEM leadership team or program advisory council to consider ongoing funding sources (e.g., community partners, sponsorships, grants); and
- promote schoolwide entrepreneurialism by students making and selling products created through integrative STEM activities to generate funds that can be used to continue adding furnishings, equipment, and inventory to the space.

Safe Environments

As educators—often from backgrounds with minimal training in STEM—transition into integrative STEM education programs and tool-based instruction, challenges may arise. Liability can reside with school and district programs when students are placed in harmful environments; therefore, a robust safety plan with appropriate policies and rules needs to be considered for integrative STEM education learning spaces (Deck, 2016; National Science Teaching Association, 2020). For example, a 3D printer should always be installed with a ventilation system to minimize student inhalation of potentially carcinogenic ultrafine particles.

School human resource offices should have guidelines and stipulations for what teaching backgrounds satisfy STEM content areas. In some instances, middle and high school job descriptions of integrative STEM education classrooms may rule out certain teaching backgrounds. Educational leaders should plan a thorough safety program for onboarding educators and developing their skills over time. This can begin with professional learning, such as safety training workshops on general lab safety and in conjunction with multiple offices (e.g., career and technical education, technology and engineering education).

The safety program should not only discuss the importance of safety in the classroom, but also model and evaluate correct tool and equipment use, showcase effective safety measures (e.g., signage, tool guards, securing of tools), and allow for resource sharing for grade appropriate classroom instruction. Educators should have ongoing safety training throughout the school year, with periodic lab evaluations by educational leaders. In addition, a strong maintenance and repair system should be in place to minimize instructional disruptions when lab equipment is serviced.

Integrative STEM education should exemplify environmentally and economically sustainable physical spaces that promote the development of healthy students and staff. Particularly important for student and educator health, when 3D printers and laser engravers are purchased to support student design projects, attention must be given to indoor air quality, exhaust systems, and waste management (United States Environmental Protection Agency, 2019).

Action steps for leaders to take to sustain safe learning environments include:

- establish policies for whom and when equipment should be used, especially as it relates to safety training, maintenance, and material requisition;
- designate a qualified individual to support the maintenance, inventory, and curriculum integration; and
- align a safety plan with recommendations from the Americans with Disabilities Act Standards, Architectural Barriers Act Standards, and Occupational Safety and Health Administration Guidelines and Standards.

Diversity and Inclusion

As integrative STEM education environments are created, educators need to foster inviting spaces for all students. Socially responsible integrative STEM programs should maintain accommodations for students' race, ethnicity, class, gender identity, sexual orientation, language, nation of origin, thinking, political, ability, tribe, and religious affiliations. For example, movable furnishings for students who are differently abled, workspace safety protocols in the language(s) of English language learners, and provisions of adequate material and technological resources for economically disadvantaged students move the program to a more equitable learning environment.

Action steps for leaders to take to sustain equitable and inclusive infrastructure and programming include:

- provide tailored professional learning opportunities for educators to differentiate instruction in hands-on activities;
- purposefully consider furnishings, equipment, and activities that accommodate diverse learners; and
- shift integrative STEM activities to small group configurations to support all students in active co-construction of meaning instead of large group configurations that may deter engagement from diverse learners.

CONCLUSION

Integrative STEM education is nested within a national and international goal to prepare our populace for a workforce that is continuously evolving, and to position all individuals as critical thinkers and problem-solvers. This chapter reviewed how the integrative STEM education school infrastructure and programming should be flexible and adaptable, promote collaboration among educators and students, and allow for critical and creative thinking.

For educational leaders to best support their educators, it is vital to continuously engage with school stakeholders in conversations of the successes and challenges of the integrative STEM program that is being implemented. Considerations for classrooms and laboratories with students and educators include accessibility, materials, supplies, space, timing, scheduling, maintenance, and investments. These decisions will need to be tailored to the current infrastructure and programming, but with acknowledgement that sustainability will require continuous work. Setting a vision, engaging in continuous improvement cycles, and celebrating the successes of the programs will foster a sustainable learning environment for all stakeholders.

REFERENCES

Brown, J. (2012). The current status of STEM education research. *Journal of STEM Education: Innovations and Research, 13*(5), 7–11. https://www.jstem.org/jstem/index.php/JSTEM/article/download/1652/1490/

Brusic, S. A., Marcum-Dietrich, N., Shettel, J., & White, J. (2019, June). *Integrative STEM for PK–4 preservice teachers*. International Society for Technology in Education (ISTE) Conference, Philadelphia, PA. https://tinyurl.com/iSTEM-for-PK-4-Teachers

Cook, K. L., & Bush, S. B. (2018). Design thinking in integrated STEAM learning: Surveying the landscape and exploring exemplars in elementary grades. *School Science and Mathematics, 118*(3–4), 93–103. https://doi.org/10.1111/ssm.12268

Deck, A. (2016). Biotechnology: Fostering a culture of chemical safety. *Technology and Engineering Teacher, 76*(3), 18–19.

Geesa, R. L., Stith, K. M., & Rose, M. A. (2020). Preparing school and district leaders for success in developing and facilitating integrative STEM in higher education. *Journal of Research on Leadership Education,* 1–21. https://doi.org/10.1177/1942775120962148

Geesa, R. L., Stith, K. M., & Teague, G. M. (2021). Integrative STEM education and leadership for student success. In F. English (Ed.), *The Palgrave Handbook of Educational Leadership and Management Discourse* (pp. 1–20). Palgrave Macmillan. https://doi.org/10.1007/978-3-030-39666-4_36-1

Grillo, K. J., Bowser, J. C., & Cooley, T. M. (2016). Leveraging technology in the coteaching model for STEM education. *The Bridge: Linking Engineering and society, 46*(2), 47–52. https://www.nae.edu/File.aspx?id=155268

Grubbs, M. E., & Deck, A. (2015). The water turbine: An integrative STEM education context. *Technology and Engineering Teacher, 75*(2), 26–30.

Kelley, T. R., & Knowles, J. G. (2016). A conceptual framework for integrated STEM education. *International Journal of STEM Education, 3*(11), 1–11. https://doi.org/10.1186/s40594-016-0046-z

Kostourou, F. (2014). We shape our building and then they shape us. In M. Angellil & R. Hehl (Eds.), *Minha Casa Nossa Cidade: Innovating Mass Housing for Social Change in Brazil* (pp. 129–31). Ruby Press.

Mizell, S., & Brown, S. (2016). The current status of STEM education research 2013–2015. *Journal of STEM Education: Innovations and Research, 17*(4), 52–56. https://www.jstem.org/jstem/index.php/JSTEM/article/view/2169/1815

National Science & Technology Council, Committee on STEM Education. (2018). *Charting a course for success: America's strategy for STEM education.* https://files.eric.ed.goc/fulltext/ED590474.pdf

National Science Teaching Association. (2020). *Safety resources.* https://www.nsta.org/safety/

Rose, M. A., Geesa, R. L., & Stith, K. (2019). STEM leader excellence: A modified Delphi study of critical skills, competencies, and qualities. *Journal of Technology Education, 31*(1), 42–62. https://doi.org/10.21061/jte.v31i1.a.3

Rosenberg, D., Daigneau, R., & Galvez, M. (2018). *Finding time for collaborative planning.* Education Resource Strategies. https://www.k12blueprint.com/sites/default/files/ERS-finding-time-for-collaborative-planning.pdf

Shively, K., Stith, K., Spoon, R., Geesa, R. L., & Rubenstein, L. D. (2021). Adopt to adapt: A multi-year case study of design thinking in elementary classrooms. In K. L. Sanzo, J. P. Scribner, J. A. Wheeler, & K. W. Maxlow (Eds.), *Design Thinking: Research, Innovation, and Implementation* (pp. 1–19). Information Age Publishing.

Shulman, L. S. (2005). Signature pedagogies in the professions. *Daedalus, 134*(3), 52–59. https://doi.org/10.1162/0011526054622015

Stith, K. M., & Geesa, R. L. (2020). Artistic biotechnology: A design thinking platform for STEAM praxis. In K. Thomas & D. Huffman (Eds.), *Challenges and Opportunities for Transforming From STEM to STEAM Education* (pp. 51–74). IGI Global. https://www.igi-global.com/chapter/artistic-biotechnology

United States Department of Education, Office of Educational Technology. (2017a). *Building technology infrastructure for learning.* https://tech.ed.gov/files/2017/07/2017-Infrastructure-Guide.pdf

United States Department of Education, Office of Educational Technology. (2017b). *Reimagining the role of technology in education: 2017 National education Technology Plan Update.* https://tech.ed.gov/files/2017/01/NETP17.pdf

United States Environmental Protection Agency. (2019). *Indoor air quality tools for schools action kit.* https://www.epa.gov/iaq-schools/indoor-air-quality-tools-schools-action-kit

5

Facilitating an Integrative STEM Curriculum

Mary Annette Rose and Krista Marie Stith

The heart of a curriculum lies at the nexus of what is planned, enacted, and experienced in our schools (Marsh & Willis, 2007). As often practiced, the curriculum is discipline-centric, separated by different content standards and learning goals, and implemented with discrete learning experiences that fragment schooling. Curriculum designers specify the sequence of learning experiences and resources in a curricular plan. Then, educators adapt the plan to the local resources and perceived needs of their students while students attempt to make meaning of the isolated facts and procedures when encountering real-world problems.

In contrast, an integrative STEM curriculum deliberatively breaks down the barriers among traditional disciplines by explicitly making *connections* among disciplinary content and ways of knowing. In other words, "discipline specific content is not divided, but addressed and treated as one dynamic, fluid study" (Brown et al., 2011, p. 6).

Integrative STEM curricula are accompanied by active learning pedagogies where students investigate phenomena, conduct experiments, troubleshoot malfunctioning systems, and design and test solutions to problems. Due to the increased relevance of these action-oriented learning experiences, students develop evidence-based reasoning needed to understand problems in their daily lives, as well as the agency and resilience needed to cope with an increasingly complex world.

Educational leaders—principals, directors, curriculum directors or specialists, and superintendents—are instrumental in facilitating the development of an integrative STEM curriculum that is intellectually rigorous, coherent, and promotes students' academic success and well-being (Geesa et al., 2020, 2021; National Policy Board for Educational Administration, 2015). To effectively facilitate the entire curriculum cycle, these leaders must understand the intended learning outcomes and cross-cutting principles of integrative STEM, as well as the processes and quality indicators for developing, implementing, and evaluating curriculum.

This chapter provides educational leaders with guidance on how to facilitate and support the development of integrative STEM curriculum at school and district levels. The discussion focuses on these essential questions:

- What are the intended learning outcomes?
- How do educational leaders facilitate the development of integrative STEM curricula?
- What are exemplars of integrative STEM curricula?

INTENDED LEARNING OUTCOMES OF INTEGRATIVE STEM

The process of developing curriculum often begins by explicating the school vision, mission, goals, and outcomes for the planned curriculum. A consensus is building that a primary aim of PK–12 STEM curriculum should be to prepare STEM-literate students. Such a curriculum would deliberatively integrate content and practices from all STEM disciplines to advance students' understandings, skills and dispositions for the transdisciplinary work of mitigating complex personal, social, and global problems (see Table 5.1 and Figures 5.1 and 5.2).

STEM literacy is "the ability to identify, apply, and integrate concepts from science, technology, engineering, and mathematics to understand complex problems and to innovate to solve them" (Balka, 2011, p. 7).

Table 5.1. National Goals and Intended Learning Outcomes for Integrative STEM

Focus	*Goals for STEM Education (National Science & Technology Council, 2018)*	*Intended Learning Outcomes (Honey et al., 2014)*
STEM literacy	Build strong foundations for STEM literacy	STEM literacy provides: • awareness of the roles of science, technology, engineering, and mathematics in modern society; • familiarity with some of the fundamental concepts from each area; and • basic level of application fluency.
Twenty-first century competencies and dispositions	Engage students where disciplines converge to promote: • adaptability and perseverance; • computational thinking; • prediction, modeling, and data analysis; • digital literacy and cyber safety; • evidence-based reasoning innovation; and • problem-finding and problem-solving.	Twenty-first century competencies, which include: • cognitive (critical thinking and innovation); • intrapersonal (flexibility, initiative, and metacognition); and • interpersonal (communication, collaboration, and responsibility).
Inclusion	Focus to increase diversity, equity, and inclusion in STEM	Focus to increase STEM interest, especially for underrepresented populations Development of STEM identity (personal relevance)
Career and college readiness	Prepare the STEM workforce for the future with career and college readiness and technical skills	Increase STEM workforce and college readiness Increase STEM course taking, educational persistence, and graduation rates

Note: Information collected from *Charting a Course for Success: America's Strategy for STEM Education*, by National Science & Technology Council, Committee on STEM Education, 2018, The White House (https://www.whitehouse.gov/wp-content/uploads/2018/12/STEM-Education-Strategic-Plan-2018.pdf); and *STEM Integration in K–12 Education: Status, Prospects, and an Agenda for Research*, by M. Honey, G. Pearson, and A. Schweingruber, 2014, The National Academies Press.

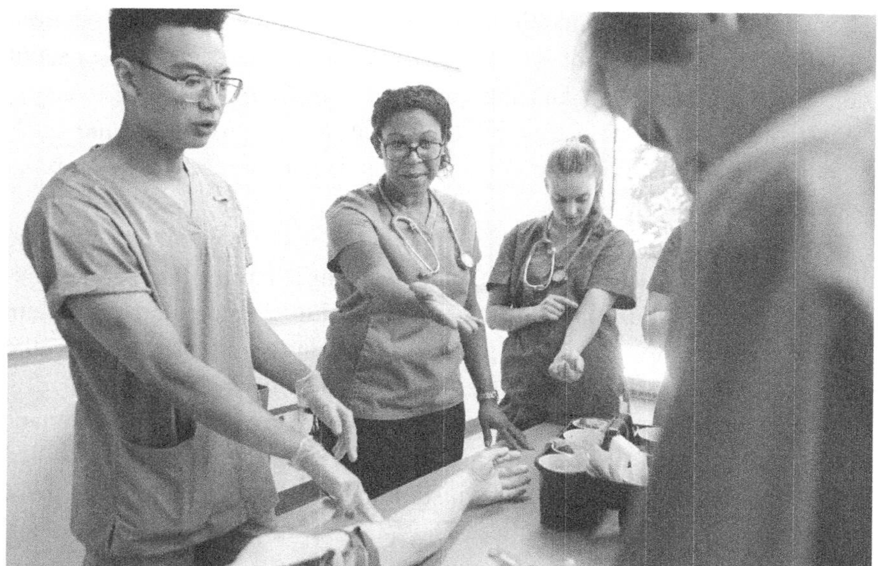

Figure 5.1. A nurse educator guiding high school students on venipuncture techniques. iStockphoto LP.

Figure 5.2. Elementary school students tinkering with a computer motherboard in class. iStockphoto LP.

Several national organizations, for example Partnership for 21st Century Learning (Battelle for Kids, 2019), also emphasize that a broad set of cognitive, interpersonal, and intrapersonal competencies (see Table 5.1) will be needed to enable students to transfer STEM principles and skills to inform personal and citizen decisions, as well as prepare them for post-secondary education and the workplace.

To advance these learning goals and outcomes, the curriculum should be horizontally integrated to enable students to meet national and state standards of the STEM disciplines (see Table 5.2). Furthermore, the curriculum should be vertically aligned to provide increasingly complex experiential learning challenges by creating well-articulated career pathways.

STEM pathways may prepare scientists, engineers, and mathematicians to drive innovation through research and development or prepare skilled professionals who select, finance, install, manage, maintain, and use these innovations in everyday practice. Thus, the entire planned curriculum—the core curriculum, advanced placement, gifted, special needs, and career and technical—could be devised to strive for integrative STEM goals and learning outcomes (see Table 5.1).

A Secondary Exemplar

The School of Engineering in Wayne County School District (2020b) is a five-year (sixth to thirteenth grade) engineering-themed school located in Goldsboro, North Carolina, with an enrollment of about 450 students. With funding from the New Schools Project, this inclusive school emerged in 2007 to provide rigorous academics with inquiry-based instruction. The district offers an honors curriculum that begins in sixth grade with an accelerated mathematics course and dedicated science and STEM courses.

Through a partnership with Wayne Community College, the high school curriculum is blended with college-level course work. Expectations for college-level course taking includes one course in ninth grade, three each in tenth and eleventh grades, and six in twelfth grade (Wayne County School District, 2020a). Courses at Wayne Community College might combine drafting and engineering courses or Intro to Derivatives and Advance Placement Calculus. This rigorous curriculum enables students to graduate in five years with an associate's degree in science or arts.

Table 5.2. Sampling of Practices and Process Skills from National STEM Standards

Science	*Technology*	*Engineering*	*Mathematics*
The Next Generation Science Standards (National Research Council, 2013)	Standards for Technological & Engineering Literacy (International Technology & Engineering Educators Association, 2020)	A Framework for Quality K–12 Engineering Education (Moore et al., 2014)	Principles and Standards for School Mathematics (National Council of Teachers of Mathematics, 2000)
1. Asking questions (for science) and defining problems (for engineering) 2. Developing and using models 3. Planning and carrying out investigations 4. Analyzing and interpreting data 5. Using mathematics and computational thinking 6. Constructing explanations (for science) and designing solutions (for engineering) 7. Engaging in argument from evidence 8. Obtaining, evaluating, and communicating information	1. Systems thinking: Designs systems considering the environments in which they operate 2. Creativity: Elaborates and articulates novel ideas 3. Making and doing: Exhibits safe, effective ways of producing products and systems 4. Critical thinking: Defends decisions based on evidence 5. Optimism: Shows persistence in addressing problems 6. Collaboration: Demonstrates productive teamwork 7. Communication: Conveys ideas through graphic, mathematical, and physical models 8. Ethics: Assesses products and systems through analysis of their impacts	1. Apply science, engineering, and mathematics 2. Processes of design • Problem and background • Plan and implement • Test and evaluate 3. Conceptions of engineers and engineering 4. Engineering thinking 5. Engineering tools 6. Teamwork 7. Issues, solutions, and impacts 8. Ethics 9. Communication skills	1. Problem-solving • Build new mathematical knowledge through problem-solving 2. Reasoning and proof • Make and investigate mathematical conjectures 3. Communication • Use the language of mathematics to express mathematical ideas precisely 4. Connections • Recognize and apply mathematics in contexts outside of mathematics 5. Representation • Use representations to model and interpret physical, social, and mathematical phenomena

Note: Quoted from *Next Generation Science Standards: For States, By States,* by National Research Council, 2013, The National Academies Press; *Standards for Technological and Engineering Literacy: The Role of Technology and Engineering in STEM Education*, by International Technology and Engineering Educators Association, 2020 (www.iteea.org/STEL.aspx); "A Framework for Quality K–12 Engineering Education: Research and Development," by T. J. Moore, A. W. Glancy, K. M. Tank, J. A. Kersten, K. A. Smith, and M. S. Stohlmann, 2014, *Journal of Pre-College Engineering Education Research (J-PEER), 4*(1), Article 2, pp. 1–15 (https://doi.org/10.7771/2157-9288.1069); and *Principles and Standards for School Mathematics,* by National Council of Teachers of Mathematics, 2000 (https://www.nctm.org/Standards-and-Positions/Principles-and-Standards/).

ACTION STEPS TO FACILITATE INTEGRATIVE STEM CURRICULUM

Whether a gradual evolution or a sweeping transition, leading curriculum change within a school requires understanding of STEM practices, as well as facilitation, coaching, and strategic planning skills. For educational leaders, this endeavor is often approached by *building the table* (Anderson-Butcher et al., 2009), which begins by coalescing a curriculum team focused on the development, implementation, and evaluation of integrative STEM curriculum and programs.

Educational leaders should assemble a curriculum team whose members are committed to advancing student achievement and possess diverse skill sets, including expertise in STEM disciplines, experiential pedagogies, curriculum development and evaluation, or community resources. The committee should be comprised of a cross-section of educators (including STEM, non-STEM, and career and technology education [CTE] educators at and across grade levels), curriculum integration specialists, and educators of students with special needs and high abilities (Rose et al., 2019).

Including representation of parents, caregivers, students, and higher education and business members will help the team stay focused on the priorities and concerns of those the curriculum will serve, as well as generate opportunities for strengthening community partnerships. Including professional staff (e.g., school counselors and financial officers) will expand the expertise to include support services.

Although the eventual goal is to coalesce around a mutual vision for improving the curriculum, it is first prudent to foster the collaborative processes and an interactive structure that will enable the formation of a *learning culture*. This culture should reflect the processes (e.g., investigating, problem-solving, modeling, designing), competencies (e.g., critical thinking, evidence-based decision-making), and practices (teamwork) engendered within integrative STEM education.

The initial stage of team formation will, invariably, take time and resources that some will perceive as inefficient, but modeling a reflective learning culture will reveal the interdependent nature of integrative curriculum work.

Self-Study: Assessing Readiness for Integrative STEM

Self-study is a critical phase of the team's work. The team should inspect the local STEM curriculum (e.g., scope and sequence maps, content outlines, resources), the results of school-level outcome measures (e.g., STEM course taking, student achievement scores on standardized mathematics and science assessments), and achievement comparisons to state-level performance targets.

Educational leaders should assist in developing an inventory of the history of STEM-based experiential learning efforts in their school and community, noting the leaders, issues, challenges, costs, and evidence of impact. Doing so will generate deeper understandings of the strengths, weaknesses, constraints, and opportunities afforded by the current STEM curricular program.

Setting Goals and Identifying Outcomes

The results of the self-study should enable educational leaders and the STEM curriculum team to judge the utility, worthiness, and readiness for a curricular shift to integrative STEM. If favorable, educational leaders should encourage the committee to either propose new or revised mission and goal statements for the school or develop a set of curricular goals compatible with the existing mission statement. See Chapter 2 for further insights.

Of particular concern is setting goals or outcomes relative to student achievement, educator performance, and desired qualities of the curriculum. In addition, measurable benchmarks, valid assessments, and a timeline should be identified to better gauge progress toward these goals. For example, a goal of Stone Mountain Middle School (2020) was to "stimulate students' interest in careers emphasizing science, technology, engineering, and mathematics disciplines." A benchmark might be a mean increase in a subscale of the STEM Career Interest Survey (Kier et al., 2014).

Investigating Possibilities

Educational leaders should encourage and enable the curriculum committee to investigate a variety of curriculum models for integrative STEM education, including career and technical education, *turn-key*, and *locally developed* models. An examination of curricula might include a review of goals, course descriptions, sequence maps, cross-curricular plans and goals, and assessments.

Visiting schools and interviewing leaders from STEM-certified schools (e.g., Indiana Department of Education, 2021) or those receiving awards or recognitions for their successful programs will yield new insights into the performances, rewards, and challenges of each model. Reviewing and recording evidence of the effectiveness, practicality, and costs associated with these curricula will generate information for a more systematic evaluation of options.

Career and Technical Education

When considering the approach to integrative STEM curriculum, educational leaders should also consider how well the curriculum fits within the future careers of all students, as well as the economic character—resources, jobs, and needs—of the region. To that end, career and technical education is a critical contributor to a comprehensive integrative STEM curriculum.

With federal funding through the *Strengthening Career and Technical Education for the 21st Century Act* (*Perkins V*) (2018), support is given to middle-grade curricular programs to explore technical careers and career pathways through problem- and project-based learning. At the secondary level, programs of study consist of a "coordinated, non-duplicative sequence of academic and technical content" that culminates in industry credentials, dual credit opportunities at local colleges, and career employability skills (Advance CTE & Association for Career and Technical Education, 2018).

The National Career Clusters Framework (Advance CTE, 2020) provides guidance for the design and development of CTE curriculum for grades 9–12 within states and school districts. Among the sixteen career clusters is the STEM cluster with two pathways commonly associated with integrative STEM: "Engineering & Technology" and "Science & Mathematics."

Both pathways include annual academic coursework in English/language arts, mathematics, science, and social studies. For the Engineering and Technology Pathway, CTE curriculum includes sequential coursework leading to engineering careers. CTE coursework for the Science and Mathematics Pathway leads to science, programming, and statistician careers. Table 5.3 offers a representative sequence of courses in these pathways.

Table 5.3. Suggested Career and Technical Courses in STEM Pathways

Grade	*Science and Mathematics Pathway*	*Engineering and Technology Pathway*
9	Introduction to Careers or Laboratory Practices and Biology Laboratory	Introduction to Engineering Design
10	Information Technology Applications or Chemistry Laboratory	Principles of Engineering or Information Technology Applications
11	Physics Laboratory	Product Engineering and Development or Digital Electronics
12	Scientific Research	Civil Engineering and Architecture or Engineering Innovation

Note: Information collected from *Science, Technology, Engineering and Mathematics: Science and Mathematics. Career Pathway Plan of Study for Learners, Parents, Counselors, Teachers/Faculty*, by League for Innovation, College and Career Transition Initiative, NCTEF, and States Career Cluster. n.d. (https://cte.careertech.org/sites/default/files/PlanPathways-CareerCluster-ST-EngineerandTech.pdf and https://cte.careertech.org/sites/default/files/PlanPathways-CareerCluster-ST-ScienceMath.pdf).

CTE curricular programs may be offered within comprehensive secondary schools as career academies or at separately administered schools often referred to as career or technical centers. To enable seamless, vertically aligned curricular programs, close relationships should be fostered among principals, curriculum specialists, and directors of CTE schools. In particular, these educational leaders should schedule biannual collaborative work sessions to evaluate existing curriculum and propose improvements by:

- analyzing the results of career programming, student achievement, and counseling services at middle or junior high schools;
- analyzing the knowledge and skill prerequisites and expectations of the introductory CTE STEM courses;
- reviewing the concerns, interests, and recommendations of staff, students, and community partners; and
- coordinating and maximizing the human capital and technical investments of each school.

Turn-Key STEM Curricula

To meet integrative STEM and CTE goals, many states and school districts have adopted *Project Lead the Way*'s (PLTW; 2020) turn-key curriculum that extends to PreK–5 (PLTW Launch), 6–8 (Gateway), and 9–12 grades with engineering, computer science, and biomedical science curricular programs. Empirical evidence suggests positive results in driving student achievement toward preferred STEM outcomes (e.g., Tai, 2012).

The annual costs associated with required educator training, equipment and expendable supplies are beyond many school budgets. Therefore, some states have approved parallel courses (e.g., Indiana Department of Education, 2020) and STEM programs that address similar learning outcomes and enable greater flexibility at the district level.

There are numerous other examples of turn-key STEM modules, courses, and programs. The Boston Museum of Science (2020) offers classroom-tested curricular units in their *Engineering is Elementary* curriculum. These begin with a realistic story where elementary learners encounter a puzzling situation. Then, they investigate science principles and apply engineering practices to propose and test a potential solution. Pitsco's (2020) sixth through ninth grades STEM Expeditions takes a customizable approach enabling educators to select from a broad set of STEM modules and whole class problem-based learning experiences.

The turn-key approach to integrative STEM curriculum is attractive to educational leaders for several reasons. Reputable curriculum developers provide a standards- and industry-aligned curriculum to match local and state academic requirements and business needs. Typically, the curricular products include a variety of educator support materials, such as lesson plans, assessments, student resources, and cloud-based learning management systems. Many provide training for educators that aims to increase the fidelity of implementing a sequence of connections; thus, enhancing educators' understanding with interdisciplinary content and confidence in implementing inquiry- and design-based pedagogies.

With educational funding increasingly volatile, educational leaders should demand *evidence that the curriculum is valid and effective* prior to investing scarce resources in turn-key curricular products. Educational leaders should carefully weigh the costs, including initial capital investment for hardware/software, maintenance, storage, and professional development required of educators to implement the curriculum with fidelity.

Evidence-based curriculum refers to several qualities of a curriculum. There is sufficient evidence that:

- the curriculum aligns with state standards and school mission statements,
- both content and instructional experts judge the content and pedagogy to be valid, and
- the curriculum consistently advances student achievement using valid and reliable assessments.

Additional considerations for the educational leader should be if the assessment items align with integrative STEM education principles, the contexts through which students investigate, and the availability of resources to share with parents and stakeholders.

Locally Developed STEM Curricula

Educational leaders should also encourage the curriculum team to investigate incremental or sweeping curricular change initiatives that are locally developed. These curricula may evolve from community needs or resources, an infusion of grant support, a professional development initiative (e.g., McFadden & Roehrig, 2017), or the guidance of a STEM curriculum specialist who works with educators daily. A locally developed curriculum is valued for its adaptability to student needs and local resources.

As Fogarty and Pete (2009) explain, there are a variety of approaches to integrating curriculum that vary in nature of staff planning, disciplinary intensity, and potential for student autonomy. The thematic or webbed approach is adaptable to localized needs and suitable for an incremental approach to curriculum change. This approach entails selecting a common theme by which disciplinary content and skill development activities can be connected.

For example, educational leaders at Maconaquah Middle School (n.d.) in Bunker Hill, Indiana employed a thematic approach for the development of a nine-week unit by:

- soliciting recommendations from students, staff, parents, and community leaders;
- leading the curriculum committee in evaluating the proposals relative to: its potential to support state standards across several disciplines, be operationalized within motivating learning experiences, demonstrate local relevance, and resource constraints; and
- providing formative feedback as the curriculum team articulated the curricular plan, especially related to perceived complexity, differentiation strategies, interdisciplinary connections, and assessment development.

One such nine-week unit focused on the themes of *processes* and *water*. Given Maconaquah's proximity to the Mississinewa Reservoir, which serves as flood control and a recreational venue, these themes were contextually relevant and lent themselves to experiential learning.

Considering the ethnically and racially diverse student populations in the United States, it is also important that curriculum developers be purposeful in building culturally relevant and responsive curriculum that equitably supports and motivates all students (Ekici et al., 2018). Culturally responsive curriculum respects the student's home culture—the dominant issues, linguistics, cultural practices, and values—supporting student's agency and voice. As examples of STEM-related culturally-responsive practices, Virgin-Islander students problem-solve invasive lionfish populations (Ekici et al., 2018) and African-American and Latinx students create computer simulations with cultural influences (Leonard et al., 2019).

Although engagement in curriculum development has positive impacts on the professional development of educators, there are costs and risks. For instance, the curriculum development process demands talented, committed staff with curriculum development and collaborative skills. However, the more extensive time for the curriculum cycle—development, implementation, assessment, and revision—increases the risk that time and resources may not result in improved learning outcomes.

SHARING FINDINGS AND ENGAGING THE COMMUNITY

After examining STEM models and conducting a self-study, educational leaders should encourage the curriculum team to organize and synthesize their findings for consideration by the broader school community. Fact sheets and graphic organizers that compare and contrast the primary differences, advantages, and challenges of various curricular options can be beneficial. Educational leaders should schedule opportunities for the curriculum team to share their findings and resources and implement a system to record and respond to concerns and recommendations with school staff and interested community members.

Eventually, educational leaders and the curriculum team should gauge the receptivity and willingness of the entire staff regarding these options, including a "status quo" option. Without the support of most staff, moving a school culture toward integrative STEM curriculum will likely require professional development for staff and new hires or other human resource interventions. For example, educational leaders have supported a cultural shift toward integrative STEM curriculum in larger school districts by enabling educators to transfer within the school district.

INSPIRING AND SUPPORTING INNOVATION

When staff members are supportive, the curriculum team begins the complex work of envisioning, designing, and developing an integrative STEM curriculum plan. Because state and national standards articulate *what students should know and be able to do* in the separate STEM disciplines, the focus of this development work is upon integration—identifying points of intersection—and examining the curriculum holistically across disciplines and grade levels.

Curriculum Mapping

Results of a study of STEM education leaders indicated that mapping the existing curriculum to identify cross-cutting concepts (e.g., systems, modeling, ethics) and common points of intersection was the most critical step toward integration (Rose et al., 2019). Curriculum mapping is a process of indexing curricular components in a database to enable inspection at the school, program, or course level for planning, monitoring, evaluation, or reporting purposes. Curriculum mapping can be done using a simple spreadsheet, however a networked mapping platform (e.g., Google Workspace) makes it a dynamic, collaborative tool.

Applied to integrative STEM, mapping may be used to trace the development of quantitative skills across STEM curricula to identify gaps and duplications (Reid & Wilkes, 2016). Mapping is also useful for assessing the vertical and horizontal alignment among elements of a curricular program by comparing the content, skills, activities, and assessments against state and national standards and other desired learning outcomes.

Assessment and Evaluation

Careful attention must be given to selecting or developing student assessments to gauge progress toward STEM learning goals, especially the assessment of reasoning, process skills, interest, and career readiness. The framework and sample tasks on the Technology and Engineering Literacy Assessment (National Assessment of Educational Progress, n.d.) offer guidance on assessing STEM reasoning and process skills. The Career and Technical Education Consortium of States (2020) offers example quizzes and modules to assess career readiness.

In addition, educational leaders should make provisions for formative evaluation of the integrative STEM curriculum, especially by engaging the STEM leadership committees and staff who implement the STEM curriculum in collaborative reflection, data review, and planning. See Chapter 9 for discussion of assessment.

FACILITATING THE DEVELOPMENT OF INTEGRATIVE STEM CURRICULUM

With determined leadership and dedicated staff, educational leaders may lead a transition to integrative STEM curriculum through incremental or sweeping change initiatives that are developed locally. Facilitating the entire cycle of curriculum—development, implementation, evaluation and revision—requires leaders to understand STEM goals, content standards, strategic leadership for each stage of the cycle, and dedication to collaborative decision-making. These understandings enable leaders to assess gaps in the horizontal and vertical alignment of content, as well as sense incongruities between the affordances and constraints of the school and community.

A variety of other tasks may fall on the educational leader as they strive to support the development of a coherent curriculum plan. Leaders may:

- propose and negotiate dual-credit courses with a local university;
- identify and develop community partnerships to support experiential learning experiences for students (e.g., internships, field trips);
- support learning management systems or curriculum mapping programs that enable collaborative planning, assessment, and communication;
- hire or appoint an innovative lead educator to serve as an integrative STEM curriculum specialist who models and supports educators in the development of integrative curriculum; and
- adjust the master schedule to maximize programming options for student learning experiences and collaborative time for integrative planning and evaluation by staff. For instance, educational leaders at Wayne School of Engineering (Peters-Burton et al., 2013) "fostered continuity and coherence across courses and grades by holding curriculum advisory meetings once a week, professional learning communities that met every day, weekly lesson tuning, weekly whole group reflections, school wide rubrics, and cross curricular instruction" (p. 18).

CONCLUSION

Integrative STEM curriculum is a purposeful attempt to fuse the bodies of knowledge and practices of the STEM disciplines into a coherent student-centered learning experience via inquiry, design, and experiential pedagogies. Seamlessly intertwining and coordinating learning experiences for students to meet grade-level learning competencies and performance targets, while also vertically sequencing these experiences to build progressively more complex STEM understandings and skills is a substantial task. Educational leaders monitor progress and coach the STEM curriculum team by providing timely, actionable feedback and support.

Prior to committing to such a task, educational leaders should convene a STEM committee to conduct a self-study and examine the advantages and disadvantages of various locally developed and prepackaged approaches to integrate STEM curriculum. Then, educational leaders should present these findings and options to the school stakeholders, gauging their receptivity to these options.

Integrative STEM curriculum—whether locally developed or preestablished—refocuses priorities for STEM learning outcomes and will likely disrupt the established patterns of curriculum development within the school. Investing in any approach to integrative STEM curriculum requires commitments from school staff, as well as costs associated with equipment, expendable materials, time for collaborative planning, and scheduling changes. However, the rewards of integrative STEM curriculum that is locally relevant and experiential are compelling, promising improved personal and citizen decision-making, improved retention, and increased career and college readiness.

REFERENCES

Advance CTE. (2020). *Career clusters.* https://careertech.org/career-clusters

Advance CTE, & Association for Career and Technical Education. (2018). *Legislative summary and analysis: Strengthening Career and Technical Education for the 21st Century Act (Perkins V).* https://www.acteonline.org/wp-content/uploads/2018/08/AdvanceCTE_ACTE_P.L.115-224Summary_Updated080618.pdf

Anderson-Butcher, D., Lawson, H. A., Iachini, A., Wade-Mdivanian, R., & Bean, J. (2009). *The Ohio community collaboration model for school improvement.* http://cayci.osu.edu/wp-content/uploads/2015/03/OCCMSIPublicReport_pressquality_reducedfilesize.pdf

Balka, D. (2011). Standards of mathematical practice and STEM. *The Math-Science Connector* [Newsletter]. School Science and Mathematics Association. https://www.ssma.org/assets/docs/MathScienceConnector-summer2011.pdf

Battelle for Kids. (2019). *Partnership for 21st century learning: A network of Battelle for kids.* https://www.battelleforkids.org/networks/p21/roadmap-21

Boston Museum of Science. (2020). *About Engineering is Elementary*. https://www.eie.org/stem-curricula/engineering-grades-prek-8/engineering-is-elementary

Brown, R., Brown, J., Reardon, K., & Merrill, C. (2011). Understanding STEM: Current perceptions. *Technology and Engineering Teacher, 70*(6), 5–9.

Career and Technical Education Consortium of States. (2020). *Practice*. https://wrs.ctecs.org/practice/

Ekici, C., Plyley, C., Alagoz, C., Gordon, R., & Santana, N. (2018). Integrated development and assessment of mathematical modeling practices for culturally responsive STEM Education: Lionfish case study. *The Eurasia Proceedings of Educational and Social Sciences, 9*, 1–10. https://dergipark.org.tr/tr/download/article-file/525604

Fogarty, R., & Pete, B. M. (2009). *How to integrate the curricula* (3rd ed.). Corwin.

Geesa, R. L., Stith, K. M., & Rose, M. A. (2020). Preparing school and district leaders for success in developing and facilitating integrative STEM in higher education. *Journal of Research on Leadership Education,* 1–21. https://doi.org/10.1177/1942775120962148

Geesa, R. L., Stith, K. M., & Teague, G. M. (2021). Integrative STEM education and leadership for student success. In F. English (Ed.), *The Palgrave Handbook of Educational Leadership and Management Discourse* (pp. 1–20). Palgrave Macmillan. https://doi.org/10.1007/978-3-030-39666-4_36-1

Honey, M., Pearson, G., & Schweingruber, A. (2014). *STEM integration in K–12 education: status, prospects, and an agenda for research*. The National Academies Press.

Indiana Department of Education. (2020). *CTE: Engineering and technology standards*. https://www.doe.in.gov/standards/cte-engineering-and-technology

Indiana Department of Education. (2021). *STEM School Certification*. https://www.in.gov/doe/students/stem-school-certification/

International Technology and Engineering Educators Association. (2020). *Standards for technological and engineering literacy: The role of technology and engineering in STEM education*. www.iteea.org/STEL.aspx

Kier, M. W., Blanchard, M. R., Osborne, J. W., & Albert, J. L. (2014). The development of the STEM career interest survey (STEM-CIS). *Research in Science Education, 44*, 461–481. https://doi.org/10.1007/s11165-013-9389-3

League for Innovation, College and Career Transition Initiative, NCTEF, and States Career Cluster. (n.d.). *Science, technology, engineering and mathematics: Engineering and technology. Career pathway plan of study for learners, parents, counselors, teachers/faculty*. https://cte.careertech.org/sites/default/files/PlanPathways-CareerCluster-ST-EngineerandTech.pdf and https://cte.careertech.org/sites/default/files/PlanPathways-CareerCluster-ST-ScienceMath.pdf

Leonard, J., Barnes-Johnson, J., & Evans, B. R. (2019). Using computer simulations and culturally responsive instruction to broaden urban students' participation in STEM. *Digital Experiences in Mathematics Education, 5*(2), 101–123. https://www.nctm.org/standards

Maconaquah Middle School. (n.d.). *Unit plan #1-7th grade*. https://mms.maconaquah.k12.in.us

Marsh, C. J., & Willis, G. (2007). *Curriculum: Alternative approaches, ongoing issues*. Pearson.

McFadden, J. R., & Roehrig, G. H. (2017). Exploring teacher design team endeavors while creating an elementary-focused STEM-integrated curriculum. *International Journal of STEM Education, 4*(21), 1–22. https://doi.org/10.1186/s40594-017-0084-1

Moore, T. J., Glancy, A. W., Tank, K. M., Kersten, J. A., Smith, K. A., & Stohlmann, M. S. (2014). A framework for quality K–12 engineering education: Research and development. *Journal of Pre-College Engineering Education Research (J-PEER), 4*(1), Article 2, 1–15. https://doi.org/10.7771/2157-9288.1069

National Assessment of Educational Progress. (n.d.). *About the TEL assessment*. https://www.nationsreportcard.gov/tel_2014/#about/focus/framework

National Council of Teachers of Mathematics. (2000). *Principles and standards for school mathematics*. https://www.nctm.org/standards/

National Policy Board for Educational Administration. (2015). *Professional standards for educational leaders*. https://www.npbea.org/wp-content/uploads/2017/06/Professional-Standards-for-Educational-Leaders_2015.pdf

National Research Council. (2013). Next Generation Science Standards: For states, by states. The National Academies Press. https://doi.org/10.17226/18290

National Science & Technology Council, Committee on STEM Education. (2018). *Charting a course for success: America's strategy for STEM education*. The White House. https://www.usinnovation.org/reports/americas-strategy-stem-education

Peters-Burton, E., Kaminsky, S. E., Lynch, S. J., Behrend, T. S., Ross, K. M., House, A., & Han, E. M. (2013). Wayne School of Engineering: A case study of an inclusive STEM-focused high school in Goldsboro, North Carolina (OSPrI Report 2013-02). George Washington University, Opportunity Structures for Preparation and Inspiration in STEM. https://ospri.research.gwu.edu/sites/g/files/zaxdzs2456/f/downloads/OSPrI_Report_2013-02.pdf

Pitsco. (2020). *Our grades 6–9 programs*. https://www.pitsco.com/Our-Programs/Grades-6-9/

Project Lead the Way. (2020). *Our preK–12 pathways: Cohesive, hands-on learning experiences*. https://www.pltw.org/our-programs

Reid, J., & Wilkes, J. (2016). Developing and applying quantitative skills maps for STEM curricula, with a focus on different modes of learning. *International Journal of Mathematical Education in Science and Technology, 47*(6), 837–852. https://doi.org/10.1080/0020739X.2016.1144814

Rose, M. A., Geesa, R. L., & Stith, K. (2019). STEM leader excellence: A modified Delphi study of critical skills, competencies, and qualities. *Journal of Technology Education, 31*(1), 42–62. https://doi.org/10.21061/jte.v31i1.a.3

Strengthening Career and Technical Education for the 21st Century Act (Perkins V), Pub. L. No. 115-224 (2018). https://www.congress.gov/bill/115th-congress/house-bill/2353

Stone Mountain Middle School. (2020). *STEM student application.* http://www.stonemountainms.dekalb.k12.ga.us/STEM.aspx

Tai, R. H. (2012). *An examination of the research literature on Project Lead the Way.* https://www.pltw.org/dr-robert-tai-report

Wayne County School District. (2020a). Anticipated course of study for WSE students. http://www.waynecountyschools.org/Instruction.aspx

Wayne County School District. (2020b). Wayne School of Engineering. https://www.waynecountyschools.org/wayneschoolofengineering_home.aspx

6

Collaboration in PK–12 Integrative STEM Instruction

Suparna Sinha, David J. Shernoff, and Cheryl Cuddihy

Today's youth will be confronted with problems that require a multidisciplinary approach and the use of new tools to solve. Although the twentieth century was based on linear engineering of complicated systems (e.g., the production of cars), proficiency with nonlinear designs and complex systems of the twenty-first century (e.g., interdependent ecosystems, the Internet) requires a global view and conceptual grasp of multiple complex factors and relationships (Boy, 2013).

There is an essential need for integrative STEM education in which multiple STEM disciplines are leveraged toward solving a single problem or fashioning a new product (Honey et al., 2014). Relatedly, advances in space exploration and many other fields illustrate that collaboration and creativity are essential to multidisciplinary achievement. There is a clear need to collaborate and coordinate more to spur innovation (Boy, 2013). Collaboration is the primary pathway by which the disciplines interact, communicate with each other, and therefore, "integrate."

The integrative STEM agenda faces several fundamental challenges including budgetary constraints and compliance mandates focusing on educator evaluation and accountability (Johnson, 2012). In addition, separate departments and class periods are typically based on traditional, disciplinary distinctions at all levels of traditional schooling. Educator preparation programs are no exception; middle and high school educators are certified to be proficient in a specific content area rather than interdisciplinary or transdisciplinary teaching and learning.

Although the application of STEM concepts was being formally recognized as desirable in education several years ago, the adoption of effective pedagogy toward the goal of a comprehensive approach to STEM education has been slow to develop and implement. There is little attention to integrating STEM and other subjects to address the need of real-life problem-solving. As a result, educational leaders are challenged in creating and sustaining integrative STEM learning environments in which educators and students are prepared to actively participate and learn through collaborative integrative STEM activities. The aim of this chapter is to provide some initial guidance toward this important instructional goal.

This chapter will discuss the characteristics of common integrative STEM pedagogies and the salience of collaboration to support integrated instruction. Next, some of the obstacles that educational leaders face in cultivating opportunities for collaboration amongst staff will be identified. This is followed by a review of several empirically-based models of collaboration in integrative STEM that may be useful in guiding future practice, research, and policy.

INTEGRATIVE STEM PEDAGOGIES AND CHARACTERISTICS

Pedagogical approaches commonly used in integrative STEM education include inquiry-based learning, problem-based learning, design-based learning, and project-based learning. These approaches promote creativity and critical thinking (Thomas, 2009), and involve collaborative problem-solving and drawing on the use of social and cooperative skills (see Table 6.1). Strategies exist for educational leaders to promote collaboration in integrative STEM. In this chapter, *collaboration* is defined as educational experiences in which educational leaders, educators, staff, students, and community partners work together to explore concepts and knowledge through integrative STEM experiences.

Table 6.1. Integrative STEM Pedagogies

Pedagogical Strategy	*Description*	*Guidelines for School Leaders*
Inquiry-based learning	Students participate in hands-on experiential learning activities to construct knowledge by testing, questioning, observing, and making predictions.	Encourage curriculum design and assessments that focus on students' understanding and application of theoretical concepts over memorization of large amounts of factual data.
Problem-based learning	Students develop problem-solving skills by going through a realistic self-directed problem-solving process.	Prepare educators for the transition from the role of an expert to that of a resource and colearner in the classroom. Provide coaching on how to integrate curricular and assessment goals in the course of problem-solving.
Design-based learning	Students gain STEM knowledge by engaging in design-based challenges combining theory, factual content, and application.	Prepare educators with pedagogical practices of explaining, questioning, demonstrating; employ strategies to help explain specific content and skills; encourage a shift in professional attitudes and values.
Project-based learning	Students explore transdisciplinary aspects of a real-life problem through inquiry, reflection, and collaboration in the context of sustained projects rooted in driving questions about the problem.	Direct educator professional development toward student-centered practices that support creating opportunities for students to work together on meaningful and complex tasks.

Inquiry-Based Learning

A signature pedagogy in integrative STEM education is positioning students to think like scientists, engineers, and other STEM professionals in a process of inquiry. In inquiry learning, students try to form explanations of phenomena based on evidence (e.g., see Figure 6.1). They often gather and analyze data as teams of investigators. The focal point of group discussions involves supporting claims and arguments with evidence.

Figure 6.1. Middle school students hypothesizing outcomes in an electronic demonstration with an electrical engineer. iStockphoto LP.

Students present, explain, communicate, and justify their explanations (Andriessen et al., 2003). Thus, group members take the role of peer investigators in presenting competing claims, which can lead to new or unexplored questions. Engaging in this kind of inquiry learning process is a primary goal of the new Next Generation Science Standards (Shernoff, Sinha, Bressler, & Schultz, 2017).

Problem-Based Learning

Problem-based learning provides opportunities for students to engage in self-directed learning experiences to solve real-world problems that often have multiple correct answers. Problem-based learning is intended to help students develop (a) flexible knowledge, (b) effective problem-solving skills, (c) self-directed learning, (d) effective collaboration skills, and (e) intrinsic motivation (Hmelo-Silver, 2004).

To facilitate problem-based learning environments, educational leaders should support educators in shifting roles to become facilitators or coaches of student learning who guide students toward appropriate resources for them to actively incorporate new knowledge into the development of viable solutions.

Design-Based Learning

Design-based learning is a form of problem-based learning that draws on design processes and practices, such as those used by architects, industrial designers, and engineers. An engineering design process is often depicted as a series of iterative stages that lead to the development of a solution to an open-ended problem. These stages begin with identifying, imagining, and empathizing with the problem from the perspective of the end-user or consumer.

This analytical process results in the formation of design goals and acknowledgement of the constraints that limit the design process and proposed solution. Further stages are followed by prototyping a solution, testing and experimenting, and improving the solution by repeating this process as needed.

Engineering design challenges can be set up by the educator to initiate the process or can emerge naturally from student-driven interests. Real engineering problems are often complex and involve a diverse team in terms of expertise. In the context of the challenge, awareness of and empathy toward concerned stakeholders is facilitated through the collaborative process to generate creative solutions.

Some schools are embracing a design-based learning approach through the integration of *makerspaces* (Sheridan et al., 2014) as a vehicle to drive increased capacity for integrative STEM education. *Makerspaces* are workspaces where people with common interests, often in computers, technology, science, and digital and electronic art, can meet and collaborate on projects. The rapidly expanding educational and artistic uses of makerspaces foster a new wave of applied multidisciplinary learning experiences. Designed to cultivate creativity and digital literacy for all learners, a maker-centered learning environment serves as a catalyst for shaping participants' involvement with a variety of technical tools.

In an elementary makerspace setting (Cuddihy, 2020), one school principal created opportunities in the school's curriculum for children to experiment with elements of coding, engineering, digital literacy, and video production through both "plugged in" (technology-based) or "unplugged" (hands-on experiences) lessons. In another school, the makerspace was designed to be an open-ended learning environment where students worked with community experts, peers, and educators through play-based learning (Britton, 2012). Chapter 4 includes more information about makerspaces.

Project-Based Learning

Project-based learning may incorporate elements of all of the pedagogies previously discussed, but refers to an instructional model that operates through sustained work on projects (Thomas, 2000). Importantly, projects are rooted in driving questions about the real world and frequently call for an integration of several disciplines, as when engineers, scientists, and mathematicians collaborate toward the solution of a complex problem (e.g., see Figure 6.2).

Students develop and refine collaboration and communication skills when doing project-based learning because these skills are crucial for group experimentation, problem-solving, discussions about conclusions, and

Figure 6.2. Elementary school students testing a wind turbine they created with plastic bottles in class. iStockphoto LP.

implications for next steps. Typically, there are numerous opportunities in which students need to rely on their social and teamworking skills as much as academic ones to effectively share and combine ideas toward solutions.

For example, to combat the lack of adequate educational materials in Rwanda, one United States elementary school project featured third- through eighth-graders creating books for Rwandan students (Cuddihy, 2020). Educational leaders coordinated efforts with their local and international partners to educate students about Rwanda. A variety of driving questions, such as characterizing the plight of rhinos, led students to make discoveries about the diversity, geography, wildlife, ecosystems, and educational settings in Rwanda. Then, students collaborated with peers to write about the various topics related to Rwanda.

Finally, the students produced different visual media through paper collaging, book illustrations, and tiles for books to be distributed in Rwanda schools. This scenario demonstrates how educational leaders can cultivate partnerships between educators to fulfill learning objectives across content areas (e.g., art, multimedia, social studies, science, literacy) while also developing global connectedness.

IMPORTANCE OF COLLABORATION IN INTEGRATIVE STEM

Collaboration among educational leaders and educators is crucial to promote integrative STEM at the level of the school. Three common models of such collaboration involve co-teaching, coaching, and community mentors.

Co-Teaching

Co-teaching can be one effective strategy for integrating subject matter expertise and pedagogical content knowledge across disciplines. Friend and Cook (2016) discuss the importance of collaboration as an essential ingredient for fostering successful co-teaching partnerships among educators who teach different content areas. In prior research, Friend et al. (2010) identify six models of co-teaching for educators and leaders to consider integrating into their practice: one teach, one observe; station teaching; parallel teaching; alternative teaching; teaming; and one teach, one assist (see Table 6.2).

Table 6.2. Models of Co-Teaching

Model Type	*Description*
One Teach, One Observe	One educator leads large-group instruction while another gathers academic, behavioral, or social data on specific students or the class group.
Station Teaching	Instruction is separated into multiple nonsequential parts and stationed at separate areas of the classroom. Students are separated into multiple groups and rotate among the stations, being taught by the educators at multiple stations and working independently at one station.
Parallel Teaching	Two educators, each with half of the class, present the same material for the primary purpose of fostering instructional differentiation and increasing student participation.
Alternative Teaching	One educator works with most students while another works with a small group for remediation, enrichment, assessment, preteaching, or another purpose.
Teaming	Both educators lead large-group instruction together by both lecturing, representing opposing views in a debate, or illustrating two ways to solve a problem.
One Teach, One Assist	One educator leads instruction while the other circulates among the students offering individual assistance.

Note: Adapted from "Co-Teaching: An Illustration of the Complexity of Collaboration in Special Education," by M. Friend, L. Cook, D. A. Hurley-Chamberlain, and C. Shamberger, 2010, *Journal of Education and Psychological Consultation, 20*(1), 9–27 (https://doi.org/10.1080/10474410903535380). Copyright 2010 by Taylor & Francis.

Teaching partnerships can support academic literacies and add value in the shift from traditional to integrative STEM models of instruction. For example, co-teaching alliances between novice and expert educators can be advantageous for both parties. Novice educators may engage in conversations about practice with an expert that can lead them to synthesize theory and practice (Roth, 1998), and expert educators benefit from fresh perspectives of new educators.

Educational leaders play an important role in facilitating co-teaching. For instance, the station model of co-teaching provides a platform for educators of STEM subjects to use their unique talents to instruct small groups of students across different content areas at the same time in the same classroom (Moorehead & Grillo, 2013), enhancing student-educator interactions and providing unique opportunities for differentiated instruction.

A challenge of co-teaching is finding the common planning time to co-design a co-teaching unit. Educational leaders can facilitate co-planning by making time available for educators to collaborate and plan with others, and encouraging the use of Google Docs, Dropbox, and other online tools for co-planning in lieu of solely synchronous, face-to-face meetings.

Coaching

A meta-analysis of more than 60 studies found a positive effect of coaching on instruction and achievement (Kraft et al., 2018). Instructional coaches can provide support to engage educators in integrative STEM learning. Ideally, instructional coaches would have a background in integrative STEM to support educators and educational leaders in content-specific knowledge, as well as to broaden connections and integrate STEM domains.

For example, literacy instructional coaches could help language arts educators to use Makedo kits to create cardboard models representing written narratives or social studies content; and mathematics instructional coaches could help educators to integrate Makey Makey kits to support the Standards for Mathematical Practice (Common Core State Standards Initiative, 2020).

There are several kinds of coaching described in the literature, including peer or team-building coaching, cognitive coaching, technical coaching, problem-solving coaching, and reform coaching (Kurz et al., 2017). Some coaching types, such as coaching for team-building or to reform educational practice, represent school-wide functions of coaching. Instructional coaches aid educational leaders to implement school-wide instructional change by gathering feedback from educators and students about their assets and areas for improvement, and contextualizing this feedback in the context of school goals (Glover, 2017; Glover et al., 2018).

Community Mentorship

Issues important to the community can provide rich context for integrative STEM projects, becoming integral to the problem to be solved in a problem-based learning approach. Students learn more about the community-based environment both by visiting community centers (e.g., zoos, libraries, museums, parks) and by inviting community-based professionals with specific expertise (e.g., environmentalists, engineers) into the classroom.

In other cases, students may choose a project to develop a solution to a problem in the community that is personally interesting or meaningful. By directly engaging in issues important to the community, or in some cases, regional, state, national, or international problems or issues, the sphere of engagement is expanded along with students' sense of relevance for learning.

Calabrese Barton and Tan (2018a, 2018b) followed the development of 41 youth-maker projects addressing issues of inequity, injustice, and other social ills within their local communities. Youth makers collaborated with maker-educators and mentors to support their communities. For example, youth in one project addressed need for safe and affordable transportation on short winter days by making a solar-powered light-up scooter.

Calabrese Barton and Tan (2018a, 2018b) found that community-based co-making legitimized youth as makers and increased their opportunities to be recognized with community mentors. Findings supported a community-centered approach to STEM-rich projects, one in which youth come to envision a more just and equitable future. Although these were not school projects, they remain an important, empirically-based model of integrative STEM community engagement and mentorship.

CHALLENGES TO IMPLEMENTING COLLABORATION IN INTEGRATIVE STEM PRACTICE

Despite the strengths of integrative STEM pedagogies, especially in terms of twenty-first century skills, there are numerous challenges to their widespread adoption in PK–12 schools. A needs-assessment study identified the greatest challenges of PK–12 educators to implementing integrative STEM, as well as supports needed to overcome those challenges (Shernoff, Sinha, Bressler, and Ginsburg, 2017). In the study, researchers interviewed educator leaders and principals knowledgeable about integrative STEM. The most frequently mentioned challenge to integrative STEM implementation was perceived lack of time for educators' collaborative planning for integrative STEM instruction, especially among middle and high school educators. Lack of administrative support for implementing integrative STEM curricula was another important challenge.

On the other hand, principals were also among the key supporters for integrative STEM that educators discussed. The extent to which school principals understood the importance of carving out the time needed to collaboratively design integrative STEM curriculum played an important role in the support educators received. Educator professional learning is also crucial. Through professional learning, educators can communicate and collaborate with other educators in a variety of disciplines to effectively implement integrative STEM.

Ideally, professional learning should reinforce integrative STEM as a collaborative, transdisciplinary process of inquiry or making in order to help educators learn pedagogical strategies, such as design- or project-based learning. Exemplar lessons are also a much-needed support for developing integrative STEM curricula. Examples of effective lessons come from school visits within or outside of an educator's district.

An important aspect of educational leaders' abilities to effectively support integrative STEM relates to embracing a collaborative, data-driven decision-making process for identifying needs, setting goals, making an action plan, monitoring the process, and evaluating the progress and needs (e.g., Glover, 2017; Glover et al., 2018). This involves using collaborative networking to conduct a self-study on the level of support needed to implement integrative STEM curricula, and analyzing and interpreting data to inform a team-generated proposal to implement needed supports. Student data is important to include in order to inform proposals of research-based practices responding to student needs.

It is also recommended to include opportunities for modeling, practice, and feedback (Glover, 2017). A team-based approach to leadership can build effective communication and a mutual understanding of team members' roles, especially when teams meet regularly. A collaborative leadership approach includes educators and staff in problem-solving and developing protocols and action plans to engage key stakeholders in integrative STEM implementation.

EVIDENCE-BASED INTEGRATIVE STEM CURRICULAR MODELS

Beyond identifying common pedagogical strategies for integrative STEM instruction, there have recently emerged several curricular models that are receiving increased attention from researchers and practitioners. Empirical support is important in this stage of integrative STEM education development in order to identify curricular models that are evidence-based and data-driven.

School-Wide Interdisciplinary Educator Planning

Recently, Shernoff et al. (2020) conducted a professional learning and research project on the creation of an integrative science, technology, engineering, art, and mathematics (STEAM) academy, designed by an interdisciplinary team of STEAM educators at one high school in a low-income district with a high Latinx population (approximately 85 percent). One of the project goals was to reduce student disengagement and dropout that was particularly problematic in the freshman year.

The professional learning program was coordinated in close partnership among the science coordinator, other professionals at the school, and a team of professional learning specialists and researchers. Participating educators included three educators of mathematics (algebra) and one educator each of English, physics, and world history/social studies. Student participants included those selected at random for the integrative STEAM academy by the school, and those who participated in a traditional, comparison academy.

The educators participated in a four-day summer institute followed by year-long, monthly professional learning community meetings. The focus of the summer institute was to help educators develop an integrative STEAM curriculum, beginning with collaborative team-building exercises for educators to experience collaborative integrative STEAM projects. Educators also participated in semistructured activities to review content standards and make curricular connections with other educators.

For the majority of the institute, educators collaboratively planned with each other. They explored possibilities of discipline integration, reviewed instructional strategies that afforded STEAM integration and supported students' problem-solving skills (e.g., inquiry-, design-, problem-, and project-based learning), and produced curricular themes that cut across subjects.

Throughout the project year, students were surveyed about their educational attitudes, especially with respect to their aspirations for future schooling both pre- and post-academy. Students in the integrative STEAM academy reported significantly greater gains in engaged learning, positive affect, interest, and intrinsic motivation from pre- to post-academy compared to students in the other academy.

There were also notable differences in patterns of student interaction, with students in the other academy reporting they spent most of their time with the educator (68 percent), while students in the integrative STEAM academy spent most of their time with students (55 percent). There was a significant difference in the desire to continue schooling between students in both academies. Whereas the educational aspirations of students in the comparison academy declined from pre- to post-academy, aspirations improved for students in the integrative STEAM academy.

Educators reported enjoying and valuing their participation in the academy and professional learning community meetings. They expressed appreciation for the opportunity to design a transdisciplinary curriculum, share ideas, and get continued feedback throughout the year. Educators also observed a positive shift in students' engagement and a sense of belonging.

Overall, this model suggests the importance of identifying an interdisciplinary team of like-minded educators to plan, question, and think deeply together about common themes to unify integrative STEM/STEAM curriculum across subjects. Interdisciplinary educator forums for collaborative planning and continuing opportunities for giving and receiving feedback appeared to be critical for implementing such a model.

Whole-Class Transdisciplinary STEAM Projects

In supporting PK–12 schools and educators to design and implement a transdisciplinary STEAM curricula and instruction, Quigley and Herro (2019) encourage educators to identify a problem or issue embedded in the surrounding community. The problem can be presented as a simple scenario with a driving question that becomes the basis for transdisciplinary project-based learning. For example, a scenario at the elementary school level may highlight the disappearance of honeybee populations. Students are then charged with researching the problem and presenting a solution to be implemented by the school.

From such a scenario, students form collaborative working groups of researchers and pollinator garden designers. The work becomes more relevant as students research the problem and learn how the decline of the honeybee population would affect school lunches and lunch choices. Students may visit a local pollinator garden space and invite various community experts, such as a garden coordinator, into the classroom.

Students learn in multiple disciplines, such as science (animal and plant dependence), technology and engineering (designing and using tools to make models of pollinator gardens), art (artistic design of gardens), language arts (presenting the solution), mathematics (measuring and calculating the garden area to inform the design), and other fields.

The key to student collaborations and community engagement is the establishment of roles, which may be based on student assets. This closely emulates how problems are solved and STEM achievements are advanced in the real world. Quigley et al. (2019) found that educators often struggle with implementing this approach initially, finding it difficult to let go of a more fact-based approach emphasizing correct answers. However, most educators were able to succeed by keeping their plans flexible and soliciting needed support from the school and educational leaders who must be prepared to foster an environment where individuals are comfortable taking risks.

Student-Led, Maker-Centered Learning

Clapp et al. (2017) from the Harvard University Agency by Design project conducted a study of maker educators in the United States. Students in maker-centered classrooms could be found using tools and resources from multiple disciplines in the process of creation. In a maker-centered classroom, teaching is a role shared by educators and their students. Often students teach each other because they are recognized as legitimate experts. Students coinspire, as well as co-critique one another.

Experts or artists from the community can also be consulted. In one example, a Portland educator referred students needing to understand how to mix fiberglass to build a boat to a local boat-builder. Educational leaders need to be proactive in building and sustaining meaningful partnerships with community members and school stakeholders to foster a wholistic learning environment for students and educators.

CONCLUSION

Preparing students for the challenges of the twenty-first century requires a multidisciplinary approach to problem-solving that promotes the development of creativity, critical thinking, and collaboration skills. Integrative STEM pedagogies foster these skills, although there are a variety of challenges that interfere with their wider adoption in PK–12 schools. Because most educators are trained to specialize in a single discipline or group of disciplines, planning integrative STEM curricula is enhanced by collaborative planning across school subjects.

Educational leaders can play a critically important role in facilitating the professional learning of educators through sharing examples of pedagogies most conducive for fostering STEM skills (e.g., inquiry-, problem-, design-, and project-based learning), as well as implementing strategies for mentoring and turn-key coaching that build upon educators' existing knowledge of STEM (Geesa et al., 2020, 2021; Rose et al., 2019). Savvy educational leaders also leverage current educator leaders and existing opportunities in the school setting to maximize their school's potential for promoting an integrative STEM agenda.

It is important for school, district, and other educational leaders to assess available resources—physical and personnel—when making plans to implement integrative STEM learning experiences. Leaders can promote integrative STEM planning by:

- scheduling time for integration planning in the school's master schedule, thereby enhancing educators' agency;
- creating physical and virtual spaces for educators, staff, and students to engage in inquiry-, problem-, design-, and project-based learning;
- advocating for resources supporting equitable opportunities for all students; and
- providing professional development programs that model collaborative processes inherent to integrative STEM activities.

Educational leaders can also help to drive instructional changes through professional learning communities that strategically create co-teaching partnerships and support STEM coaches to cultivate opportunities within the current school.

Promoting effective integrative STEM programs cannot rest on the shoulders of STEM educators alone; educational leaders play a vital role in promoting and anchoring a culture of student-centered integrative STEM pedagogy and bridging connections. Evidence-based models of whole-class, transdisciplinary STEAM problem-solving suggest that the boundaries of collaboration can expand beyond the classroom, to include organizations, settings, and experts in the community, and address issues important to the community or broader society (Quigley & Herro, 2019).

Student-led maker projects are receiving growing attention (Clapp et al., 2017) because they illustrate student collaboration as central to integrative STEM. This is in part because students are a legitimate source of expertise, and their continual feedback enhances the learning process. All such models point to the observation that collaboration among educators, leaders, staff, students, and stakeholders in the community is an active and essential ingredient to providing authentic educative experiences preparing students to drive positive change in the real world.

REFERENCES

Andriessen, J., Baker, M., & Suthers, D. (Eds.). (2003). *Arguing to learn: Confronting cognitions in computer-supported collaborative learning environments*. Springer. https://doi.org/10.1007/978-94-017-0781-7

Boy, G. A. (2013, August). *From STEM to STEAM: Toward a human-centered education, creativity & learning thinking*. European Conference on Cognitive Ergonomics, Toulouse, France. https://doi.org/10.1145/2501907.2501934

Britton, L. (2012). The makings of maker spaces, part 1: Space for creation, not just consumption. *Library Journal*, *137*(16), 20–23. https://www.libraryjournal.com/?detailStory=the-makings-of-maker-spaces-part-1-space-for-creation-not-just-consumption

Calabrese Barton, A., & Tan, E. (2018a). A longitudinal study of equity-oriented STEM-rich making among youth from historically marginalized communities. *American Educational Research Journal*, *55*(4), 761–800. https://doi.org/10.3102/0002831218758668

Calabrese Barton, A., & Tan, E. (2018b). *STEM-rich maker learning: Designing for equity with youth of color.* Teachers College Press.

Clapp, E. P., Ross, J., Ryan, J. O., & Tishman, S. (2017). *Maker-centered learning: Empowering young people to shape their worlds.* Jossey-Bass.

Common Core State Standards Initiative. (2020). *Standards for mathematical practice.* http://www.corestandards.org/Math/Practice/

Cuddihy, C. (2020). *Once upon a makerspace: Elementary students document the stories of their thinking* (Publication No. 27544508) [Doctoral Dissertation, Rutgers University]. ProQuest Dissertations Publishing. https://doi.org/doi:10.7282/t3-8bqm-ws37

Friend, M., & Cook, L. (2016). *Interactions: Collaboration skills for school professionals* (8th ed.). Pearson.

Friend, M., Cook, L., Hurley-Chamberlain, D. A., & Shamberger, C. (2010). Co-teaching: An illustration of the complexity of collaboration in special education. *Journal of Education and Psychological Consultation*, 20(1), 9–27. https://doi.org/10.1080/10474410903535380

Geesa, R. L., Stith, K. M., & Rose, M. A. (2020). Preparing school and district leaders for success in developing and facilitating integrative STEM in higher education. *Journal of Research on Leadership Education*, 1–21. https://doi.org/10.1177/1942775120962148

Geesa, R. L., Stith, K. M., & Teague, G. M. (2021). Integrative STEM education and leadership for student success. In F. English (Ed.), *The Palgrave Handbook of Educational Leadership and Management Discourse* (pp. 1–20). Palgrave Macmillan. https://doi.org/10.1007/978-3-030-39666-4_36-1

Glover, T. A. (2017). A data-driven coaching model used to promote students' response to early reading intervention. *Theory Into Practice, 56*(1), 13–20. https://doi.org/10.1080/00405841.2016.1260401

Glover, T. A., Reddy, L. A., & Kurz, A. (2018). Use of an online platform to facilitate and investigate data-driven instructional coaching. *Assessment for Effective Intervention, 44*(2), 95-103. https://doi.org/10.1177/1534508418811593

Hmelo-Silver, C. (2004). Problem-based learning: What and how do students learn? *Educational Psychology Review, 16*(3), 235–266. https://doi.org/10.1023/b:edpr.0000034022.16470.f3

Honey, M., Pearson, G., & Schweingruber, H. (Eds.). (2014) *STEM integration in K–12 education: Status, prospects, and an agenda for research.* National Academies Press. https://doi.org/10.17226/18612

Johnson, C. C. (2012). Implementation of STEM education policy: Challenges, progress, and lessons learned. *School Science and Mathematics, 112*(1), 45–55. https://doi.org/10.1111/j.1949-8594.2011.00110.x

Kraft, M. A., Blazar, D., & Hogan, D. (2018). The effect of teacher coaching on instruction and achievement: A meta-analysis of the causal evidence. *Review of Educational Research, 88*(4), 547–588. https://doi.org/10.3102/0034654318759268

Kurz, A., Reddy, L. A., & Glover, T. A. (2017). A multidisciplinary framework of instructional coaching. *Theory Into Practice, 56*(1), 66–77. https://doi.org/10.1080/00405841.2016.1260404

Moorehead, T., & Grillo, K. (2013). Celebrating the reality of inclusive STEM education: Co-teaching in science and mathematics. *Teaching Exceptional Children, 45*(4), 50–57. https://doi.org/10.1177/004005991304500406

Quigley, C. F., & Herro, D. (2019). *An educator's guide to STEAM: Engaging students using real-world problems.* Teachers College Press.

Quigley, C. F., Herro, D., & Baker, A. (2019). Moving toward transdisciplinary instruction: A longitudinal examination of STEAM teaching practice. In M. S. Khine & S. Areepattamannil (Eds.), *STEAM education: Theory and practice* (pp. 143–164). Springer. https://doi.org/10.1007/978-3-030-04003-1_8

Rose, M. A., Geesa, R. L., & Stith, K. (2019). STEM leader excellence: A modified Delphi study of critical skills, competencies, and qualities. *Journal of Technology Education, 31*(1), 42–62. https://doi.org/10.21061/jte.v31i1.a.3

Roth, W.-M. (1998). Science teaching as knowledgeability: A case study of knowing and learning during coteaching. *Science Education, 82*(3), 357–377. https://doi.org/10.1002/(sici)1098-237x(199806)82:3<357::aid-sce4>3.0.co;2-b

Sheridan, K. M., Halverson, E. R., Litts, B. K., Brahms, L., Jacobs-Priebe, L., & Owens, T. (2014). Learning in the making: A comparative case study of three makerspaces. *Harvard Educational Review, 84*(4), 505–531. https://doi.org/10.17763/haer.84.4.brr34733723j648u

Shernoff, D. J., Bressler, D. M., Massaro, I., & Sinha, S. (2020). The influence of a freshman iSTEAM academy on student engagement and educational attitudes. *Journal of Higher Education Theory and Practice, 20*(7), 33–54. https://doi.org/10.33423/jhetp.v20i7.3150

Shernoff, D. J., Sinha, S., Bressler, D. M., & Ginsburg, L. (2017). Assessing teacher education and professional development needs for the implementation of integrated approaches to STEM education. *International Journal of STEM Education, 4*(13), 1–16. https://doi:10.1186/s40594-017-0068-1

Shernoff, D. J., Sinha, S., Bressler, D. M., & Schultz, D. (2017). Teacher perceptions of their curricular and pedagogical shifts: Outcomes of a project-based model of teacher professional development in the Next Generation Science Standards. *Frontiers in Psychology, 8*(989), 1–16. https://doi.org/10.3389/fpsyg.2017.00989

Thomas, I. (2009). Critical thinking, transformative learning, sustainable education, and problem-based learning in universities. *Journal of Transformative Education, 7*(3), 245–264. https://doi.org/10.1177/1541344610385753

Thomas, J. W. (2000). *A review of research on project-based learning.* The Autodesk Foundation. http://www.bobpearlman.org/BestPractices/PBL_Research.pdf

7

Extended Learning Opportunities in Integrative STEM

Kate Shively

This chapter is about extended learning opportunities—the need, examples of programs, and leadership strategies—that promote and enhance community partnerships to support PK–12 students' engagement, interests, and curiosities in integrative STEM education. In addition, this chapter provides guidance to educational leaders to support extended learning opportunities in integrative STEM, with the goal to design sustainable programs.

The National Education Association (NEA; 2008) defines extended learning opportunities as "a broad range of programs that provide children with academic enrichment and/or supervised activities beyond the traditional school day and, in some cases, beyond the traditional school year" (p. 1). These programs are often offered and accessed before, during, and after school hours. Examples of extended learning opportunities include, but are not limited to apprenticeships, community service, independent studies, internships, online learning, and programming offered by community service organizations, museums, and libraries.

Organized by age or grades, gender, or thematic topics (e.g., integrative STEM experiences), extended learning opportunities may afford students more time to engage with their interests, sharpen talents, or have extra academic practice. For instance, young participants interested in robotics may engage in competitive programming, such as Vex Robotics (2020) where teams of students apply engineering concepts to create robotic solutions to problems.

Arguably, extended learning environments are possible venues for improving student STEM-related achievement when they enable opportunities for students to apply the content and skills they encountered during the school day. More effective extended learning opportunities combine three components to facilitate and engage students through (a) academic enrichment, (b) cultural activities, and (c) recreational opportunities (NEA, 2008, p. 2).

Beyond these varied purposes, PK–12 students may build leadership skills, enhance career awareness, and prepare for higher education or careers through engagement with community initiatives and programs (Meeder & Pawlowski, 2020). Due to the multiple benefits extended learning opportunities might offer, it is prudent for educational leaders to forge partnerships with community members that enable integrative STEM experiences across all grade levels.

INTEGRATIVE STEM EXTENDED LEARNING OPPORTUNITIES

For the purposes of this chapter, extended learning are opportunities to explore integrative STEM capabilities, knowledge, and curiosities while encompassing an interdisciplinary, multidisciplinary, or transdisciplinary approach beyond traditional classrooms. Scholars call to develop, improve, and innovate integrative STEM education due to rapidly rising demands to attract student interest in STEM fields (Honey et al., 2014; Kelley & Knowles, 2016).

Instrumental to this endeavor are *supportive* educational leaders (e.g., principals, deans, directors, specialists, superintendents, community partners) who inform, develop, model, and promote integrative STEM extended learning opportunities to their local student populations (Owens Jr. et al., 2015). Because school and district-level leaders make decisions about designing and facilitating educational programming in schools (Owens Jr. et al., 2015), it is important to acknowledge how they build a strong infrastructure to support extended learning opportunities relative to integrative STEM.

Scholars, as well as educational leaders, recognize three necessary foundational steps for leadership to implement in schools and communities:

1. Develop a budget and fund integrative STEM programs, organize crowdfunding events and fundraisers, write grants, and inform parent-teacher organizations or associations about needs for support (Kladifko, 2013);
2. Promote extended learning opportunities via media, branding, and public relations with educators, staff, families, and community members; and
3. Create programs and schedules designed to combine, reimagine, and consider different methods and environments (e.g., makerspaces, eLearning), travel opportunities, and community service (Ferrandino, 2006; National Science Teachers Association, 2018).

Furthermore, *supportive* school, district, and community leaders may engage in the practices to maintain and extend integrative STEM opportunities, such as continuously assessing needs and opportunities, practicing community-engagement, developing partnerships, and promoting a philosophy of mentoring and coaching. The next sections offer strategies for leaders to implement these practices of establishing integrative STEM extended learning opportunities for *all* students.

Assessing Needs and Opportunities

Developing an extended learning program to support integrative STEM should begin with an assessment of needs, existing programs, and future opportunities. In the needs assessment, one goal should be for leaders to identify gaps between school programming and student needs and interests. These insights can then guide a community-level assessment whereby leaders catalog the needs, priorities, programming, and resources of community organizations.

Leaders should create specific assessments for their school and community. As leaders collect information and examine community resources, they can create a community profile (Kladifko, 2013) of potential partners and weigh these against school and student needs. The profile may include venues where students and families give or obtain services, learn together, or work with businesses, higher education institutions, public libraries, zoos, museums, the media, youth organizations (e.g., Boys and

Girls Clubs), foundations, service organizations (e.g., soup kitchens, hospitals, humane society), and technology and informatics organizations.

Take Action for Assessing Needs and Opportunities

- Assess gaps in school programming and student interests toward integrative STEM education.
- Assess community needs and assets with the aim to build relationships beyond the school district.
- Compile a general community profile, including diverse integrative STEM learning opportunities.
- Conduct an assessment of community strengths and potential partnerships to match with integrative STEM curricular and programmatic goals.

Community-Engaged Practices

A central tenet of creating successful extended learning opportunities in integrative STEM is community engagement (e.g., see Figures 7.1 and 7.2). Bandy (2011) recognizes community engagement as service learning defined by the National Service Learning Clearinghouse as "a teaching and learning strategy that integrates meaningful community service with instruction and reflection to enrich the learning experience, teach civic responsibility, and strengthen communities" (para 1). Through community engagement, school and community partnerships may form that can lead to a mutually beneficial relationship for communities and schools, addressing the needs of all involved.

Community engagement positions educational leaders in a reciprocal relationship with a network of potential partners. For instance, educational leaders can lead or attend community meetings and luncheons offered by local organizations, interact with community leaders at public events, invite nonprofit and social services leaders to school events, and identify ways to mutually benefit from a collaborative partnership.

Developing relationships with community stakeholders is important to generate and sustain STEM-related interest (Merrill & Daugherty, 2010; Owens Jr. et al., 2015; Watters & Diezmann, 2013). Thus, a community

Figure 7.1. High school students working in a community garden. iStockphoto LP.

Figure 7.2. Middle school students taking action in a service learning project at a public park. iStockphoto LP.

profile should include the needs of potential partners. Understanding the needs of the school and the community informs the type of relationship. Leaders can better understand the needs of their potential partners by administering community assessment to determine needs (Blank & Langford, 2000; Stefanski et al., 2016).

Take Action for Community Engagement

- Develop a clear plan of action for integrative STEM extended learning opportunities.
- Coordinate a schedule for attending local events and hosting community meetings.
- Refer to Table 7.1 for a longer list of nationally recognized integrative STEM extended learning organizations created for children and youth.
- Identify sites for students to volunteer or intern in the local STEM partnership network and design a plan to encourage students to participate.

Table 7.1. Exemplar Organizations Supporting Integrative STEM Extended Learning Opportunities

Name	*Description*
Code Nation https://codenation.org/	Offers opportunities for schools and organizations to apply for courses and/or clubs taught by volunteers who are experts in STEM fields.
CSTEM Challenge https://www.cstem.org/	Offers integrated STEM learning experiences via curriculum and instruction for educators, caregivers, and students.
DREAM—Achievement Through Mentorship https://dream.rice.edu/	Serves as a model for developing STEM mentors, as university students who study STEM-related fields act as mentors for underrepresented populations.
Education Development Center https://www.edc.org/body-work/stem	Offers resources (e.g., curricula, digital games and applications) to engage students in new media and technology.
Family Engineering https://familyscienceandengineering.org/	Provides affordable elementary curriculum for hands-on experiences for families.
FIRST Robotics https://www.firstinspires.org/robotics/frc	Provides LEGO robotics leagues for multiple age groups with online registration.

Table 7.1. *(Continued)*

Name	*Description*
Girls, Inc.: Girls in STEM https://girlsinc.org/impact-categories/girls-in-stem/	Offers out-of-school programming to supplement STEM learning beyond school hours.
Girls Who Code https://girlswhocode.com/	Provides a free club related to computer science, programming, and coding to start at nonprofit organizations.
Maker Faires https://makerfaire.com/	Hosts annual events with communities, schools, or other organizations featuring hands-on, integrative STEM activities and experiences.
Million Women Mentors https://www.millionwomenmentors.com/	Recruits women and girls to pursue STEM careers through networking and mentoring.
National Girls Collaborative Project https://ngcproject.org/about-ngcp	Brings organizations together to connect girls to STEM-related careers.
National Inventors Hall of Fame https://www.invent.org/	Offers invention clubs, camps, and programs.
Olympics of the Mind https://www.odysseyofthemind.com/start-your-odyssey/	Hosts annual competitions engaging PK–12 students in STEM creative problem solving for schools and out-of-school programs.
Resilient Educator https://resilienteducator.com/collections/steam-teaching-resources/	Provides research, resources, STEM and STEAM scholarship, education grants, events and conferences, and professional learning.
Science Olympiad https://www.soinc.org/	Hosts annual STEM tournaments and professional learning workshops with emerging and innovative STEM content.
SMILE https://web.uri.edu/smile/	Offers afterschool programs for children and youth in fourth to twelfth grades across and is a model for future integrative STEM afterschool programs.
Technovation https://www.technovation.org/	Offers program models for a club, chapter, mentors and worldwide competitions.

Table 7.1. *(Continued)*

Name	*Description*
Technology Student Association https://tsaweb.org/	Offers competitions, conferences, and resources to connect high school students to STEM career pathways.
Verizon Innovative Learning https://www.verizon.com/about/responsibility/verizon-innovative-learning	Provides free technology and internet access and a next-gen, technology-infused curriculum delivering, and works with nonprofit organizations to coordinate and facilitate STEM-focused programs to attract students to STEM career pathways.
Vex Robotics https://www.vexrobotics.com/	Provides STEM products (e.g., curriculum and kits), educator certification, resources, and lab models to implement nationwide.

Community-Engaged Integrative STEM Committees

In addition to creating a community profile, *supportive* school and community leaders often create integrative STEM committees to foster relationships with existing organizations at local, state, and national levels to network with museums, businesses, organizations, and foundations (Gunn, 2020). These committees are comprised of caregivers, educators, and community members—all of whom demonstrate interest, experience, or expertise in the STEM fields.

The community-engagement committee may explore new avenues for extended learning, such as considering opportunities to learn more about career pathways and long-term compensation offered in the STEM fields (e.g., work-based learning or internships). Committee members may encourage, create, and sustain student organizations (e.g., Technology Student Association) and competitive teams/events (e.g., Science Olympiad, Maker Faires, Science Fairs, FIRST Robotics, Olympics of the Mind, 4-H).

Furthermore, educational leaders and integrative STEM committees can prioritize funding, plan for integrative STEM field trips (e.g., in-person, virtually), host integrative STEM fairs, workshops, or competitions, and sponsor integrative STEM before and after school programs (Owens Jr. et al., 2015). For instance, Million Women Mentors is an organization that assists in introducing students who identify as female to integrative STEM career opportunities and networking with mentors in the field.

Take Action for Community Engagement Committees

- Identify, invite, and appoint educators, staff, family members, and community members to an integrative STEM committee focused on extended learning.
- Empower committees to develop and monitor programming through program development, outreach, event planning, fundraising, advocacy, and marketing.
- Collaboratively establish a framework for extended learning opportunities to coordinate and maximize resources (NEA, 2008).
- Protect time and dates on school and district calendars related to the extended learning events, activities, and programs.

Integrative STEM Partnerships

As educational leaders strengthen their network by creating a community profile and integrative STEM committees, they begin developing partnerships via active engagement. NEA (2008) argues effective extended learning opportunities require "partnerships between community organizations that share the goals of promoting learning and community engagement" (p. 2). A partnership means that the school and the community benefit and honor reciprocity via the sharing of resources.

Expectations of community leaders are important to understand when developing relationships toward partnerships. By definition, reciprocity situates partners to expect something in return; and what school and community leaders offer should reinforce the commitment, roles, operations, and goals for both parties.

For example, school and community members share an interest in employability, which includes students (i.e., future workers) to meet expectations toward achievement. As a result of this shared interest, career standards were implemented across the nation as essential to prepare students for career pathways; thus, arguing the necessity to design an effective STEM education system across all grade levels (United States Department of Education, n.d.).

Take Action for Partnerships

Kladifko (2013) offers six general recommendations to cultivate and sustain community partnerships with schools. The following actions are revised and extended from Kladifko's suggestions to specifically correlate to integrative STEM.

- Acknowledge and announce school success with the larger community, directly connecting student achievement, growth, and interests related to STEM to the community partners that support extended learning experiences.
- Send regular communication, such as newsletters, school newspapers, and brochures about integrative STEM events, programming, and activities to contacts indicated on the community profile, and invite community partners to integrative STEM extended learning events.
- Schedule an integrative STEM-related visit or presentation with local businesses, government leaders, and legislators; invite educators, staff, and fellow leaders to participate in this visit, and send correspondence after the visit to show gratitude and to recap the purpose of the visit.
- Engage with the community in various ways, including but not limited to participating in community service, attending chambers of commerce meetings, cultivating relationships, and volunteering with students for community events.
- Ask local businesses, athletic teams, and government leaders to sponsor or adopt learning opportunities.
- Make the school accessible for general and integrative STEM community activities, such as town hall meetings, special business or foundation events, public service breakfasts, invention fairs, video game or robotic competitions, computer science and informatics conferences, etc.

Integrative STEM Professional Learning and Certifications

The successful implementation and sustainability of extended learning programs for integrative STEM education is a commitment that requires buy-in from multiple stakeholders, as well as becoming familiar with additional concerns leaders have discovered when incorporating integrative STEM in PK–12 (Ejiwale, 2013; Shernoff et al., 2017). It is important to consider the need for PK–12 educators who serve as integrative STEM facilitators and have access to professional learning opportunities and certifications. As a result, institutions of higher education are another important partnership to foster and establish.

Universities and colleges offer schools resources to develop "professional communities" (Merrill & Daugherty, 2010, p. 24), which provide expertise as a component of professional learning for integrative STEM education. These professional communities can form as a result of informal opportunities or as formal coursework. Educational leaders can advocate, lobby, and call for the coursework to count toward new licensure or certifications in integrative STEM leadership (Kladifko, 2013; Geesa et al., 2020; Rose et al., 2019). Their influence can motivate program leaders in higher education to innovate their existing coursework.

In addition, educational leaders can coordinate and offer integrative STEM leadership and continuing professional learning at their schools (NEA, 2008), outline educator professional learning requirements, and provide voluntary training options (Merrill & Dougherty, 2010). Leaders should ensure the professional integrative STEM trainings for educators demonstrate an "alignment and pooling of resources, so that there is no duplication but instead a filling of the gaps in service provision" (Kladifko, 2013, p. 55) to ensure the design is a reciprocal benefit for schools and higher institutions.

Educational leaders can arrange professional learning opportunities by presenting examples of effective integrative STEM extended learning lessons, activities, pedagogical approaches, and curricula (Geesa et al., 2021; Shernoff et al., 2017). Additionally, observing video recordings of effective integrative STEM facilitators implementing extended learning opportunities are also identified as best practices in professional learning (Shernoff, et al., 2017).

Professional learning experiences focused on the extended learning program should improve participants' career advancement goals. These experiences may incentivize educators and community partners to become more involved with facilitating integrative STEM extended learning. Additionally, identifying opportunities that offer continuing education, degree, or licensure credits may attract educators to participate.

Continuing professional learning courses can be offered through a business, with consultants, or in partnerships with institutions of higher education.

Take Action for Professional Learning

- Outline professional learning opportunities focused on extended learning in integrative education.
- Determine integrative STEM extended learning requirements for educators and facilitators.
- Schedule professional learning and offer resources and information for career advancement opportunities.
- Network with legislators and higher education leaders to advocate for leadership certifications and licensure opportunities for educators in integrative STEM.

Integrative STEM Mentorship

Access to professional and peer mentorship is central to the effectiveness of extended learning opportunities in support of integrative STEM (Karcher, 2005). Mentors may enrich and complement school curricula and serve to attract, recruit, and sustain students' interest in STEM fields (Honey et al., 2014).

Kupersmidt et al. (2018) offer three recommendations for effective mentors include (a) having STEM education backgrounds or are currently employed in a STEM-related position, (b) demonstrating technical skills needed for the program activities, and (c) developing relationships with children and youth not only to help them learn content, but also to observe and learn how to enter STEM fields.

Organizing a mentorship program may resemble the following plan of action. First, leaders through the practice of partnerships and community engagement can locate STEM mentors via the school's network with the local population. Then, a parent volunteer network can be established for identifying STEM mentors directly from the STEM field. Caregivers with established careers in STEM can be recruited to share their expertise either as a mentor for educators or students involved in integrative STEM extended learning opportunities.

When community-based partners are identified, educational leaders can pair integrative STEM facilitators with a STEM mentor, providing additional support and resources (Honey et al., 2014) to develop extended learning programs. Then, leaders can help match STEM mentors to service roles based on their expertise and interests. Mentors can be guest speakers, act as advisors to share their journey with students, or inform students about career and college opportunities (Honey et al., 2014). Offering incentives to volunteers (e.g., complimentary meals and products from community partners) may attract and connect volunteers to the larger community.

Finally, leaders can encourage students with strong interests, passions, or elevated understandings of STEM-related topics to volunteer as peer mentors (Honey et al., 2014). As a result, peer mentors and mentees may form relationships pertaining to their area of interest, launching their personal and professional network for their future. Supportive educational leaders can assist integrative STEM extended learning programs by recommending peer mentors according to previously determined criteria with school stakeholders, such as educators.

The educational leaders can appoint educators, staff, and school stakeholders to develop and facilitate a leadership program that focuses on finding peer mentors, which may also provide trainings to inform and support integrative STEM learning. Trainings may focus on procedures for identifying student participants, types of learning opportunities, and recruitment strategies.

Take Action for Mentorship

- Identify professional mentors in the local community via a survey of caregivers and community members and compile a list of professional integrative STEM mentors.
- Facilitate the creation of a parent or caregiver volunteer network with help from school stakeholders.
- Introduce and pair professional mentors with facilitators of extended learning programs.
- Provide professional training related to the role of professional and peer mentors related to informing, attracting, and supporting students in integrative STEM extended learning opportunities.

EVALUATE SCHOOL-COMMUNITY PARTNERSHIPS FOR IMPROVEMENT

Effective school-community partnerships are needed to ensure sustainable and successful extended learning opportunities. Thus, educational leaders and integrative STEM committees should establish a plan to assess the formation and performance of extended learning experiences with the aim of determining areas for improvement and informing decisions regarding continuance and future growth.

Evaluation should be embedded at the onset of planning for extended learning. As with the design of effective curriculum, success is dependent on articulating clear goals that align to program activities and lead to measurable short- and long-term outcomes. Popular among professional evaluators and funders of STEM education programs, a logic model is a valuable planning tool for clarifying essential data, sources of information, and measurement tools to inform the evaluation (Wilkerson & Haden, 2014).

Educational leaders may want to examine the intersections of performance, engagement, and school-STEM professional partnerships (Tytler et al., 2015) by gathering performance and perception data from the spectrum of participants (i.e., facilitators, community leaders, students and school staff) using interviews, focus groups, observational rubrics, and questionnaires.

Central to successful partnerships is leaders' and stakeholders' level of involvement and willingness to change practices (Watters & Diezmann, 2013, p. 53). As educational leaders look to the future, recommendations for growth may focus on the authentic pedagogical practices that engage students in meaningful experiences, possibly inspiring careers in STEM fields (Watters & Diezmann, 2013, p. 53).

CONCLUSION

This chapter offers educational leaders key strategies for implementing integrative STEM extended learning opportunities. Establishing partnerships with community members and businesses with integrative STEM interests and expertise can extend learning opportunities for educators, staff, families, and students. Supportive educational leaders should begin by assessing gaps between school programming, student interests, and community needs and resources.

The results should inform the work of a collaborative committee that plans, fosters, monitors, and evaluates an integrative STEM extended learning program that includes community-engaged practices, partnerships, and mentorship. By fostering continuous improvements in extended learning programs, educational leaders can motivate student interests in integrative STEM and enhance and coordinate school and community resources for the common goal of preparing youth for STEM careers.

Rhode Island SMILE: An Example of Extended Learning in Integrative STEM

Carol Marcus Englander

Science and Math Investigative Learning Experiences (SMILE) is an afterschool program that addresses the nationwide need to increase students' science and mathematics interest and knowledge through hands-on, inquiry-based activities in different states. The program's focus is to increase the number of under represented and educationally underserved students who are well-prepared to enter college and pursue STEM careers.

Established in 1994, the Rhode Island SMILE program was modeled after the Oregon State University SMILE Program, which began in 1986 under the direction of Dr. Miriam Orzech. With funding from a local technology company, American Power Conversion (now Schneider Electric), Rhode Island participants have not been financially responsible for any part of the program.

SMILE leads fourth- to twelfth-grade students into postsecondary education opportunities. With school district approval, teacher leaders identified children for the program with the approval of their parents. The SMILE acceptance criteria includes students: working at grade level, having grades of "C" or better, desiring to be in a STEM club, and having good SMILE attendance and school citizenship. Historically, SMILE membership has been comprised of 60 percent ethnic subgroups and 65 percent female (Rhode Island SMILE Database, 2019).

SMILE is a multifaceted program designed to increase student interest in a variety of areas. Students are exposed to mentor-based STEM activities and develop appreciation for how science and mathematics are used in everyday life. Students consider how STEM disciplines have potential to be used to solve complex problems in the world, and the curriculum includes units that are approximately 10 weeks long in engineering, environmental, and stewardship strands. Each grade-level curriculum rotates yearly, so students do not repeat activities.

Features of the SMILE Program

SMILE includes several features that align with characteristics of integrative STEM, which include college and career exploration, afterschool club and field trip involvement, family and community engagement, and sustainability planning.

College and Career Exploration

SMILE curricula are aligned with the state education standards and extend student learning beyond what they are acquiring in their classes. High school students are required to take four years of college-track mathematics and science. For students participating in SMILE for one year or more, the high school graduation rate is 93 to 100 percent (Rhode Island SMILE Database & Rhode Island Department of Education, Office of Data and Technology Services, 2018).

In 2017 and 2018, 75 percent of SMILE seniors immediately enrolled in college (National Student Clearinghouse, 2018). SMILE students have attended 345 colleges and universities in the United States, and several students pursue STEM-related majors (National Student Clearinghouse, 2018). Between 1998 and 2017, 322 SMILE alumni enrolled at University of Rhode Island, with 70 percent pursuing STEM-related career paths (University of Rhode Island Office of Institutional Research, 2018).

SMILE combines academic experiences with career explorations and university experiences from early ages. Curricula are developed specifically to be hands-on with concrete applications and career-oriented field trips. Mentors from sponsor corporations and student organizations from University of Rhode Island are actively involved in SMILE; these volunteers serve as role models of academic success and encourage students to aim for college success.

Students gain exposure to integrative STEM-related fields throughout their SMILE experience from fourth to twelfth grades. Engineering Challenge Weekends are events where middle and high school SMILE students come to the University of Rhode Island's campus and work in mixed school teams on an engineering project. Industry representatives introduce each engineering challenge, establishing a real-world experience by emphasizing their company's own relevant experiences, and motivating student engagement to complete the challenge.

Middle school challenges include designing, building, and testing bridges, cranes, maglev trains, and wind turbines. High school design challenges include biotechnology forensics, solar racing car, SeaPerch remotely operated underwater vehicles, and bioengineering a football helmet.

SMILE students have an "on-campus" college experience because they see college students who look like them when touring the campus, visiting labs, learning about college admission requirements, and using the recreation facilities. A SMILE student has many opportunities to visit the university campus by their senior year, which demystifies the college experience and makes it seem more like an attainable goal.

Afterschool Club and Field Trip Involvement

Weekly afterschool clubs are the core of SMILE. These clubs establish continuity, provide context for learning, and build a sense of community for students and leaders. Clubs of approximately 20 students are organized by grade level at elementary, middle, and high schools.

SMILE students meet weekly for one and a half to two hours after school for hands-on science and mathematics enrichment activities.

SMILE club leaders are educators at the same school with strong mathematics and science knowledge. Leaders receive continuous support through professional development workshops, networking, curriculum materials, and equipment. SMILE workshops for leaders are conducted three times a year and are led by University of Rhode Island resource faculty and SMILE staff. Curricular materials and contact information of other SMILE educators and staff are available through a shared online storage drive. SMILE staff visit each club, and leaders submit activity logs and attendance after each meeting.

SMILE educators conduct report card celebrations during club meetings. Educators review each student's grades, praise the students, and have "special snacks." If any student has a grade less than "C," they agree to a contract to improve the deficiency within two weeks or be suspended from the club. SMILE educators notify the parents and discuss the problem with the classroom teacher to determine ways to support the student.

In addition to club meetings at school, field trips give students the opportunity to explore careers, interact with professionals, and learn about scientific principles in the real world. SMILE raises money to support the transportation costs associated with trips. An example of a career-oriented field trip for SMILE students is a facility tour of Toray Plastics (America), Inc. where students learn how thin film plastic is made and changed into usable products (e.g., potato chip bags).

SMILE also sponsors a two-day overnight camp for fifth-grade students. The event focuses on field-based curriculum using science equipment. Activities integrate science and mathematics topics designed to foster an appreciation for the natural environment. Also, the fourth-grade ecology field day brings students to the University of Rhode Island campus to learn about marine science, soils and plants, and vernal pools (e.g., see Figure 7.3), which extends their experiences in integrative STEM and provides them more opportunities to explore the connections among STEM, higher education, and careers.

Figure 7.3. SMILE students determining permeability of different soils.
Rhode Island SMILE Program.

Community and Family Engagement

Local corporations are an integral part of SMILE because they provide long-term financial commitments and volunteer staff who serve as presenters and mentors to SMILE students. SMILE benefits from higher education institutions, as well. The University of Rhode Island provides scientific expertise, access to equipment, facilities, and administrative support. University students, faculty, corporate employees, and SMILE educators act as mentors to SMILE students.

In addition, parents, caregivers, and family members are involved in SMILE. Family science nights occur yearly in each school district for all three school levels. These nights bring students, families, and community members together for an engaging evening of science exploration and discovery. SMILE students act as instructors, engage participants in hands-on activities, explain their observations and data, and generate conclusions. College planning materials and financial aid information are also available for families to review.

Sustainability Planning

Data are needed in order to sustain the program. SMILE, the Rhode Island Department of Education Office of Data and Technology Services, the National Student Clearinghouse, and the Office of Institutional Research at University of Rhode Island enable the tracking of most students who have been in SMILE through their state identification number, school district, and date of birth. SMILE participant statistics focus on high school graduation, college entrance, and college majors and graduation rates.

SMILE has established a successful model of collaboration among a diverse group of people from schools, families, and local communities, universities, and corporations. This model has allowed SMILE to design and implement exciting programs for students that provide them access to scientific expertise, mentoring opportunities, financial and administrative support, and community involvement.

Each school district has made commitments to the program by facilitating club meetings and providing funding for educator stipends and, in some cases, late buses for SMILE students to attend meetings. The sustainability of SMILE and other extended learning programs requires multiple sources of funding, as SMILE staff continue to seek additional support and improve funding strategies.

Leadership Strategies

Leadership strategies, such as stakeholder communication, community partnerships, and support for experiential learning, have been critical for SMILE to be successful from support of educational leaders.

Stakeholder Communication

SMILE personnel coordinate meetings with superintendents, school committee members, and cooperating agencies each year to disseminate data regarding the past year's SMILE program. This information includes number of participants at each club level, number of returning students, participants' ethnicities and gender, high school graduation rate, number of students currently in college, college names and majors, and number of high school SMILE seniors selected for a SMILE scholarship. These statistics show partners how effective the program is, and why SMILE is worth allocating funds for educator stipends.

SMILE supports each district with a 3-to-1 ratio of dollars spent. These statistics are also communicated to additional stakeholders in each district. Inviting corporate and foundation partners, funding agencies, administrators, caregivers, parents, and extended family members to annual SMILE family science nights and potlucks in each school district is one successful strategy. These events bring students, families, community members, and partners together for a fun evening of ethnic foods and integrative STEM learning.

Community Partnerships

Establishing connections with current and potential partners in technology and manufacturing industries to introduce SMILE and plan field trips to the career site is another successful strategy to facilitate extended learning opportunities for students. SMILE staff develop club pre-activities to acquaint students with each community partner prior to their visit. This results in excellent workplace experiences for the SMILE students and new funding opportunities for the extended learning program.

For example, becoming acquainted with personnel from the Environmental Protection Agency and National Oceanic and Atmospheric Administration enhanced partnerships and curricula with these organizations. Scientists from these groups present areas of interest to SMILE educators and students. Additionally, SMILE clubs visit their labs and SMILE writes grants to these agencies to help fund the program.

Support of Experiential Learning

To enhance awareness of careers in STEM, SMILE students are introduced to hands-on inquiry-based activities at an early age, encouraged to understand the need for and usefulness of mathematics, and see STEM learning disassociated from test-taking strategies. Students say they learn more in SMILE without tests than they learn in their regular classes. Students enter their SMILE room at the end of the regular school day, and they are greeted by their teachers, fortified by a snack, and ready to understand a new concept through experiential learning.

Summary

For more than a quarter of a century, SMILE has provided full-year afterschool programming to students in fourth to twelfth grades in Rhode Island. Through mentoring opportunities, field trips, and hands-on engineering projects, students have developed a positive connection to schools and the teacher leaders who support them.

SMILE students are introduced to STEM activities, some of which are of great interest, so much so that they take the deemed "hard" science and mathematics courses in high school that prepare them to pursue STEM-related majors in higher education. SMILE students enjoy learning concepts and skills beyond the mainstream curriculum ahead of other students, and they become STEM-literate, lifelong learners through the program. Features and strategies of this program may be replicated by educational leaders throughout the nation.

REFERENCES

Bandy, J. (2011). *What is service learning or community engagement?* Vanderbilt University. https://cft.vanderbilt.edu/guides-sub-pages/teaching-through-community-engagement

Blank, M., & Langford, B. H. (2000). *Strengthening partnerships: Community school assessment checklist.* Coalition for Community Schools, & The Finance Project. https://phennd.org/wp2014/wp-content/uploads/2020/04/assessment_cs.pdf

Ejiwale, J. A. (2013). Barriers to successful implementation of STEM education. *Journal of Education and Learning*, *7*(2), 63–74. https://doi.org/10.11591/edulearn.v7i2.220

Ferrandino, V. L. (2006). *Leading after-school learning communities: What principals should know and be able to do.* National Association of Elementary School Principals. https://www.naesp.org/sites/default/files/docs/leading-after-school-learning-communities-executive-summary.pdf

Geesa, R. L., Stith, K. M., & Rose, M. A. (2020). Preparing school and district leaders for success in developing and facilitating integrative STEM in higher education. *Journal of Research on Leadership Education*, 1–21. https://doi.org/10.1177/1942775120962148

Geesa, R. L., Stith, K. M., & Teague, G. M. (2021). Integrative STEM education and leadership for student success. In F. English (Ed.), *The Palgrave Handbook of Educational Leadership and Management Discourse* (pp. 1–20). Palgrave Macmillan. https://doi.org/10.1007/978-3-030-39666-4_36-1

Gunn, J. (2020). *Building a partnership between your school and a STEAM organization*. Resilient Educator. https://resilienteducator.com/classroom-resources/steam-organizations-school-partnership/

Honey, M., Pearson, G., & Schweingruber, H. A. (Eds.). (2014). *STEM integration in K–12 education: Status, prospects, and an agenda for research*. National Academies Press. https://doi.org/10.17226/18612

Karcher, M. J. (2005). The effects of developmental mentoring and high school mentors' attendance on their younger mentees' self-esteem, social skills, and connectedness. *Psychology in the Schools*, *42*(1), 65–77. https://doi.org/10.1002/pits.20025

Kelley, T. R., & Knowles, J. G. (2016). A conceptual framework for integrated STEM education. *International Journal of STEM Education*, *3*(11), 1–11. https://doi.org/10.1186/s40594-016-0046-z

Kladifko, R. E. (2013). Practical school community partnerships leading to successful educational leaders. *Educational Leadership and Administration: Teaching and Program Development*, *24*, 54–61. https://files.eric.ed.gov/fulltext/EJ1013145.pdf

Kupersmidt, J., Stelter, R., Garringer, M., & Bourgoin, J. (2018). STEM mentoring: Supplement to the elements of effective practice for mentoring. *MENTOR: National Mentoring Partnership*. https://www.mentoring.org/new-site/wp-content/uploads/2018/10/STEM-Supplement-to-EEP.pdf

Meeder, H., & Pawlowski, B. (2020). *Preparing our students for the real world: The education shift our children and future demand*. National Center for College and Career Transitions. https://www.nc3t.com/wp-content/uploads/2020/02/Preparing-Our-Students-for-the-Real-World-021720.pdf

Merrill, C., & Daugherty, J. (2010). STEM education and leadership: A mathematics and science partnership approach. *Journal of Technology Education*, *21*(2), 21–34.

National Education Association (NEA). (2008). *Closing the gap through extended learning opportunities*. https://www.icareby.org/sites/www.icareby.org/files/ClosingGap.pdf

National Science Teachers Association. (2018). *The role of e-learning in science education.* http://files.eric.ed.gov/fulltext/ED520338.pdf

National Student Clearinghouse. (2018). *SMILE students enrolled in college, and colleges attended* [Unpublished raw data].

Owens Jr., E. W., Shelton, A. J., Bloom, C., & McClinton, J. (2015). Comparing principals' support of STEM education in public and private high schools: A National Study. *Journal of Contemporary Issues in Higher Education, 1*(1), 30–42.

Rhode Island SMILE Database. (2019). *Statistics internal query, 1995-2019* [Unpublished raw data].

Rhode Island SMILE Database & Rhode Island Department of Education, Office of Data and Technology Services. (2018). *SMILE high school graduates* [Unpublished raw data].

Rose, M. A., Geesa, R. L., & Stith, K. (2019). STEM leader excellence: A modified Delphi study of critical skills, competencies, and qualities. *Journal of Technology Education, 31*(1), 42–62. https://doi.org/10.21061/jte.v31i1.a.3

Shernoff, D. J., Sinha, S., Bressler, D. M., & Ginsburg, L. (2017). Assessing teacher education and professional development needs for the implementation of integrated approaches to STEM education. *International Journal of STEM Education, 4*(13), 1–16. https://doi.org/10.1186/s40594-017-0068-1

Stefanski, A., Valli, L., & Jacobson, R. (2016). Beyond involvement and engagement: The role of the family in school-community partnerships. *School Community Journal*, *26*(2), 135–160. https://files.eric.ed.gov/fulltext/EJ1124001.pdf

Tytler, R., Symington, D., Williams, G., White, P., Campbell, C., Chittleborough, G., Upstill, G., Roper, E., & Dziadkiewicz M. N. (2015). Building productive partnerships for STEM education: Evaluating the model and outcomes of the scientists and mathematicians in schools program 2015. *STEME Research Group*. https://www.csiro.au/~/media/Education-media/Files/STEM-Prof-Schools/Productive-Partnerships-STEM-Education-PDF.pdf

University of Rhode Island Office of Institutional Research. (2018). *SMILE alumni enrollment and majors at URI, 1998-2017*. https://web.uri.edu/ir/reports-and-surveys

United States Department of Education. (n.d.). *College- and career-ready standards*. https://www.ed.gov/k-12reforms/standards

Vex Robotics. (2020). *Competition brings STEM skills to life.* https://www.vexrobotics.com/competition

Watters, J. J., & Diezmann, C. M. (2013). Community partnerships for fostering student interest and engagement in STEM. *Journal of STEM Education: Innovations and Research, 14*(2), 47–54.

Wilkerson, S. B., & Haden, C. M. (2014). Effective practices for evaluating STEM out-of-school time programs. *Afterschool Matters*, *19*, 10–19. https://files.eric.ed.gov/fulltext/EJ1021960.pdf

8

Promoting Professional Learning for Integrative STEM

Ginger Mink Teague, Krista Marie Stith, and Rachel Louise Geesa

As the world continues to grow more complex, so does the need for citizens to be equipped with the problem-solving skills necessary to navigate the demands of the twenty-first century. To meet this challenge, PK–12 students must gain competencies in the STEM disciplines of science, technology, engineering, and mathematics. Additionally, they need transportable skills that include problem-solving, critical thinking, communication skills, and STEM literacy. With knowledge and technologies growing at exponential rates, "there is an ever-increasing need for well-prepared teachers who can help all children learn for the complex world they are entering" (Darling-Hammond & Oakes, 2019, p. 1).

Whether or not students plan to enter STEM-related fields, it is essential for them to develop the thinking and literacy skills, often associated with integrative STEM education, to successfully meet the complexities of an increasingly technological world. This necessity calls for PK–12 schools to rethink traditional approaches to education and identify ways to build STEM competencies. Exposing students to integrative STEM opportunities requires educational leaders and educators to build their own educational and instructional capacity to navigate this challenge.

Thus, the question looms—in what ways can educational leaders support their own learning and educators' learning in integrative STEM content and practices through professional learning? This chapter explores ways to plan and implement professional learning opportunities that build the capacity of educators and leaders to lay groundwork for students to develop STEM literacy.

First, it is important to consider the a) shifts needed for educators and their leaders to include integrative STEM education in schools and b) shifts in developing content knowledge and pedagogical practices. Then, characteristics of integrative STEM professional learning and exemplars of promising strategies and best practices to establish and maintain professional learning are discussed.

A PRAXIS SHIFT FOR EDUCATORS THROUGH PROFESSIONAL LEARNING

The implementation of integrative STEM education calls for new teaching and learning approaches, pedagogical skills, and deeper conceptual understanding within and across the STEM disciplines (Shernoff et al., 2017). Educational leaders and educators with limited cross-disciplinary knowledge and experience with integrating academic disciplines may struggle (Brown et al., 2011; Dare et al., 2018).

The literature provides many examples of PK–12 educator STEM content knowledge and pedagogy gaps that leaders and educators identify as barriers for crafting environments conducive to support students thinking and communicating as scientists, technologists, engineers, and mathematicians (Cunningham & Carlsen, 2014, Li & Schoenfeld, 2019; Margot & Kettler, 2019). Professional learning opportunities may address barriers identified, such as educators' unfamiliarity with design, engineering, and technology (Hsu et al., 2011) and lower capacities in technology and online tools (Handal et al., 2013).

STEM Content

New learning for educators may include building their own understanding of STEM content and increasing awareness of standards from other disciplines. In our technological and scientifically driven society, STEM content is constantly evolving. Content taught 20, 15, 10, or even five years ago may no longer be accurate or relevant to today's youth. As educators are academics and lifelong learners, their learning of STEM content should be considered when planning professional learning.

STEM Pedagogy

Expanding from content alone, professional learning may incorporate new learning in mathematical and scientific inquiry, engineering practices, computational thinking, design thinking, and integrative practices to foster these understandings in their own classrooms.

Professional learning can support educators to become impactful facilitators, building their capacity to ask probing questions, assess conceptual development, address misconceptions, and work within instructional teams (e.g., see Figures 8.1 and 8.2). Professional learning in STEM content or pedagogy may be available through professionals in higher education, online classes and modules, conferences and summits, guest speakers, educator-centric field trips, and in-house presentations.

Figure 8.1. Educators participating in professional learning about design plans in a makerspace. iStockphoto LP.

Figure 8.2. Educators engaging in professional learning on 3D printer applications for their classes. iStockphoto LP.

Pedagogical Content Knowledge

Educational leaders should also emphasize professional learning opportunities that enhance educators' pedagogical content knowledge of integrative STEM learning experiences. As pedagogical content knowledge is the intersection of content knowledge and pedagogy (Shulman, 1987), with strong pedagogical content knowledge, educators should be able to think and teach as professionals in STEM fields.

For example, the development of pedagogical content knowledge in scientific inquiry should involve "experiencing authentic science investigations and experimentation practices" (Kelley & Knowles, 2016, p. 5) to teach students to think and practice as scientists. Problem- and project-based learning approaches have been considered successful ways to contextualize learning within STEM fields (Nadelson & Seifert, 2013) because situated learner-centered STEM activities can seamlessly integrate scientific inquiry, mathematical thinking, technological literacy, and engineering design.

In learner-centered classrooms, facilitators employ guided and self-directed learning strategies while providing opportunities for students to make decisions, design solutions to problems, and test hypotheses. The task to facilitate this type of learning becomes even more complex as educators navigate building both content-specific knowledge and skills while also making connections among the STEM content areas (National Academy of Engineering & National Research Council, 2014).

A Shifting School Exemplar

To begin addressing the goal of improving STEM outcomes for their students, Yorktown Community Schools in Indiana created a STEAM ("A" for the arts) leadership team, including their director of educational initiatives, STEM specialist, technology specialist, and literacy coach. The leadership team was tasked to develop and implement high-quality professional learning in STEM for their educators.

The district's STEM professional learning was delivered two ways: (a) a project-based learning cohort model and (b) a personalized professional learning model. The first cohort of 20 educators participated in a five-day program delivered throughout the summer and school year. Each educator completed at least one high-quality project-based learning unit or project with their students during the year and mentored one educator in the succeeding year.

The district moved to a personalized professional learning model to ensure that all educators and staff were getting the support and training that they needed rather than focusing on a one-size-fits-all model. These personalized professional learning offerings were delivered in several formats (e.g., in person before and after school, lunch-and-learns, book studies, and online modules presented in their learning management systems).

Sessions consisted of a variety of topics, such as STEM implementation, introduction to project-based learning, technology integration, literacy and STEM, social-emotional learning, as well as educator requested sessions. Educators earned credits for participation and those that received at least 10 credits received a stipend for their work. By allowing educators choice, educational leaders continued to build capacity and educator buy-in for programming and instruction that addressed both STEM content and pedagogy.

LEARNING IMPACT FOR EDUCATIONAL LEADERS

Educational leaders play a valuable role in building the capacity of educators, staff, and fellow leaders to face and embrace new challenges. To successfully implement integrative STEM, leaders must foster the growth of students and educators in addition to their own professional learning. Similar to professional learning for educators, professional learning for leaders is needed to provide a conceptual understanding of the knowledge, skills, and dispositions required for supporting STEM literacy, exposure to STEM career pathways, and community-integrated experiences (Geesa et al., 2020, 2021; Rose et al., 2019).

For example, professional learning with a community partner may lead to established learning experiences that build students' awareness of local career prospects while also enriching the curricula with real-world applicability. Effective leaders determine ways to build their own capacity to make decisions and collaborate with others to develop and enact policies that open doors to empowering educators to take on new challenges.

Educational leaders should build their own understanding of what an integrative approach requires of their educators and staff, such as unpacking standards, incorporating problem- and project-based strategies, gaining content understanding, and building new instructional practices. Leaders can also have knowledge about individual educator's capacity for new pedagogies, content, and change, as it "is essential to creating programs that meet their needs while attending to the agendas of STEM initiatives" (Nadelson & Seifert, 2013, p. 260).

Educational leaders should consider alternative ways to approach many traditional aspects of school, especially in considering effective professional learning practices. Having familiarity with professional learning practices of other integrative STEM programs, incorporating community needs, and working with STEM specialists and consultants may provide the initial directions to make well-informed professional learning decisions to benefit all stakeholders.

Educational leaders' engagement in their own professional learning builds their capacity to effectively address the demands of an integrative STEM program. Exploration of successful programs, examination of effective professional learning practices, and consideration of their own school and district are key areas of learning. External supports, such as conferences and summits, scholarly literature, and formal coursework, are also available.

LEARNING IMPACT FOR EDUCATORS

Professional learning can promote positive attitudes about integration of disciplines and collaboration with colleagues, leading to a willingness to change their own practice (Al Salami et al., 2017). When faced with the task of implementing integrative STEM, educators may be skeptical. They may fear their ability to facilitate content from multiple disciplines or question the impact for students. Both educators and educational leaders can address concerns by exploring successful programs through school visits, participating in online opportunities for learning, or reviewing relevant educational literature.

Educators and leaders may experience changes in paradigms and new conceptual understanding and pedagogical practices when bringing integrative STEM into schools. Together, they should decide what they deem as effective professional learning activities. Educators should have opportunities to share their professional growth needs and barriers that stand in the way with educational leaders as they consider professional learning needs.

Integrative STEM requires collaboration among educators to ensure that programs, courses, and units of study are designed to achieve the goals set by the school or district. This calls for educational leaders to build awareness of strategies that foster collaboration, such as creating a culture that is built on shared values and vision, encouraging collective learning and application, and valuing shared practice among educators (Hipp & Huffman, 2003).

PERCEPTIONS OF PIONEERING EDUCATORS

Although the research on STEM professional learning is emerging, some studies indicate that transitioning into an integrative STEM program is often not a seamless shift for educators (e.g., see Table 8.1). Avery and Reeve (2013) found that teachers who participated in the National Center

Table 8.1. Educator Perceptions of Benefits and Challenges after STEM Professional Learning Participation

Researchers	*Benefits*	*Challenges*
Avery & Reeve (2013)	STEM professional learning benefits in the classroom include *students*: • experiencing facilitated instruction, • increasing their motivation for STEM learning, • maintaining engagement with subject matter, • increasing their appreciation for science and mathematics, • improving their thinking and problem-solving skills, and • improving their learning strategies.	Challenges with implementing STEM content in the classroom include *educators*: • evaluating group projects, • aligning learning to standards, • providing available authentic engineering design challenges, and • developing STEM lessons.
Margot & Kettler (2019)	STEM professional learning benefits in the classroom include *students*: • applying learning, • participating in cross-curricular STEM education, • being inherently motivated by STEM instruction, and • experiencing struggles and failures as valuable components of the engineering design process.	Challenges with implementing STEM professional learning include educators: • having limited knowledge and comfort with STEM contributing to activities in STEM professional development, • lacking understanding of why STEM should be included in curricula, • changing practices to facilitate integrative STEM, • working around typical school structures, • believing students are unable or unwilling to be successful in STEM education, and • not having quality assessment tools, planning time, and knowledge of STEM disciplines.

Note: Information collected from "Developing Effective STEM Professional Development Programs," by Z. K. Avery, and E. M. Reeve, 2013, *Journal of Technology Education, 25*(1), 55–69 (http://files.eric.ed.gov/fulltext/EJ1020199.pdf); and "Teachers' Perception of STEM Integration and Education: A Systematic Literature Review," by K. C. Margot, and T. Kettler, 2019, *International Journal of STEM Education, 6*(2), 1–16 (https://doi.org/10.1186/s40594-018-0151-2).

for Engineering and Technology Education professional development perceived increased motivations, engagement, and appreciation for STEM subjects. These teachers also reported difficulties with evaluation of collaborative projects and the development of STEM lessons.

As shown in Table 8.1, Margot and Kettler (2019) identified six categories of challenges and barriers to educators implementing STEM professional development content, which include (a) pedagogical challenges, (b) curriculum challenges with integration, (c) structural challenges, (d) student concerns, (e) assessments concerns, and (f) teacher supports, time, and subject-matter knowledge.

ADDITIONAL CONSIDERATIONS FOR PROFESSIONAL LEARNING

An integrated approach to learning requires educational leaders to review and reconsider the design and implementation of scheduling, assessments, and evaluation practices relative to educators and curricular programs. Leaders must consider allocation of fiscal and time resources to support student and educator learning. The cost for training educators and staff and providing ongoing support may be far different than expenses related to traditional approaches in professional learning.

For example, traditional professional learning opportunities may only be for a few hours or a day while ongoing training and professional learning experiences may last a few weeks, months, or semesters for educators and staff. Educational leaders may consider funding instructional coaches or peer mentors and providing structured time for educators to have extended learning opportunities in the schools.

Educators may need blocks of time to address multiple disciplines within one class, or class schedules may need to be redesigned for educators of different disciplines to develop integrated curricula and meaningful assessments. Content silos should also be reexamined if scheduling cannot support the autonomy of elementary educators to integrate the STEM disciplines into their required mathematics and reading scheduled blocks of time.

Educational leaders may need to reconsider their current evaluation processes. Effective leaders of integrative STEM programs build their own capacity to recognize what successful teaching and learning looks like in an environment where students are engaged in project- and problem-based learning activities and integrated curricula. Educational leaders must become aware of the need to build assessments that address both content knowledge and the *process* of problem-solving, instead of assessing students on the end products alone (Shively et al., 2018).

For program evaluation, consultants and STEM specialists from institutions of higher education, STEM organizations, state-level education departments, scholarly literature, and feedback from stakeholders may be helpful in providing evaluative feedback and new lenses for educational leaders to consider programming innovations.

IMPACTFUL PROFESSIONAL LEARNING

Implementation of integrative STEM education necessitates the need for ongoing professional growth opportunities that empower educators to effectively facilitate powerful STEM learning. Professional learning is needed to meet the rising needs for students to build "conceptual understandings and procedural skills and abilities that individuals need to address STEM-related personal, social and global issues" (Bybee, 2018, p. 138). As educational leaders and educators consider how to address their learning needs, consideration should be given to what is known about effective professional learning.

Professional Learning Characteristics

Understanding research-based professional learning practices can serve as the foundation for educational leaders to create professional learning plans that effectively meet the needs of a school or district. Researchers (e.g., Avery & Reeve, 2013; Combs & Silverman, 2016; and Darling-Hammond et al., 2017) have identified characteristics of impactful professional learning that is situated within the context of the actual content and evidence-based pedagogical practices (see Table 8.2).

Table 8.2. Research-Based Characteristics of Impactful Professional Learning

Characteristic	*Description*
Active learning-focused	Participants are actively involved in developing or practicing teaching strategies.
Aligned to school goals, state and district standards, and assessments	Professional learning is coherent with stated expectations for teaching and learning.
Content-focused	Professional learning is directly tied to the curriculum or program.
Collaborative	Educators work collaboratively and learn collectively with other educators.
Embedded with feedback and reflection	Professional learning opportunities incorporate high-quality feedback mechanisms and opportunities for reflecting on learning and new practices.
Job embedded	Professional learning is contextualized within the classroom and includes learning and practice within the regular teaching environment.
Provides coaching and expert support	Professional learning includes modeling and sharing of evidence-based practices.
Sustained for a duration of time	Professional learning takes place over an extended period, longer than a one-day session or workshop.

Impactful professional learning occurs when educators are afforded the time necessary to learn, practice, implement, and then reflect on learning new strategies that call for changes in their practice (Darling-Hammond et al., 2017). Although research does not offer exact amounts of time necessary for a professional learning experience to be effective, the literature indicates extended time of 20 hours or more is favorable with professional learning spread over the course of a semester or intense professional learning sessions including follow-up as educators return to their classrooms (Desimone, 2009).

The duration of the professional learning experience and ongoing learning must be significant, allowing time for educators to learn new practices and determine how best to implement their new or redefined learning (Gulamhussein, 2013). Intensive sessions in the summer can be scheduled to include follow-up sessions over the course of a school year. Instructional coaches or peer mentors may provide regular support to educators on planning, implementing, and reflecting on the classroom outcomes.

Ongoing professional learning may include groups of educators working together in professional learning communities (PLCs) to share their practices as they co-plan and evaluate the effectiveness of lessons. PLCs offer a format for collaborative work, collective learning, and innovation among educators in the same school or across schools (Brown et al., 2018). Learning arises naturally from their shared experiences and is sustained as colleagues collaborate in learning that is embedded in their work. Being intentional to include groups of educators, interdisciplinary colleagues, instructional coaches, staff, and educational leaders in professional learning experiences is a positive step toward successful implementation.

Collaboration among educators, staff, and leaders with instructional coaches or professional learning facilitators is a hallmark of effective professional learning. Collaboration recognizes learning as "an active, interactive, constructive, and iterative process" (Darling-Hammond & Oakes, 2019, p. 14). When educators learn together, "the value of co-construction is that each participant contributes his or her own experience and thinking in a way that can lead to synergistic insight" (Combs & Silverman, 2016, p. 22).

Learning collaboratively means that educators are open to sharing practices, planning together, observing one another, and collectively solving problems (Darling-Hammond & Oakes, 2019). For example, educators in a PLC may participate in weekly collaboration meetings to reflect on and plan integrative STEM learning experiences and revisit roles and responsibilities in their collaborative group.

Developing Effective STEM Professional Learning Opportunities

Leaders' roles in planning for effective professional learning focused on integrative STEM content and practices is critical and challenging. With purposeful multidisciplinary teaching, professional learning constructs should include pedagogical content knowledge and skills. With standardized testing pressures impacting the amount of time available for educators, STEM professional learning should be relevant in addressing standards-based STEM lessons.

Avery and Reeve (2013) recommend STEM professional development to (a) provide a supportive professional development environment,

(b) provide an exemplar of an engineering design challenge, (c) provide training on managing group projects and evaluating student contributions, (d) consider standards-based pressures the impact STEM learning, (e) train teachers to develop their own standards-based, engineering design challenges, and (f) train teachers on how to integrate STEM concepts into their instructional materials (pp. 12–13).

Different strategies can support educators in building a sense of integrative STEM learning by actively engaging them in developing conceptual understanding and problem-solving skills. One strategy is to facilitate professional learning in which educators roleplay as students. In Havice et al. (2018), leaders participated in an integrative STEM education institute along with teachers. Results from pre-post questionnaires indicated immediate and long-term changes in pedagogy and self-efficacy.

As part of leaders' and educators' professional learning, participating educators played the roles of young students and solved engineering design challenges. In Project Lead The Way professional development experiences, participants spend portions of the training in the role of a student in PK–12 grades (Project Lead The Way, Inc., 2020). While participating in these training experiences, educators explore evidence-based instructional practices, such as activity-, project-, and problem-based learning, and the use of scientific inquiry and engineering design.

Another strategy is to fund instructional coaches or peer mentors to support job embedded professional learning. Palmyra Area School District in Pennsylvania, for example, employs a STEM instructional coach to support elementary educators in the development and implementation of integrative STEM learning experiences.

The coach collaborates with classroom teachers by identifying integrative intersections within upcoming units of instruction, as well as exploring possible visions for integrative STEM learning. After identifying a potentially valuable focus, the partners collaboratively develop and implement an integrative STEM learning experience with students. The coach models preferred STEM pedagogy. Then, the two evaluate and revise the experience for future implementation with another group of students.

Alternatively, a professional learning plan can include shared learning opportunities with others outside of the school or district. Summer workshops or institutes of sustained duration offer a way to engage educators and staff in learning that is active and directly connected to the content and pedagogical practices necessary to effectively implement integrative STEM education in schools. However, extending learning beyond in-school events calls for additional considerations of budget, resources, and time allotments.

Establishing professional learning opportunities that enable collaboration among educators, staff, and instructional leaders can also facilitate lifelong learning. With the amount of new teaching and learning strategies and changes in practice necessary for educators to implement integrative STEM, working with others removes the isolation typical within the teaching profession.

Bringing together "interdisciplinary teams of educators to engage in engineering design activities can help promote connections within and across STEM domains" (Donna, 2012, p. 7), and educators have opportunities to share resources and develop strategies to engage students in innovation through collaboration. Educational leaders can lead change by uncovering educators' needs for professional learning, providing necessary resources, and tracking professional development experiences and their impact on teaching and learning (Louis et al., 2010).

Professional Learning Providers

Aside from institutions of higher education, there are multiple providers that may provide integrative STEM education professional learning. Examples of providers include:

- Buck Institute for Education's Project Based Learning Program (2020): Provides project-based learning workshops for educators in one or three day timelines with sustained support on site and online
- International Technology and Engineering Educators Association's (ITEEA) STEM Center for Teaching and Learning (2020): Provides summer institutes, trainers, and STEMinars for elementary education programs
- Project Lead The Way, Inc. (2020): Provides face-to-face and online training in the areas of engineering, biomedical science, and computer science through their activity-, project-, and problem-based learning approach

- TeachThought Professional Development (2020): Provides project-based strategies that align with content standards and offers workshops for educational leaders

CONCLUSION

Implementation of integrative STEM education holds great promise for developing STEM-literate students who are equipped to navigate the demands of an ever-changing global society. This approach calls for new learning and new practices for educators and educational leaders. Educators face challenges as they build capacity to integrate the STEM disciplines and other disciplines while also developing problem-solving, critical thinking, communication skills, ethical behavior, and STEM literacy.

Building supportive conditions and cultivating a culture that promotes professional learning are critical ways that leaders can foster educator growth (Teague, 2012). Supportive conditions include both structural conditions (e.g., time, resources) and relational conditions (e.g., trust, communication, recognition, caring support). Educational leaders "can have a significant influence on teachers' classroom practices through their efforts to motivate teachers and create workplace settings compatible with instructional practices known to be effective" (Louis et al., 2010, p. 103).

Sharing practices and learning collectively depends on allowing time for educators to collaborate, observe others teaching and facilitating instruction, and engage in reflective practice. This time must be built into the educators' schedules through shared planning periods, release times, or professional learning days devoted to PLC work. Many school districts have also found success in providing instructional coaches or mentors, in addition to educational leaders, to provide integrative STEM education support and modeling for educators.

As educators take on the challenges of implementing integrative STEM learning, mechanisms for feedback and assessment of progress are needed. Professional learning models that have been tied to student learning gains include time devoted to reflecting on practice and receiving feedback (Darling-Hammond et al., 2017).

Educational leaders need to provide opportunities for reflection, authentic feedback, and evaluation among educators and staff. They must also find ways to be involved in the process. Observing learning, facilitating lessons, and discussing practices with educators should be frequent and used to uncover what students are learning to gain insight into educators' practice.

Professional growth opportunities grounded in evidence-based professional learning practices can set the stage for ongoing learning necessary to effectively integrate STEM disciplines. Educational leaders must reexamine current practices for professional learning, scheduling, and use of resources. Educational leaders play a critical role as they cultivate a culture that promotes ongoing professional growth through professional learning opportunities focused on active learning of content and pedagogical practices.

REFERENCES

Al Salami, M. K., Makela, C. J., & de Miranda, M. A. (2017). Assessing changes in teachers' attitudes toward interdisciplinary STEM teaching. *International Journal of Technology & Design Education, 27*(1), 63–88. https://doi.org/10.1007/s10798-015-9341-0

Avery, Z. K., & Reeve, E. M. (2013). Developing effective STEM professional development programs. *Journal of Technology Education, 25*(1), 55–69. http://files.eric.ed.gov/fulltext/EJ1020199.pdf

Brown, B. D., Horn, R. S., & King, G. (2018). The effective implementation of professional learning communities. *Alabama Journal of Educational Leadership, 5,* 53–59. https://files.eric.ed.gov/fulltext/EJ1194725.pdf

Brown, R., Brown, J., Reardon, K., & Merrill, C. (2011). Understanding STEM: Current perceptions. *Technology and Engineering Teacher, 70*(6), 5–9.

Buck Institute for Education. (2020). *Project Based Learning for all.* https://www.pblworks.org/

Bybee, R. W. (2018). *STEM education now more than ever*. NSTA Press.

Combs, E., & Silverman, S. (2016). *Bridging the gap: Paving the pathway from current practice to exemplary professional learning*. Frontline Research & Learning Institute. https://www.frontlineinstitute.com/reports/essa-report/

Cunningham, C. M., & Carlsen, W. S. (2014). Teaching engineering practices. *Journal of Science Teacher Education, 25*(2), 197–210. https://doi.org/10.1007/s10972-014-9380-5

Dare, E. A., Ellis, J. A., & Roehrig, G. H. (2018). Understanding science teachers' implementations of integrated STEM curricular units through a phenomenological multiple case study. *International Journal of STEM Education, 5*(4), 1–19. https://doi.org/10.1186/s40594-018-0101-z

Darling-Hammond, L., & Oakes, J. (2019). *Preparing teachers for deeper learning*. Harvard Education Press.

Darling-Hammond, L., Hyler, M. E., & Gardner, M. (2017). *Effective teacher professional development.* Learning Policy Institute. https://learningpolicyinstitute.org/sites/default/files/product-files/Effective_Teacher_Professional_Development_REPORT.pdf

Desimone, L. M. (2009). Improving impact studies of teachers' professional development: Toward better conceptualizations and measures. *Educational Researcher, 38*(3), 181–199. https://doi.org/10.3102/0013189X08331140

Donna, J. D. (2012). A model for professional development to promote engineering design as an integrative pedagogy within STEM education. *Journal of Pre-College Engineering Education, 2*(2), 1–8. https://doi.org/10.5703/1288284314866

Geesa, R. L., Stith, K. M., & Rose, M. A. (2020). Preparing school and district leaders for success in developing and facilitating integrative STEM in higher education. *Journal of Research on Leadership Education*, 1–21. https://doi.org/10.1177/1942775120962148

Geesa, R. L., Stith, K. M., & Teague, G. M. (2021). Integrative STEM education and leadership for student success. In F. English (Ed.), *The Palgrave Handbook of Educational Leadership and Management Discourse* (pp. 1–20). Palgrave Macmillan. https://doi.org/10.1007/978-3-030-39666-4_36-1

Gulamhussein, A. (2013). *Teaching the teachers: Effective professional development in an era of high stakes accountability*. National School Boards Association, Center for Public Education. http://conference.ohioschoolboards.org/2017/wp-content/uploads/sites/17/2016/07/1pm111317A114Job-embedPD.pdf

Handal, B., Campbell, C., Cavanagh, M. Petocz, P., & Kelly, N. (2013). Technological pedagogical content knowledge of secondary mathematics teachers. *Contemporary Issues in Technology and Teacher Education, 13*(1), 22–40. https://citejournal.org/wp-content/uploads/2016/04/v13i1mathematics1.pdf

Havice, W., Havice, P., Waugaman, C., & Walker, K. (2018). Evaluating the effectiveness of integrative STEM education: Teacher and administrator professional development. *Journal of Technology Education, 29*(2), 73–90. http://files.eric.ed.gov/fulltext/EJ1182375.pdf

Hipp, K. K., & Huffman, J. B. (2003, January 5–8). *Professional learning communities: Assessment—development—effects* [Paper presentation]. International Congress for School Effectiveness and Improvement, Sydney, Australia. http://files.eric.ed.gov/fulltext/ED482255.pdf

Hsu, M.-C., Purzer, S., & Cardella, M. E. (2011). Elementary teachers' views about teaching design, engineering, and technology. *Journal of Pre-College Engineering Education Research, 1*(2), 31–39. https://doi.org/10.5703/1288284314639

International Technology and Engineering Educators Association. (2020). *STEM Center for Teaching and Learning.* https://www.iteea.org/STEMCenter.aspx

Kelley, T. R., & Knowles, J. G. (2016). A conceptual framework for integrated STEM education. *International Journal of STEM Education, 3*(11), 1–11. https://doi.org/10.1186/s40594-016-0046-z

Li, Y., & Schoenfeld, A. H. (2019). Problematizing teaching and learning mathematics as "given" in STEM education. *International Journal of STEM Education, 6*(44), 1–13. https://doi.org/10.1186/s40594-019-0197-9

Louis, K. S., Leithwood, K., Wahlstrom, K. L., & Anderson, S. E. (2010). *Investigating the links to improved student learning: Final report of research findings.* Center for Applied Research and Educational Improvement, University of Minnesota. https://www.wallacefoundation.org/knowledge-center/Documents/Investigating-the-Links-to-Improved-Student-Learning.pdf

Margot, K. C., & Kettler, T. (2019). Teachers' perception of STEM integration and education: a systematic literature review. *International Journal of STEM Education, 6*(2), 1–16. https://doi.org/10.1186/s40594-018-0151-2

Nadelson, L. S., & Seifert, A. (2013). Perceptions, engagement, and practices of teachers seeking professional development in place-based integrated STEM. *Teacher Education and Practice, 26*(2), 242–265.

National Academy of Engineering & National Research Council. (2014). *STEM integration in K–12 education: Status, prospects, and an agenda for research.* The National Academies Press. https://doi.org/10.17226/18612

Project Lead The Way, Inc. (2020). *PLTW.* https://www.pltw.org

Rose, M. A., Geesa, R. L., & Stith, K. (2019). STEM leader excellence: A modified Delphi study of critical skills, competencies, and qualities. *Journal of Technology Education, 31*(1), 42–62. https://doi.org/10.21061/jte.v31i1.a.3

Shernoff, D. J., Sinha, S., Bressler, D. M., & Ginsburg, L. (2017). Assessing teacher education and professional development needs for the implementation of integrated approaches to STEM education. *International Journal of STEM Education, 4*(13), 1–16. https://doi.org/10.1186/s40594-017-0068-1

Shively, K., Stith, K. M., & Rubenstein, L. D. (2018). Measuring what matters: Assessing creativity, critical thinking, and the design process. *Gifted Child Today, 41*(3), 149–158. https://doi.org/10.1177/1076217518768361

Shulman, L. (1987). Knowledge and teaching: Foundations of the new reform. *Harvard Educational Review, 57*(1), 1–23. https://doi.org/10.17763/haer.57.1.j463w79r56455411

TeachThought Professional Development. (2020). *TeachThought: We grow teachers.* https://wegrowteachers.com/

Teague, G. M. (2012). *The principal's role in developing and sustaining professional learning communities: A mixed methods case study* (Publication No. 1356). [Doctoral dissertation, University of Tennessee - Knoxville]. Tennessee Research and Creative Exchange. https://trace.tennessee.edu/cgi/viewcontent.cgi?article=2336&context=utk_graddiss

9

Assessment and Data-Informed Decision-Making in Integrative STEM

Mary Annette Rose, Krista Marie Stith, Rachel Louise Geesa, and Jim Egenrieder

Integrative STEM is the intentional fusion of knowledge and practices of the STEM disciplines for educational purposes. The aim is to assist students in developing the interdisciplinary and transdisciplinary competencies required to explain phenomena and confront complex, real-world problems. A successful integrative STEM program prepares career- and college-ready students and STEM-literate citizens.

Educators plan and implement student assessments to inform decisions about instruction, curriculum, and school improvement. For students, the assessment processes and data should provide actionable feedback to support learning progress, enhance the development of their self-directed learning skills, and inform their decisions regarding educational and career pathways.

Developing an effective assessment system can be a challenging endeavor. The potential combinations of knowledge and practices that may emerge during authentic STEM learning experiences often do not align with well-established assessments (Honey, et al., 2014). The development and evaluation of integrative assessment approaches are still emerging (Gao et al., 2020). Educators are less familiar with assessment approaches that reveal students' integrated reasoning while engaged in interdisciplinary or transdisciplinary STEM practices.

Educational leaders play a central role in developing and supporting "intellectually rigorous and coherent systems of curriculum, instruction, and assessment to promote each student's academic success and well-being" (National Policy Board for Educational Administration, 2015, p. 12). This chapter summarizes promising approaches for assessing students' achievement and progress toward integrative STEM goals while highlighting the role of educational leaders in assessment planning, using data to monitor student progress, and making informed curricular and instructional decisions based on the data.

ASSESSMENT PLANNING

Educational leaders *set the stage* for the synergistic work required to develop coherent assessment plans through establishing collaborative STEM leadership teams, department or grade-level teams, or professional learning communities (PLCs). As discussed in greater detail in Chapter 8, the structure and processes of PLCs promote collective learning among educators and can have significant use in supporting integrative STEM programs.

For example, collaborative meetings among teams or PLCs provide educators the space and time to build common understandings about discipline-specific assessment practices and coordinate assessment plans across disciplines and grade levels. Because educators have different strengths in STEM knowledge and skills, discussions within teams will build consensus as to what constitutes proficiency and what assessment data are important to inform educational decisions.

Initially, leaders should encourage educators to reflect on the purpose and desired outcomes of integrative STEM; the questions in Table 9.1 may assist in this process.

Measuring What Matters

Curriculum and assessment developers often take a backward-planning approach (Wiggins & McTighe, 2005) that begins with goal setting and the identification of standards, followed by assessment planning, and then developing learning activities and experiences. These learning goals and standards focus on enduring conceptual understandings that cut across multiple STEM disciplines and reflect the process skills and practices of STEM professionals.

Table 9.1. Reflective Questions for Planning Process

Number	*Questions*
1.	What is the purpose of *integrative STEM* in the school or district?
2.	What do you expect students to know and be able to do *in relation to integrative STEM* by the time they leave school? (Standards)
3.	What do you expect students to know and be able to do *in relation to integrative STEM* by the end of each year? (Benchmarks)
4.	How well will students be able to do what they want to do with the knowledge and skills they acquire *in integrative STEM* by the time they leave school? (Performance)
5.	Why are you getting the *integrative STEM* results you are getting? Why are you not getting the *integrative STEM* results you want?
6.	How will you use the *integrative STEM* data you gather?
7.	How will you disseminate *integrative STEM* assessment data to stakeholders?

Note: Information tailored from questions in *Data Analysis for Comprehensive Schoolwide Improvement* (2nd ed., p. 15), by V. L. Bernhardt, 2004, Routledge.

As noted in Chapter 5 (see Table 5.1), the practices of professionals within each STEM discipline often overlap but maintain unique differences. Some practices are discussed as *habits of mind* (e.g., persistence, responsible risk-taking, thinking interdependently, metacognition) (Costa & Kallick, 2008), whereas other skills are expressed as the twenty-first century skills (i.e., collaboration, communication, critical thinking, and creativity).

The development of expertise in the use of practices and process skills does not occur in isolation from knowledge construction and conceptual development. Integrative STEM combines understandings that were likely formed from a variety of experiences (e.g., previous courses, out-of-school contexts). An integrated network of knowledge is needed for students to investigate and understand a problem or phenomenon and then use evidence-based reasoning to formulate and evaluate their explanations and design solutions.

Educational leaders should monitor the development of assessment plans and ensure that connections among core concepts and practices are explicitly stated within learning goals. Furthermore, learning goals should target higher-order cognitive skills that reveal integrative reasoning through expressions of analysis, synthesis, and evaluation. Then, specific assessment strategies should be matched to each goal.

An Example

A student-driven experiment (a science practice) focused on alternative fuels produced from an anaerobic bioreactor as a scalable solution to minimize fossil-fuel dependency is an example of a high school lesson. As noted in Table 9.2, conceptual learning goals may relate to a variety of STEM concepts and the relationships among them. To understand how this complex system works, students likely synthesize understandings from all STEM disciplines. During the experiment, students assemble a bioreactor complete with microorganisms (e.g., yeast) that convert the sugar in corn into ethanol through fermentation.

Table 9.2. Conceptual Understandings of an Alternative Fuels Experiment

Science	*Technology/Engineering*	*Mathematics*
Anaerobic microbes	Bioprocessing	Bivariate measurements
Carbon dioxide	Bioreactor	Graphing
Fermentation	Fuel	Mathematical model
Enzyme/Catalyst	Material conversion processes	Patterns of association
Ethanol	Sensors and instruments	Statistical analysis

Students develop hypotheses and then manipulate and measure variables (e.g., temperature, time) to observe the effect of these manipulations on the volume of ethanol produced. Without these conceptual understandings, students would not understand what is happening, how the variables are related, and how it could be further innovated.

An adequate assessment plan likely requires multiple strategies to gauge the accuracy and depth of students' conceptual understandings, as well as their facility in executing these practices. Most importantly, students' integrative reasoning should be assessed as it relates to planning, implementing, evaluating their methods, and interpreting the results.

Therefore, the approach should assess the accuracy of the students' understanding of concepts and their relationships, the interpretation of data, as well as the soundness and defensibility of their conclusions. The outcomes of these assessments inform educators' instructional decisions (formative assessment) during learning experiences and summative decisions of students' readiness to continue at the end of units or semesters.

PURPOSE OF ASSESSMENTS

A variety of assessment strategies should be employed to support and validate the growth of all students at all academic ability levels. Formal and informal assessments can have different purposes and occur frequently or infrequently (see Table 9.3).

Table 9.3. Types and Purposes of Assessments in Integrative STEM

	Diagnostic	*Interim*	*Formative*	*Summative*
Description	Identifies readiness for certain skill sets	Monitors progress over time	Assesses for learning	Assesses for learning
Type	Formal and Informal	Formal	Formal and Informal	Formal
Occurrence	• Before learning • Infrequent	• Quarterly, semesterly, or yearly • Infrequent	• During learning • Frequent	• End of learning process • Infrequent
Purpose	• Focuses on one area of knowledge • Identifies student knowledge, skills, and attitudes prior to instruction	• Tracks student progress toward mastery • Informs instruction for summative assessments	• Determines student progress and areas of need • Enhances instructional techniques while learning occurs	• Evaluates achievement and academic progress • Measures understandings in disciplines and mastery of standards
Assessment examples	• Discussions • Pretests • Career interest inventories • Reviews of prior STEM work • Student or family interviews	• Standardized tests aligned with grade-level standards • Survey, test, or exam • Unit or chapter tests • Performance assessment	• Authentic tasks • Checks for understanding • Discussions • Entry slips • Exit tickets • Observations • Performance assessments • Portfolios • Reflective questioning • Student interviews	• College entrance exams • Final exams • State exams used for accountability • Standardized assessments (e.g., Advanced Placement exams) • Unit or chapter tests • Performance assessment

Note: Performance assessments may be used for various purposes (i.e., diagnostic, interim, summative, or formative).

Diagnostic Purpose

The level of student preparation for more rigorous learning experiences and higher-level courses is an important concern for all educators. Diagnostic assessments can be used to measure students' retention of previous STEM learning, skills in self-regulation, and interests in STEM education and careers. The results will be useful to school counselors and students. Counselors will be better informed to recommend educational and career pathways to students. Students will gain a better understanding about how their interests and aspirations compare to prerequisites for educational coursework and career pathways.

When educators know students' strengths and areas for growth, they are better prepared to plan and scaffold student learning experiences. For instance, the Student Attitudes toward STEM (S-STEM) Survey (Friday Institute for Educational Innovation, 2012) is appropriate for students in grades 4–5 and grades 6–12. S-STEM assesses students' confidence and attitudes toward science, engineering and technology, mathematics, and twenty-first century learning.

Items also gauge students' attitudes toward STEM career areas, their expected performance in STEM in the coming year, potential postsecondary school plans, and if they have connections with adults in STEM fields. Results may inform educational leaders of the need for or efficacy of integrative STEM programming.

Formative Purpose

Formative assessments are used to reveal progress or identify learning obstacles that might affect students' capacities during problem-solving, design, and inquiry learning experiences. The results provide actionable feedback to both students and educators. Educators use a variety of formative assessments to determine if students are:

- identifying the concepts and principles critical to analyzing the problem or design challenge,
- transferring preexisting understandings they have learned in other contexts,

- interpreting the concepts or principles in a manner consistent with the conditions of the context, and
- applying the concepts or principles in an integrative manner.

Strategies for formative assessment can be discreet as educators watch and listen to student teams. For example, educators could use checklists to quickly record observations and make notes for future reference. Assessments may be quick and spontaneous interventions where students use hand signals or sticky notes to respond to question prompts. Alternatively, assessment rubrics may prompt students to evaluate their own progress or that of their peers during collaborative learning experiences.

Interim and Summative Purposes

Interim or benchmark assessments are typically given to multiple classes within schools to track student progression and mastery prior to the summative tests. According to Herman et al. (2010), these assessments support educators when (a) communicating expectations for learning, (b) planning curriculum and instruction, (c) monitoring and evaluating instructional or program effectiveness, and (d) predicting future performance.

Summative assessments are associated with end-of-course or end-of-year exams or standardized exams provided by state, national, or international organizations. Assessment results may indicate a students' readiness to move to the next grade level or participate in higher-level courses. For example, students must display sufficient mathematics skills to take chemistry or physics courses in which higher-level algebra is important for success.

Educational leaders are often tasked with collecting and sharing data from summative assessments with stakeholders. The Massachusetts Comprehensive Assessment System, for example, assesses students in grades 5, 8, 9, and 10 in the content areas of earth and space science, life science, physical science, and technology/engineering. The purpose is to assess "the skills, scientific practices, and subject matter" established by the state's curriculum framework (Massachusetts Department of Elementary and Secondary Education, 2020, para. 1). Students are tested in winter/early spring and action steps are recommended by the state for students who perform partially or do not meet expectations.

Large-Scale

A review of large-scale national and international assessment data may be helpful to leaders when comparing school or state-level data by core subjects. Achievement results may be analyzed relative to students' race, ethnicity, gender, (dis)ability status, English language learner status, socioeconomic status, school location, region or country, and highest level of parental education. Thus, educational leaders may compare disaggregated results to identify and address shortfalls in equity and inclusion in STEM.

In the United States, educators can access the National Assessment of Educational Progress (NAEP; 2020) that measures what students know and can do in a variety of disciplines (e.g., mathematics, science, technology and engineering). As an international example, the Trends in Mathematics and Science Survey (TIMSS; Mullis et al., 2020) monitors trends in mathematics and science skills and knowledge at fourth and eighth grades every four years across more than 60 countries and with insight from teachers, families, and leaders.

Performance Assessment

Tests with constructed response-item are helpful for assessing student abilities to recall normative ideas, recognize patterns, and classify concepts. Integrative STEM learning experiences are typically more complex and include authentic problems, issues, and contexts that require extensive time and resources to pursue. Integrative assessments help educators to identify and understand students' ability to apply knowledge, practices, and skills during multiple stages of extended problem-solving.

STEM education leaders recommend performance assessment when students engage in design-, inquiry-, and project-based learning tasks (e.g., Rose et al., 2019). Performance assessments enable students to demonstrate their competence while engaged in a performance task—a procedure, practice, or process that is authentic to a STEM context. These open-ended, complex tasks result in a live performance or the development of a discrete product, lab report, or plan that serves as evidence of learning (see Table. 9.4).

Table 9.4. Examples of Performance Assessments 

Assessment	*Description*
Design and science notebooks, observation reports, and other journaling/portfolio tools	Students record observations, hypotheses, understandings, curiosities, and tentative solutions
Discussions, debates, and speeches	Students demonstrate facility with STEM concepts and principles, as well as evidence-based reasoning as it relates to controversial issues
Plans, 2D drawings, and schedules	Students demonstrate their understandings and skills by proposing action steps for the future and predicting future scenarios
Predictions through mathematical models	Students predict and model future scenarios based on trends in data
Presentations, poster sessions, exhibitions, drama enactments, and performances	Students present their work to the instructor and others providing an authentic audience for students to demonstrate their understanding
Prototypes and 3D models	Students demonstrate their design skills by developing and modeling products that can be used to test a design concept
Psychomotor skills and processes	Students demonstrate facility in assembling, using, or troubleshooting technological processes and equipment
Role-playing and simulations	Students provide evidence of thinking and doing as STEM professionals by using or simulating processes and practices

Exemplary performance tasks enable students at multiple ability levels to transfer, blend, and apply their learning from STEM disciplines (Gotwals & Songer, 2013). For example, elementary students may apply their new understandings of Newton's Laws of Motion, simple machines, cost projections, and design practices when they redesign their playground that was damaged after a storm. The students demonstrate these understandings as they present their proposals to the local board of education.

In a middle school, teams may apply principles of user-centered design and 3D modeling as they modify and test a new control device of a ride-on-car for children ages birth to three who experience limited mobility problems (International Technology and Engineering Educators Association, n.d.). While at the high school level, precalculus students apply Law of Sines and right triangle trigonometry and digital communication skills as they simulate a disaster relief mission where they take on the role of air traffic controllers and pilots to rescue those in need (Edutopia, 2015).

Performance assessments also complement differentiated instruction and assessment for students with special needs, (dis)abilities, advanced academic opportunities, and diverse backgrounds, and students who are English language learners. Students benefit from differentiated performance assessments that allow flexibility, student voice and choice, and hands-on, inquiry-driven learning that also provides for calculated risk, individualized pacing, and options for groupwork (e.g., see Figures 9.1 and 9.2).

Performance tasks are also employed within large-scale, computer-administered assessments. NAEP (2020) employs simulation-based performance tasks that enable students to demonstrate the range of knowledge and skills they possess by completing both problem-solving situations and discrete constructed-response questions. NAEP administers these interactive assessments for science, mathematics, and technology and engineering literacy (TEL).

Several tasks administered in the 2014 NAEP TEL assessment are available for educators to use as practice items, such as Chicago and Iguana Home (The Nation's Report Card, n.d.). Educational leaders can use the NAEP resources—tasks, frameworks, and data tools—to show the logic of assessment development. For example, TEL Item Maps align each description of the knowledge and skill that was assessed by the test item and show the description within a difficulty progression.

Figure 9.1. Microbiology teacher providing feedback to high school students as they interpret their observations. iStockphoto LP.

Figure 9.2. Elementary school students presenting their model volcano and explaining how it works. iStockphoto LP.

Performance Assessment Rubrics

The assessment of performance tasks should be guided by a pre-established set of criteria that aligns to integrative STEM learning goals, outcomes, and standards. For assessing procedural tasks (e.g., adjusting a microscope, coding a loop, calculating a mean), educators typically conduct a task analysis then devise a checklist of key benchmarks on which they record evaluations of performances.

However, when assessing essential understandings and transferrable process skills, rubrics are often used to describe key criteria along a continuum of achievement or expertise. For example, Microsoft Corporation (n.d.) developed rubrics to assess six dimensions of twenty-first century learning (see Table 9.5). Within the "Knowledge Construction" section, it is indicated that "the strongest student work demonstrates that students applied the knowledge they constructed to a different context and connects information and ideas from two or more academic disciplines" (p. 10).

Table 9.5. Twenty-First Century Student Work Rubric Dimensions and Indicators

Dimension	*Big Idea*	*Strong Rubric Indicators for Individual Students*
Collaboration	Students work together in pairs or groups to: • discuss an issue, • solve a problem, or • create a product.	Student: • shares responsibility fairly, • makes substantive decisions together, and • creates a product that is coherent and interdependently designed with others.
Knowledge construction	Students generate new ideas and understandings and build knowledge when they: • interpret, • analyze, • synthesize, or • evaluate information or ideas.	Student: • focuses on knowledge construction as the main effort, • demonstrates conceptual understanding, • applies their knowledge, and • creates interdisciplinary work.
Real-world problem-solving and innovation	Students demonstrate problem-solving as they: • develop a solution to a new problem, • complete a task without instructions, or • design a complex product with set requirements.	Student: • provides a successful solution that addresses a real-world problem, and • innovates and implements a solution in the real world.
Use of ICT for learning	Students use ICT to support knowledge construction.	Student: • uses ICT as a requirement in constructing knowledge, and • designs a product that demonstrates attention to authentic users.
Self-regulation	Students are aware of learning goals and associated success criteria of an activity and provide evidence of progress and success in the activity.	Student: • is aware of learning goals and associated success criteria in advance, • successfully plans and monitors their own work, and • improves the quality of their work based on feedback.
Skilled communication	Students participate in extended communication that represents a set of original, connected ideas discussed in: • written work, • audio or visual media, or • video media.	Student communication: • is extended or multimodal, • contains sufficient supporting evidence, and • is designed appropriately for a particular audience.

ICT, information and communication technology.

Note: Information collected from *21CLD Student Work Rubrics*, by Microsoft Corporation, n.d., (https://msenmediastorage.blob.core.windows.net/asset-8712445d-1500-80c5-a30e-f1e51444b5fe/efa53621-d578-482a-a81c-c60ecdc84936.pdf). CC by 3.0.

When assessing collaborative problem-solving skills, Herro et al. (2017) developed the Co-Measure rubric of sixth- through eighth-grade students during STEAM ("A" for the arts) activities. The rubric includes six dimensions that incorporate approaches and content from multiple disciplines: peer interaction, positive communication, inquiry rich with multiple paths, authentic approach and tasks, and transdisciplinary thinking.

Some assessments track the stages of students' process while engaged in inquiry, experimentation, project development, or engineering design. An Engineering Design Process Portfolio Scoring Rubric (Groves et al., 2014), for example, includes a set of rubrics with 12 elements about the process and two elements related to a presentation of the project. These elements articulate knowledge and skills required to complete activities of an engineering design process (see Table 9.6).

Table 9.6. Components and Elements of an Engineering Design Process Portfolio Scoring Rubric

Component	*Element*
I: Presenting and Justifying a Problem and Solution Requirements	• Presentation and justification of the problem • Documentation and analysis of prior solution attempts • Presentation and justification of solution design requirements
II: Generating and Defending an Original Solution	• Design concept generation, analysis, and selection • Application of STEM principles and practices • Consideration of design viability
III: Constructing and Testing a Prototype	• Construction of a testable prototype • Prototype, testing, and data collection plan • Testing, data collection, and analysis
IV: Evaluation, Reflection, and Recommendations	• Documentation of external evaluation • Reflection on the design project • Presentation of a designer's recommendations
V: Documenting and Presenting the Project	• Presentation of the project portfolio • Writing like an engineer

Note: Quoted from *Using an Engineering Design Process Portfolio Scoring Rubric to Structure Online High School Engineer Education*, by J. F. Groves, L. R. Abts, and G. L. Goldberg, 2014, Presentation at the 121st ASEE Annual Conference & Exposition, Indianapolis, IN, (https://peer.asee.org/using-an-engineering-design-process-portfolio-scoring-rubric-to-structure-online-high-school-engineering-education.pdf).

Raising Understanding and Support for Integrative Assessment

Educational leaders and STEM teams should take deliberate steps to help all stakeholders understand the rationale for integrative STEM outcomes, the value of using a broader spectrum of assessment strategies, and the value of collectively analyzing STEM assessment data. Multiple venues—program and course descriptions, orientations, conferences, and the school website and newsletters—should be used to raise awareness of this shift in assessments and provide opportunities for stakeholders to discuss concerns. Integrative STEM data should be discussed and shared with students, parents, caregivers, educators, and community partners (Geesa et al., 2021).

DATA COLLECTION, ORGANIZATION, AND ANALYSIS

Educational leaders should provide a system-wide perspective on the quality of assessment planning, the methods for data collection, and the data analysis and interpretation that leads to informed decision-making. Educational leaders could monitor and assist educators in analyzing their assessment instruments and process to ensure that they meet well-established quality criteria. Rider-Bertrand (2015) identified four criteria for evaluating assessments used within STEM programming:

- *Alignment to standards.* Assessments are aligned with state and district-level content and practice standards.
- *Cognitive rigor.* Performance expectations for conceptual understandings, practices, and process skills should be appropriately challenging for students.
- *Congruence with curriculum.* Assessments should correspond with the planned curriculum to ensure standards are addressed.
- *Balance for formative and summative assessment.* A balanced assessment system is essential for meeting federal and local mandates, while also recognizing the need to inform teachers' instructional decisions and students' self-directed learning decisions.

However, educational leaders might also emphasize that the qualities of assessments vary by their purpose. When the purpose is formative, concerns for authenticity, contextual relevance, and utility should take precedence over the technical criteria normally associated with achieving generalizability and comparability of tests used for accountability.

Leaders should welcome alternative assessment approaches, especially performance assessment, and encourage teams of teachers to experiment as they strive to measure advancements of integrative learning and skill development. Leaders can assist in this process by encouraging peer review and a pilot study of assessment rubrics to enhance alignment with multiple STEM learning goals and scoring reliability.

Data Collection

Educational decision-makers should collect data from multiple types of assessments and sources (e.g., informal classroom observations, peer assessments) to inform decisions about effective integrative STEM education instruction and assessment planning. Efficient systems for collecting and organizing assessment data are needed to help educators identify strengths and areas for improvement. Although some educational leaders and educators may already have specific training in data collection, organization, and analysis, specialists in assessment should be accessed when additional expertise is needed.

Data Organization and Analysis

To optimize the value of assessment data, it should be shared and collectively analyzed by STEM teams. Educational leaders should ensure that systematic procedures and tools for monitoring student progress enable iterative analyses at a variety of levels (e.g., student, classroom, grade, department, school, district). Leaders should provide spaces and training for the confidential and collaborative analysis and interpretation of assessment data within grade levels, departments, PLCs, and the STEM leadership team. Data may be disaggregated by (dis)ability, ethnicity, gender, grade level, language, race, school, and socioeconomic status to better identify the unique needs of different populations of students.

When viewing assessment data from multiple sources, a more holistic representation of student, class, program, and school needs may be revealed. A data wall or digital database can be used to visually display student achievement levels and proficiency targets (Sharratt & Planche, 2016). Educational leaders should help educators focus upon patterns in the data (trends) and seek out root causes they can target with adjustments in instruction.

Collective assessment data analysis and data-informed decision-making require a *culture of trust* where all educators feel comfortable looking at, sharing, and questioning data without fear of accusation or blame. Educational leaders should promote a culture of trust by respecting the contributions of teachers and staff, respecting the school's legacy, and sharing intentions backed by a clear rationale (Modoono, 2017).

DATA-INFORMED DECISION-MAKING

After assessment data are analyzed, STEM teams or PLCs should make decisions about how to better support students in preparing them for success in life, higher education or training, and the workplace. Trend data may underscore a defensible rationale to make changes in the scope, sequence, and pace of curriculum and instruction, as well as resources that support these endeavors. Educational leaders should develop structures and schedules that promote consistent educator communication that focuses on targeted STEM goals and outcomes and routine use of data to inform adjustments to curriculum, instruction, and assessment strategies.

A School-Wide Exemplar

Brownsburg High School includes ninth through twelfth grade with more than 2,700 students and 140 teachers in Brownsburg, Indiana. To better support the social, emotional, academic, and career- and college-readiness needs of these students, educational leaders implement leadership teams for each grade level. These teams work with the same group of students throughout their four years of high school to allow team members to build relationships with students and better address their career- and college-readiness needs. Each team consists of an assistant principal, two school counselors, an academic coach, an administrative coordinator, and two special education teachers of record.

The high school also uses PLCs with educators in all departments, including a STEM PLC, thus providing students, educators, and families consistency in recognizing students' current successes and needs for the future. Brownsburg school leaders set clear expectations for educators to consistently collaborate regarding instructional, curricular, and assessment planning; data analyses; and decision-making based on assessment results.

Using Data to Inform Decisions

All staff, including STEM educators and educational leaders, participate in PLC meetings in a common meeting space at Brownsburg High School each week for 45 minutes. All educators discuss assessments, data, instructional strategies, and student needs. Educational leaders facilitate the meetings and communicate the purpose, goals, and deliverables expected from each meeting. PLC members share data presentations with district-level leaders on a quarterly basis and school-level leaders on a monthly basis. These data reviews allow all teachers to engage in collective decisions regarding student, classroom, program, and school improvement to promote more interdisciplinary and transdisciplinary learning opportunities.

CONCLUSION

Developing a coherent system to assess student progress toward integrative STEM learning goals and outcomes is complex and requires the collaboration of many professionals. There is a need for multiple types of assessments to capture information regarding integrative STEM conceptual understandings, practices, higher-order reasoning, and attitudes for a variety of assessment purposes, including diagnostic, interim, formative, and summative purposes.

Performance assessment provides opportunities for students to demonstrate their proficiency in transferring and interconnecting disciplinary principles and practices. Leaders should welcome alternative assessment approaches that align with school goals and curriculum standards, yet encourage teachers to experiment as they strive to measure integrative learning and skill development advancements.

Educational leaders should promote a culture of assessment by establishing STEM leadership teams and helping all stakeholders understand the rationale for integrative learning goals and integrative assessments. Educational stakeholders need a robust understanding of assessment, strategies for implementing performance assessment, and collaborative analysis of assessment data that informs planning for integrative STEM education.

REFERENCES

Bernhardt, V. L. (2004). *Data analysis: For comprehensive schoolwide improvement* (2nd ed.). Routledge.

Costa, A. L., & Kallick, B. (Eds.). (2008). *Learning and leading with habits of mind: 16 essential characteristics for success*. Association for Supervision and Curriculum Development.

Edutopia. (2015). *Performance-based assessment in math*. George Lucas Educational Foundation. https://www.edutopia.org/practice/performance-based-assessment-making-math-relevant

Friday Institute for Educational Innovation. (2012). *Student attitudes toward STEM (S-STEM) survey: Development and psychometric properties*. https://www-data.fi.ncsu.edu/wp-content/uploads/2020/11/28143332/S-STEM_FridayInstitute_DevAndPsychometricProperties_2015.pdf

Gao, X., Li, P., Shen, J., & Sun, H. (2020). Reviewing assessment of student learning in interdisciplinary STEM education. *International Journal of STEM Education, 7*(24), 1–14. https://doi.org/10.1186/s40594-020-00225-4

Geesa, R. L., Stith, K. M., & Teague, G. M. (2021). Integrative STEM education and leadership for student success. In F. English (Ed.), *The Palgrave Handbook of Educational Leadership and Management Discourse* (pp. 1–20). Palgrave Macmillan. https://doi.org/10.1007/978-3-030-39666-4_36-1

Gotwals, A. W., & Songer, N. B. (2013). Validity evidence for learning progression-based assessment items that fuse core disciplinary ideas and science practices. *Journal of Research in Science Teaching, 50*(5), 597–626. https://doi.org/10.1002/tea.21083

Groves, J. F., Abts, L. R., & Goldberg, G. L. (2014). *Using an engineering design process portfolio scoring rubric to structure online high school engineer education*. Presentation at the 121st ASEE Annual Conference & Exposition, Indianapolis, IN. https://peer.asee.org/using-an-engineering-design-process-portfolio-scoring-rubric-to-structure-online-high-school-engineering-education.pdf

Herman, J. L., Osmundson, E., & Dietel, R. (2010). *Benchmark assessment for improved learning.* Assessment and Accountability Comprehensive Center. https://files.eric.ed.gov/fulltext/ED524104.pdf

Herro, D., Quigley, C., Andrews, J., & Delacruz, G. (2017). Co-Measure: developing an assessment for student collaboration in STEAM activities. *International Journal of STEM Education, 4*(26), 1–12. https://doi.org/10.1186/s40594-017-0094-z

Honey, M., Pearson, G., & Schweingruber, H. (Eds.). (2014). *STEM integration in K–12 education: Status, prospects, and an agenda for research.* National Academies Press.

International Technology and Engineering Educators Association. (n.d.). *ITEEA dream ride . . . Go Baby Go style: A guide for educators.* https://www.iteea.org/File.aspx?id=148379&v=f36a7e44

Massachusetts Department of Elementary and Secondary Education. (2020). *Science and technology/engineering test design and development.* https://www.doe.mass.edu/mcas/tdd/sci.html

Microsoft Corporation. (n.d.). *21CLD student work rubrics.* https://msenmediastorage.blob.core.windows.net/asset-8712445d-1500-80c5-a30e-f1e51444b5fe/efa53621-d578-482a-a81c-c60ecdc84936.pdf

Modoono, J. (2017). The trust factor. *Educational Leadership, 74*(8), 30–34. http://www.ascd.org/publications/educational-leadership/may17/vol74/num08/The-Trust-Factor.aspx

Mullis, I. V. S., Martin, M. O., Foy, P., Kelly, D. L., & Fishbein, B. (2020). *Highlights: TIMSS 2019 international results in mathematics and science.* https://timssandpirls.bc.edu/timss2019/international-results/wp-content/themes/timssandpirls/download-center/TIMSS-2019-Highlights.pdf

National Assessment of Educational Progress. (2020). *Assessment frameworks.* National Center for Education Statistics. https://nces.ed.gov/nationsreportcard/assessments/frameworks.aspx

National Policy Board for Educational Administration. (2015). *Professional standards for educational leaders 2015.* https://ccsso.org/sites/default/files/2017-10/ProfessionalStandardsforEducationalLeaders2015forNPBEAFINAL.pdf

Rider-Bertrand, J. (2015). *A K–12 STEM program audit of the Radnor Township School District.* https://www.rtsd.org/cms/lib/PA01000218/Centricity/Domain/1/RTSD_STEM_Audit_Report_with_annotations6.9.15.pdf

Rose, M. A., Geesa, R. L., & Stith, K. (2019). STEM leader excellence: A modified Delphi study of critical skills, competencies, and qualities. *Journal of Technology Education, 31*(1), 42–62. https://doi.org/10.21061/jte.v31i1.a.3

Sharratt, L., & Planche, B. (2016). *Leading collaborative learning: Empowering excellence*. Corwin.

The Nation's Report Card. (n.d.). *NAEP technology & engineering literacy (TEL) report card: Sample scenario-based tasks and discrete questions.* https://www.nationsreportcard.gov/tel/tasks/

Wiggins, G., & McTighe, J. (2005). *Understanding by design* (2nd ed.). Association for Supervision and Curriculum Development.

10

Evaluation of Integrative STEM Education

Rachel Louise Geesa, Mary Annette Rose, Krista Marie Stith, and Marilynn Marks Quick

The nine competencies of integrative STEM education discussed in this book form a network that is essential for creating a coherent school culture that consistently advances core STEM outcomes for students. Gauging the relevance and worth of these competencies in the context of the local school or educational program is an act of evaluation.

Making informed judgments about how well these competencies are harmonized to advance student preparation for the future is a fundamental goal in evaluation of integrative STEM education. In this chapter, systems of program, curriculum, and educator evaluation are highlighted to assist educational leaders and integrative STEM leadership teams in identifying quality indicators, metrics, and strategies to improve integrative STEM education.

BUILDING EVIDENCE-BASED EVALUATIONS

As "agents of continuous improvement," educational leaders hold the primary responsibility for assuring that evidence-based evaluation processes are embedded within cycles of school management, curriculum development, and supervision of personnel (National Policy Board for Educational Administration, 2015). When STEM leaders are mutually committed to a culture of evidence-based decision-making, self-reflective educators may organically and informally generate evaluative questions (see Table 10.1) and gather evidence to inform educational decisions.

Table 10.1. Examples of Integrative STEM Evaluation Questions

Domain	*Example Questions*
Mission and Culture	To what extent are the values and aspirations of the local community supportive of integrative STEM education in schools?
Equity, Diversity, and Inclusion	In what ways are inclusive practices embedded in the school culture? How are students' attitudes and interests in integrative STEM education experiences measured and subsequent data used to make decisions?
Infrastructure and Programming	To what extent do educators have a common work time to plan integrative STEM lessons?
Curriculum	To what extent is curriculum horizontally integrated (i.e., infusing multiple STEM standards across disciplines)?
Instruction	To what extent are educators using student-directed instructional strategies that focus on real-world problems?
Extended Learning	In what ways do leaders and educators foster community partnerships that provide integrative STEM experiences beyond the classroom?
Professional Learning	To what extent are educators self-assessing and peer assessing their integrative STEM practices?
Assessment	To what extent do student assessments enable students to demonstrate what they know and can do?
Evaluation	What evidence indicates that students are ready for the workforce, higher education, and STEM-literate citizenship?

However, to maximize the benefits of evaluation, effective leaders also formalize evaluation processes. Leaders coordinate and empower integrative STEM teams, educators, and other school stakeholders to collaboratively establish formal evaluation plans, gather and analyze data, and use this evidence to make decisions and improve programming.

Program evaluations may be approached as a separate, discrete activity from standard daily practice that culminates in adapting, adopting, or eliminating a program (summative evaluation) or as a standard practice of continuous improvement (formative evaluation). These evaluative results may be used to celebrate achievements, build support, seek funding, fulfill accountability requirements, identify problems, set new goals, and assist in making defensible program changes.

Outcomes and Criteria to Evaluate Integrative STEM

Evaluative goals are inherently linked to educational stakeholders' values and roles, the structure and cultural norms of the school, and the accountability criteria and curriculum standards. Educational leaders should periodically and collaboratively examine the expectations of stakeholders to identify the valued outcomes and criteria to evaluate integrative STEM programs and elements.

Educational decision-makers—school board members, administrators, and state-level educational leaders—will likely be concerned about budget constraints, personnel performance, and student performance on state tests. Educators and staff who implement integrative STEM curriculum and programs may emphasize the resources and the need for co-planning to support authentic learning experiences. The recipients of integrative STEM education—students, their families, and community members—may value opportunities for advanced courses or personalized career development experiences.

Educational values can differ among STEM-focused schools that explicitly forward STEM goals in their mission and vision statements. For example, a school enrollment process that selects students based on interest and motivation in STEM disciplines (i.e., an *inclusive* STEM school) often strives to increase the percentage of "underrepresented youth for the successful pursuit of advanced STEM studies" (Peters-Burton et al., 2014, p. 64). In contrast, selective schools with competitive enrollment standards tend to serve primarily high-achieving students by maximizing the amount of Advanced Placement courses completed by students.

Educational leaders should also compare local perspectives against broader perspectives; numerous examples of integrative STEM-related goals and outcomes are offered by state departments of education, nonprofit organizations, and schools (e.g., see Table 10.2). To clarify and support evaluation, educational leaders and STEM leadership teams should state goals as measurable outcomes, identifying indicators, performance targets, or benchmarks to further communicate success.

A variety of evaluation rubrics identify assessment indicators and metrics and may serve as frameworks to guide an evaluation plan. Several state departments of education (e.g., Arizona, Colorado, Georgia, Indiana, North Carolina, Ohio, Tennessee, Texas, Washington) offer or endorse

Table 10.2. Examples of State, Organization, and School Integrative STEM Goals

Structure	*Example*	*Integrative STEM Goals*
State	STEM Education Goals in Wisconsin Wisconsin Department of Public Instruction (2020)	• Actively invite, engage, motivate, and inspire all students in these subject areas and related career pathways. • Raise the achievement of all students so that they are prepared to create and use technology in their learning, college, community, and careers. • Close the achievement and technical skill gaps between economically disadvantaged students, ELLs (English language learners), students of color, and their peers. • Increase the number and diversity of students who aspire and succeed at the highest levels of academic and technical achievement in these subject areas and related career pathways. • Inspire learning which benefits the common good, resulting not only in individual gains in STEM skills, but also in stronger communities as a result of students applying their skills to solve relevant community issues.
Organization	Chicago STEM Ecosystem Outcomes, Illinois Chicago STEM Pathways Cooperative (2015)	• Program Outcomes: An increase in the intensity, duration and quality of STEM learning opportunities. • Staff outcomes: An increase in the confidence, competence, and motivation in offering STEM learning opportunities. • Student outcomes: An increase in engagement, interest, and applied knowledge of STEM content and processes. • Initiative outcomes: The documentation of promising practices and the sharing of this information with the field in ways that can effectively guide program improvement and expansion efforts.
School	STEM Program Goals, Georgia Stone Mountain Middle School (2020)	• Promote connections among STEM disciplines through authentic project-based lessons. • Facilitate students' use of the engineering design process in order to solve real-world problems. • Stimulate students' interest in careers emphasizing science, technology, engineering, and mathematics disciplines. • Develop students' creativity, communication, collaboration, critical thinking, and comprehension skills. • Cultivate community, business, and parent partnerships that support students' participation in the STEM program and pursuit of STEM careers.

Note: Quoted from *STEM education goals in Wisconsin*, by Wisconsin Department of Public Instruction, 2020 (https://dpi.wi.gov/stem/goals); Chicago STEM Ecosystem Logic Model, by Chicago STEM Pathways Cooperative, 2015 (https://stemchicago.wordpress.com/stem-learning-ecosystems-rfq-information/stem-learning-ecosystems-logic-model-as-of-71515/); and *STEM Brochure, 2020–2021*, by Stone Mountain Middle School, 2020 (http://www.stonemountainms.dekalb.k12.ga.us/STEMBrochure.aspx).

a STEM certification or designation process to promote and recognize STEM implementation within schools. For most states, the process begins by conducting a self-assessment within the school prior to submitting an application that includes evidence to support the achievement claims and STEM practices.

The application process is rigorous and often involves the work of teams of educators and community members to ensure the school fulfills the expectations set by the state's department of education to receive this recognition of achievement. Schools recognized in STEM education may leverage this evidence of successful programming in grants and external fundraising, as well as publicize this achievement to current families, potential families, and other stakeholders.

For schools and districts in states that do not have a similar process, the evaluation rubrics typically provided on the websites of the state departments offer educational leaders a valuable framework for evaluating the level of STEM implementation of a school. Intended for use at all grade levels, Indiana Department of Education (2021) organizes its STEM School Certification Rubric into four domains that include 25 elements (criteria) (see Table 10.3), four levels of indicators for each criterion (i.e., Investigating, Developing, Approaching, and Innovating), and suggestions for school-based evidence to support each level.

Table 10.3. Domains and Elements of Indiana STEM School Certification Rubric

Domain	*Elements*
1. Culture	Decision-making, continuity of learning, common work time, sustainability plan, measurement of students' attitudes/interests, student/parent feedback data, STEM instructional feedback, instructional support, STEM communications, and equity (10 elements)
2. Curriculum	Curriculum integration, computer science, employability skills, equity, and assessments (five elements)
3. Instruction	STEM instructional approach training, STEM instructional approach implementation, student instructional work groups, technology in instruction, and STEM integration (five elements)
4. Partnerships	Community partner feedback, STEM career exploration, community engagement, extended learning, and equity (five elements)

Note: Information collected from *STEM School Evaluation Rubric 2021–2022,* by Indiana Department of Education, 2021 (https://www.in.gov/doe/students/stem-school-certification/)

The STEM certification rubric of Tennessee Department of Education and Tennessee STEM Network (2018) characterizes a "Model STEM School" as offering annual "work-based learning experiences" for students. The Tennessee Department of Education rubric emphasizes student participation in self-evaluation and goal setting, STEM classrooms designed for collaborative student work, connections to STEM experts, and exhibitions through virtual learning experiences.

College and Career Readiness Models

College- and career-readiness are valued outcomes of integrative STEM education. Educational leaders should ensure that readiness programs are evaluated regularly. Leaders should catalog all school-supported college-readiness programs, such as on-site counseling services, online college-readiness systems, summer bridge programs, Advanced Placement and dual-credit courses, and collaborative programs with colleges.

The short- and long-term outcomes of these programs could be evaluated along three dimensions, including academic preparedness, academic tenacity, and college knowledge (John W. Gardner Center for Youth and Their Communities, 2014). Indicators of academic preparedness might include participation and completion of Advanced Placement and dual-credit STEM courses, as well as scores on state-level and college entrance exams. Students' academic tenacity—participation and perseverance through adversity—could be measured through self-report questionnaires. Indicators of students' college knowledge could include campus visitations, meeting with college advisors, and completion of college applications.

Relative to career readiness, educational leaders should ensure that an evaluation plan assesses the frequency and extent to which all students have access to career development information and learning experiences. This should include examining career development resources within the entire PK–12 curriculum, counseling programs, and extended learning opportunities beyond school.

At the elementary level, career awareness experiences enable students to identify their own strengths, interests, and preferences, as well as begin to develop an understanding of the relationship between school and the workforce. Students may engage in career-focused games, interact with

STEM workers during career days or fairs, or participate in career-related classroom and community projects.

At the middle school level, students are provided with opportunities to assess their own career interests and explore career options, as well as begin to consider career goals and educational pathways to reach these goals. School counselors might administer career assessments or use computer-based systems to help students reflect on and develop a career and educational plan. Educators and community organizations may provide opportunities for students to interview professionals, take field trips, or participate in job shadowing experiences.

In high school, STEM programming should include a variety of opportunities for students to immerse themselves in STEM careers. These immersive experiences may include participation in career-related clubs and after school activities, internships and cooperative education placements, capstone projects, after-school jobs, and community-based volunteer work.

Metrics of career-readiness programs' measures of success or areas that need improvement may be quantitative measurements of participation by gender, ethnicity, or socioeconomic status; changes in STEM course enrollments; and the results of career awareness and interest questionnaires. Instruments to support data collection on career awareness may include the Teacher Efficacy and Attitudes Toward STEM survey (T-STEM) and Student Attitudes Toward STEM (S-STEM) surveys developed by Friday Institute for Education Innovation (2012, 2021).

Integrative STEM Curriculum Evaluation

Curricula should also be evaluated in terms of their potential to achieve learning goals and standards from two or more STEM disciplines. Formative evaluation should be embedded in the cycle of curriculum planning development and implementation. One of the more transparent strategies to evaluate curricular interconnectedness is through curriculum mapping. When mapping, educational leaders and teachers deliberatively identify the intersections of curriculum (e.g., see Figure 10.1). This promotes curricular coherence at and across grade levels by emphasizing mutually supportive learning goals and practices, instructional approaches, and assessments.

Figure 10.1. Middle school educators evaluating and revising curriculum maps. iStockphoto LP.

When evaluating the STEM curriculum, examining and collaboratively reflecting on a curriculum map is especially helpful for identifying gaps and opportunities for strengthening the integration of content and learning progressions. Educational leaders can introduce and demonstrate the process of curriculum mapping, explain its usefulness for evaluating integrative connections, and establish a central database to document and continuously refine curriculum and evaluation decisions.

If evaluation has not been embedded in the curriculum development process, educational leaders might employ several strategies for evaluating alignment of the planned curriculum with school-level STEM goals and STEM standards. Evaluators could conduct content analyses of instructional materials, especially assessments, to ascertain the extent the curriculum is horizontally articulated (i.e., aligned at grade level to achieve multiple standards). Such an analysis could provide insights into the relative balance of the discipline-centric versus the integrative curricular components.

Furthermore, the assessment plan and implementation should be evaluated in terms of its balance of assessment strategies (e.g., performance, constructed response, essay response). A variety of assessment strategies should enable students to demonstrate what they know and can do relative to STEM learning goals and outcomes. Evaluators should also review if assessments align with state and district-level content and practice standards.

EVALUATING EDUCATORS

Translating STEM curriculum and programming into engaging, authentic learning experiences is the responsibility of educators. Educational leaders who are well-versed in preferred STEM pedagogical practices and effective personnel evaluation can support educators by providing actionable feedback to inspire and inform instructional improvements (Geesa et al., 2020, 2021; Rose et al., 2019). Such strategies as reflection, classroom walk-throughs, and clinical observation can help structure an effective process to supervise and evaluate educators in integrative STEM. These pillars of evaluation are each described briefly in the following sections.

Reflection/Self-Evaluation

Because even the best educational leaders serving as evaluators may only have time for brief classroom walk-throughs one to two times a week, it is imperative that leaders build capacity in their schools by fostering reflective, collaborative practitioners. A team of reflective educators should be individually and collectively thinking about ways to continually improve instruction through reflective self-evaluation.

At the heart of self-evaluation is a collaborative process of establishing expectations about the behaviors educators and leaders should see and hear in an integrative STEM classroom. During small group discussions in whole staff meetings, grade-level or content meetings, and common planning times, leaders can facilitate the development of a shared set of preferred behaviors and outcomes related to integrative STEM goals and outcomes.

A sample T-chart of what may be seen and heard in an effective integrative STEM classroom is highlighted in Table 10.4. Educators can create such a T-chart after they have researched best practices as a committee, participated in professional development, or implemented effective

Table 10.4. Examples of What is Seen and Heard in Effective Integrative STEM Classrooms

What is *seen*	*What is heard*
• Students are introduced to new lesson topic by watching a video • Students document reflections in their journals • Small group work with hands-on activities • Students use safety precautions with tools and instruments • Digital devices are available for student use in recording and analyzing data from product testing • Classroom activity is appropriately challenging • Students briefly visit outside of school building to collect materials for activity • Teacher is co-teaching with colleagues to integrate STEM disciplines into activity	• Teacher asks students about previous experiences with topic • Students ask questions and teacher helps guide them to answer their questions • Teacher talks with a small group about collaboration as one student is dominating the conversation and not considering potential solutions of others • Students are engaged in solving a local, authentic problem • Local scientists virtually visits classroom to describe their work pertaining to activity • Students are talking with one another about the design of their prototype

Note. The items listed are contextual examples of what could be seen and heard in an integrative STEM classroom observation. The items should be interpreted as a realistic scenario as opposed to what would occur in a "model" integrative STEM classroom observation.

STEM strategies for a period of time. With a T-chart, educators can conduct peer reviews or evaluators may conduct walk-throughs and formal observations and detail what they see and hear as they visit classrooms.

Self-evaluation can be promoted in varied ways. When conducting a formal post-observation conference, the evaluator should begin the conference asking the educator, "How do you think the lesson went?" (Glickman et al., 2018). When facilitating small- or whole-group meetings, the evaluator can ask educators to share something they are proud of in terms of what students were doing and saying. New ideas from the sharing can be added to the T-chart.

The power of self-evaluation stems from doing evaluation *with* educators, not *to* them. Evaluators who customize reflective questions for those they supervise will engage in high-level discussions that encourage further thought and result in improved practice. Reflective questions should focus on the goals and practices of integrative STEM, such as:

- When teaching interdisciplinary lessons, to what extent is student agency (e.g., voice, choice) used?

- When planning integrative STEM units, how do you include STEM principles in your instruction?
- When promoting twenty-first century skills in your instruction, in what ways do you prompt students to identify potential design solutions and make data-informed decisions?

Walk-Throughs

Regular walk-throughs in classrooms may help provide authentic observations of teaching behavior, which increase the accuracy of educator evaluation. Downey et al. (2004) created one well-known framework of a three- to five-minute walk-through that informs evaluators what to focus on during a clinical observation. Trained evaluators can readily determine patterns based on these walk-throughs that can guide individual conferencing, as well as school-wide professional learning based on observed needs.

The steps of the Downey et al. (2004) walk-through can provide a comprehensive structure for evaluators. As leaders visit classrooms, they collect and analyze classroom data to monitor the quality of instruction based on the principles of effective integrative STEM instruction. During a walk-through, the evaluator quickly notes each step of the model (i.e., orientation to work; curriculum content, context, and cognitive levels; and instructional decisions). These steps have been simplified to provide an introductory guide to Downey et al.'s walk-through model as follows.

Orientation to Work

Educators readily understand that student engagement is related to student achievement. Too many students who are off-task can alert the evaluator that a problem may exist because of a lack of sound management practices or educator planning. If students are not oriented to the work or distracted from being fully engaged, learning is not optimized. For students who complete integrative STEM activities (e.g., design challenges) earlier than their classmates, educators can challenge those students to further assess the potential impacts of their design solutions or innovate their solutions to authentic problems.

Curriculum Content, Context, and Cognitive Levels

First, instruction must provide access to the materials that will be tested for students, yet integrate *curriculum content* for rich experiences. In an integrative STEM classroom with purposeful curriculum mapping, the content can be design-, inquiry-, problem-, or project-based while also constructed for student success in state-level assessments.

The *context of learning* can contribute to a student's engagement and interest. If the context is always whole-group and worksheets, student interest can wane. Learners typically respond to a variety of contexts to keep motivation high and to a wide variety of learning styles that tap into the way they learn best. Authenticity, problem-solving, and educators serving as *guides on the side* to facilitate learning provide a rich context for integrative STEM learning.

The *cognitive levels* that are monitored during Downey et al.'s (2004) walk-through align with Bloom's Taxonomy for Teaching, Learning, and Assessment. If students are only exposed to lower levels of Bloom's Taxonomy (i.e., remember, understand, and apply), content often is forgotten in a few months. However, when classroom activities stretch students to analyze, evaluate, and create content, the probability of long-term mastery is enhanced. A common expectation in integrative STEM classrooms is for students to apply knowledge and skills at the higher levels of Bloom's Taxonomy (i.e., analyze, evaluate, and create). Table 1.3 provides examples of knowledge and skill sets in STEM education that align with these higher levels.

Instructional Decisions

After noting the curricular decisions that an educator has made, the evaluator then turns to observing the instructional decisions evident in the lesson. These instructional decisions include *teaching practices*, *alignment with school or district goals*, and *content-area best practices*. Important teaching practices in a STEM classroom include the educator asking not telling, using a variety of materials, and providing opportunities for students to solve authentic problems as scientists, technologists, engineers, and mathematicians. Chapter 6 provides greater detail on powerful teaching strategies and instructional approaches in integrative STEM.

When all classrooms strive to meet *school or district goals*, that synergy of focus can elevate learning throughout the educational unit. For example, when an educator applies instructional decisions to support a school's writing goal in STEM and non-STEM classes, the students of that classroom deepen their understandings of the writing process and gain an appreciation of how writing can be approached from a variety of perspectives depending on the content, purpose, and audience.

Agreeing on integrative STEM instructional decisions as a school is vital to promote STEM knowledge and practices. If only isolated classrooms focus on an integrative STEM model, students are unlikely to value knowledge and practices (e.g., innovation, mathematical representation, collaborative discussion of constraints and design goals, data gathering and analysis) that require consistent experiences to refine strategies as students mature.

Zemelman et al. (2012) provide educators with subject area best practices in all content areas. For example, it is understood that best practices in an elementary learner's mathematics environment include the use of manipulatives, metacognition, and nonroutine problem-solving. During a walk-through, the evaluator would also include the best practice of culturally relevant pedagogy to deliberately ensure that integrative STEM content is readily accessible to all students regardless of gender, race, sexual orientation, religion, language, gender identity, or (dis)ability.

As educational leaders conduct classroom walk-throughs, leaders should look for indicators of student engagement and application of STEM practices (see Table 5.2), authentic performance assessments, community engagement, opportunities for extended learning, and equitable access to STEM experiences. Through several short walk-throughs in all classrooms during the academic year, educational leaders can better understand of schoolwide patterns of integrative STEM curriculum and instruction. Leaders should see students engaged in design-, inquiry-, problem-, and project-based teaching and learning activities (e.g., see Figure 10.2).

Clinical Observations

A typical classroom observation model consists of some form of a clinical observation, which includes a pre-observation conference, an observation,

Figure 10.2 An educational leader talking with elementary school students as they test their 3D models. iStockphoto LP.

and a post-observation conference. Glickman et al. (2018) have outlined a collaborative and formative developmental approach to clinical observation that informs improvements. During the pre-observation conference, the evaluator should ask the educator what they would like to have observed.

The primary objective of a clinical observation is to support the educator's professional growth in integrative STEM. Unlike a walk-through, which is typically three to five minutes long, a clinical observation includes extended amounts of time for the educator and leader to focus on specific objectives. The evaluator serves as another pair of eyes to collect either quantitative or qualitative data for the educator during a twenty- to thirty-minute observation. During the post-observation conference, the focus is on the integrative STEM educator, who is asked to self-evaluate the lesson. The evaluator then shares the collected data and supports the educator in analyzing the data.

A wise evaluator often gifts the observed educator with a reflective question to promote ongoing growth, such as, "When planning future STEM lessons as you consider social and emotional learning of your students, how will your instructional approach enhance student self-directed learning, persistence, and risk-taking?" When clinical observations are conducted collaboratively and skillfully, the professionalism and reflection of those being observed leads to continual growth.

A critical component of clinical observation includes meaningful, useful feedback. Useful feedback commonly includes criteria of specificity, timeliness, and delivery in a nonjudgmental way. For example, right after an observation, an educator could be left a short affirming note that indicates: "During your science lesson today, you integrated several best practices, such as integrating mathematics and art, small group work, hands-on activities, journaling, and authentic problem-solving."

Marzano et al. (2021) have claimed that "effective, focused feedback is the main ingredient in the instructional coaching process" (p. 39). The authors recommend a process that involves three phases: describing, acknowledging, and coaching.

The *describing* phase describes as precisely as possible what has been seen and heard during the observation.

During the *acknowledging* stage, the evaluator can acknowledge growth and provide recognition for what worked well for the person being observed.

In the *coaching* stage, self-appraisal questions can support the educator's progress by determining the current status and a two-way discussion of what the educator would like to strive for next. An example question Marzano et al. (2021) provided for coaching is, "What worked well with this strategy from your perspective, and is there anything you would do differently?" (p. 40).

A comprehensive evaluation acknowledges the strengths and areas of growth of the person as their performance is evaluated. Such evaluations provide useful feedback and encourage educational leaders to confront personnel problems when minimum standards have not been met. An integrative STEM educator who does not perform to expectations should be given a detailed improvement plan with clear goals and objectives necessary to meet the school or district standards and remedial support.

Evaluating Student Services Personnel and Support Staff

In addition to serving as instructional coaches to educators, leaders may also supervise student services personnel (e.g., school counselors, social workers, nurses, psychologists, other certified personnel) and other support staff (e.g., secretary, registrar, janitor). Although these individuals may not directly teach integrative STEM content and skills with a team of educators, they serve integral roles in the school and should share the integrative STEM mission, vision, and goals in supporting all students to be STEM-literate citizens who are career and college ready.

School counselors, for example, should spend at least 80 percent of their time providing direct or indirect services to students (American School Counselor Association [ASCA], 2019). *ASCA Mindsets & Behaviors for Student Success: K–12 College- and Career-Readiness for Every Student* serve as a guide for evaluators when working with school counselors to determine the effectiveness of comprehensive school counseling programs in academic, social/emotional, and career development. School counselors should also use data to analyze program results and determine systemic change in schools for all students to be ready for the workforce and higher education upon high school graduation (ASCA, 2019).

Evaluating School or District Leaders

The supervision of school and district leaders includes evaluator support and guidance that is similar to the evaluation of educators, but at a larger scale (e.g., school or district-wide). Evaluators should refer to the Professional Standards for Educational Leaders (National Policy Board for Educational Administration, 2015) and the alignment with the nine competencies identified for educational leaders in integrative STEM (see Table 1.5) as they observe leaders, review data and supporting documents, and discuss current leadership strategies and plans for the future.

Evaluators should offer school and district leaders reflective questions to ponder as they strive to address all of the leadership standards and integrative STEM competencies, provide collaborative leadership opportunities, and develop, implement, and sustain coherent integrative STEM programming (see Figure 1.2). Additionally, evaluators may provide feedback to leaders related to their work in guiding educators, student services personnel, support staff, and other stakeholders in creating and fostering a STEM learning ecosystem that is culturally relevant, socially responsible, equitable, and inclusive for all students to thrive within. Leaders should also perform personal reflection and self-evaluation in meeting the STEM mission, vision, and goals.

Systems Thinking

An organization will only make limited progress unless the process of self-evaluation, supervision, and program evaluation are approached systemically. When school personnel engage in systems thinking about their responsibilities for continuous improvement through educator, curriculum, and program evaluation processes, they will ensure that evidence-based decision-making drives improvement in the design and implementation of integrative STEM programming.

First, key stakeholders should be involved in researching effective evaluation models and jointly agreeing on the policies that will be implemented. Policies should reflect current federal, state, and local laws and guidelines to promote fair, unbiased, and consistent evaluation practices. These stakeholders will determine if the evaluation system can properly support those being evaluated in reaching the school or district mission, vision, and goals.

The follow-up from evaluation data can be used to establish individual, small group, school, or district-wide professional learning initiatives. Collaboration can be scheduled with key personnel during planning or release times, before or after school, lunch meetings, and other identified times. Because of the important role of family and community involvement in integrative STEM classrooms, educators can be encouraged to develop ongoing relationships with an advisory council or community partners and communicate evaluation results with them.

CONCLUSION

Evaluation is a critical component to informing adjustments during the implementation of integrative STEM initiatives (formative evaluation), as well as ensuring the extent program goals are met (summative evaluation) and best practices are continuously pursued in educator instruction, curriculum, and programming. Integrative STEM programming promotes a variety of desired outcomes, including career and college readiness.

A strong evaluation program includes multiple strategies for gathering information and providing formative feedback to improve the integration of STEM content and practices, as well as STEM-preferred approaches to teaching and learning. Educational leaders should arrange times for educators and staff to collaborate and share challenges and best practices, evaluate one another, and support each other to enhance their curriculum and instruction.

Program-level evaluation assesses the value of integrative STEM programming, informs areas of opportunities and strengths, and helps to inform decision-making for future direction. Though evaluations can be organically created, state-created rubrics can provide a starting framework for schools and districts as well.

Curriculum mapping is an impactful approach to evaluate curriculum goals and alignment with STEM standards. Curricular coherence across grade levels, which is integrative, requires purposeful collaboration and opportunities for refinement. Leaders can support, develop, and evaluate integrated curricula to support student-centered learning. Given the focus on career and college readiness and STEM-literate citizenship, evaluation should assess the extent to which curricular components support extensive opportunities to explore and increase knowledge and skills for career development and advanced studies in science, technology, engineering, and mathematics.

REFERENCES

American School Counselor Association. (2019). *ASCA National Model* (4th ed.).

Chicago STEM Pathways Cooperative. (2015). *Chicago STEM ecosystem logic model.* https://stemchicago.wordpress.com/stem-learning-ecosystems-rfq-information/stem-learning-ecosystems-logic-model-as-of-71515/

Downey, C. J., Steffy, B. E., English, F. W., Frase, L. E., & Poston, Jr., W. K. (2004). *The three-minute classroom walk-through: Changing school supervisory practice one teacher at a time.* Corwin Press.

Friday Institute for Educational Innovation. (2012). *Student Attitudes Toward STEM (S-STEM) Survey instrument & codebook middle/high school (6-12th).* https://www.fi.ncsu.edu/resources/student-attitudes-toward-stem-s-stem-survey-instrument-codebook-middle-high-school-6-12th/

Friday Institute for Educational Innovation. (2021). *About the Teacher Efficacy and Attitudes Toward STEM Surveys (T-STEM).* https://www.fi.ncsu.edu/pages/about-the-teacher-efficacy-and-attitudes-toward-stem-surveys-t-stem/

Geesa, R. L., Stith, K. M., & Rose, M. A. (2020). Preparing school and district leaders for success in developing and facilitating integrative STEM in higher education. *Journal of Research on Leadership Education,* 1–21. https://doi.org/10.1177/1942775120962148

Geesa, R. L., Stith, K. M., & Teague, G. M. (2021). Integrative STEM education and leadership for student success. In F. English (Ed.), *The Palgrave Handbook of Educational Leadership and Management Discourse* (pp. 1–20). Palgrave Macmillan. https://doi.org/10.1007/978-3-030-39666-4_36-1

Glickman, C. D., Gordon, S. P., & Ross-Gordon, J. M. (2018). *SuperVision and instructional leadership: A developmental approach* (10th ed.). Pearson.

Indiana Department of Education. (2021). *STEM School Evaluation Rubric 2021–2022.* https://www.in.gov/doe/students/stem-school-certification/

John W. Gardner Center for Youth and Their Communities, Stanford University. (2014). *Menu of college readiness indicators and supports.* College Readiness Indicator Systems Resource Series. Bill & Melinda Gates Foundation.

Marzano, R. J., Rains, C. L., & Warrick, P. B. (2021). *Improving teacher development evaluation: A guide for leaders, coaches, and teachers.* Marzano Resources.

National Policy Board for Educational Administration. (2015). *Professional standards for educational leaders 2015.* https://ccsso.org/sites/default/files/2017-10/ProfessionalStandardsforEducationalLeaders2015forNPBEAFINAL.pdf

Peters-Burton, E. E., Lynch, S. J., Behrend, T. S., & Means, B. B. (2014). Inclusive STEM high school design: 10 critical components. *Theory Into Practice, 53*(1), 64–71. https://doi.org/10.1080/00405841.2014.862125

Rose, M. A., Geesa, R. L., & Stith, K. (2019). STEM leader excellence: A modified Delphi study of critical skills, competencies, and qualities. *Journal of Technology Education, 31*(1), 42–62. http://doi.org/10.21061/jte.v31i1.a.3

Stone Mountain Middle School. (2020). *STEM brochure.* http://www.stonemountainms.dekalb.k12.ga.us/STEMBrochure.aspx

Tennessee Department of Education & Tennessee STEM Innovation Network. (2018). *Tennessee STEM school designation self-assessment.* https://www.tsin.org/designation-step-1

Wisconsin Department of Public Instruction. (2020). *STEM education goals in Wisconsin.* https://dpi.wi.gov/stem/goals

Zemelman, S., Daniels, H., & Hyde, A. (2012). *Best practice: Bringing standards to life in America's classrooms* (4th ed.). Heinemann.

Conclusion: Leading the Future Generation to Success through Integrative STEM Education

Krista Marie Stith, Rachel Louise Geesa, and Mary Annette Rose

Since the 1980s, there have been calls from government and industry sectors to prepare learners to participate successfully in a globally competitive environment as responsible citizens throughout the workforce and community. An integrative exposure to STEM from an early age is essential for students to stay competitive. Additionally, exposure to integrative STEM further prepares students to build lifelong STEM literacy and become democratically responsible citizens. The preparation for students to be able to personally and professionally thrive after their formal PK–12 education is a central tenet to education.

EDUCATIONAL LEADER COMPETENCIES IN INTEGRATIVE STEM

Initiatives have been launched at local, state, and federal levels to include STEM literacy as a desired goal. However, these initiatives must be balanced with many other demands placed on educational leaders. This book may be used as a resource for educational leaders with strategies to interweave integrative STEM programming throughout nine referenced competencies within an educational organization.

Of note, the broad range of skills that are highlighted throughout this book are not expected to reside in a sole leader of an organization. Even the strongest leaders will find difficulty in navigating such a complex process by themselves. It is recommended that leaders pursue a shared leadership style where multiple stakeholders (e.g., teachers, community partners) participate in decision-making and responsibilities. With the cumulative strengths of individuals, integrative STEM can be interwoven through different roles and responsibilities to contribute to a coherent culture.

Descriptions of integrative STEM programming and leader roles and responsibilities throughout the book are summarized through the following nine competencies: mission and culture; equity, diversity, and inclusion; infrastructure and programming; curriculum; instruction; extended learning; professional learning; assessment; and evaluation (see Figure 1.4).

Mission and Culture

An integrative STEM culture within a school or district requires intentional focus, time, and dedication to build, implement, and sustain. Educational leaders form and guide a STEM leadership team to share information and collaborate with school stakeholders to facilitate a shared mission that includes continuous improvement through family-school-community partnerships in integrative STEM. Leaders provide opportunities for stakeholder involvement in decision-making, professional learning, and ongoing refinement of integrative STEM educational experiences that are inclusive and equitable.

Equity, Diversity, and Inclusion

Creating and sustaining inclusive integrative STEM programs require intersectional data analysis and deliberate decisions to ensure that all students have equal access to STEM resources and learning opportunities. Educational leaders provide clear expectations and collaborative strategies for purposeful and routine reviews of the social, emotional, academic, and career- and college-readiness needs of their diverse student populations. To promote social responsibility, school stakeholders welcome all students in equitable STEM learning environments.

Infrastructure and Programming

For students to engage in real-world problem-solving and hands-on learning experiences in integrative STEM, proper access to materials, supplies, facilities, and educational spaces is critical. Educational leaders engage with educators, school counselors, staff, and stakeholders to develop and implement schedules and programs that promote collaborative learning opportunities in integrative STEM. Educators identify and use technologies, classroom spaces, laboratories, and outside learning environments for students to experiment, explore, test, and engineer solutions in authentic educational learning experiences.

Curriculum

Through integrative STEM learning, PK–12 students experience inclusive opportunities to develop as career- and college-ready and STEM-literate citizens with twenty-first century skills and competencies. Educational leaders encourage educators to use inquiry, design, and experiential pedagogies across multiple academic disciplines. Leaders and educators commit time, resources, and professional learning related to embedding STEM curricula throughout the program, school, or district.

Instruction

Integrative STEM education experiences include transdisciplinary teaching and learning approaches. Educators need to collaboratively design and implement authentic educational opportunities that promote critical thinking, creativity, collaboration, and communication for students. Educational leaders set expectations for design-, inquiry-, problem-, and project-based instructional approaches to engage students in solving real-world problems.

Extended Learning

Equitable experiences for students to engage in integrative STEM learning that takes place outside of the regular school day are imperative in inclusive learning environments. Educational leaders cultivate partnerships with community and business leaders in integrative STEM fields to provide students with workforce opportunities and exposure to authentic connections in STEM disciplines. Leaders and educators embed career development, higher education exploration, and employability skills in learning activities with external partners in the classroom and through the educational organization.

Professional Learning

Methods to effectively implement integrative STEM content and instructional strategies may require formal training or ongoing professional learning experiences for educators. Educational leaders work with educators to identify areas of need in professional growth related to integrative STEM materials, curriculum, schedules, teaching techniques, and assessment. Educators participate in professional learning communities (PLCs) as a form of continuous collaboration to co-plan, co-teach, implement, and evaluate interdisciplinary, multidisciplinary, and transdisciplinary lessons (see Figure 1.1) that address the needs of their diverse learners.

Assessment

Students are assessed in their knowledge, skills, and competencies in integrative STEM through diagnostic, interim, formative, and summative forms. This variety of student assessments provides data for educational leaders, educators, and stakeholders to make informed decisions about successes and areas of focus for continuous improvement in integrative STEM. Educational leaders provide educators autonomy to be creative and intentional in their development and use of equitable and authentic performance assessments for all students.

Evaluation

For integrative STEM programming to be impactful throughout the learning ecosystem, systems for evaluation with meaningful shared feedback need to be in place. Educational leaders serve as observers and guides as they regularly visit classrooms and offer reflective questions related to integrative STEM for teachers and staff and to consider. Program, school, and district evaluations assist educational leaders and stakeholders to recognize the status of STEM programming and set future goals.

FOCUS ON THE FUTURE

Educational leaders should consider how integrative STEM could manifest in the future. Integrative STEM curricular and teaching approaches are rich and rigorous experiences where students have access to complex, open-ended problems in formal and informal settings. For integrative STEM to fully integrate into educational systems, educators need to develop a greater fusion of disciplines that move from intradisciplinary to interdisciplinary and transdisciplinary approaches. Educators also need to use a broad range of instructional approaches, such as design-, inquiry-, problem-, and project-based teaching.

Therefore, as more schools and districts facilitate integrative STEM with curricular and instructional approaches, local and global programs should be meaningful and relevant to the specific set of learners in each situation. The transformations of students into problem-solvers should be documented and disseminated to others to further support the paradigm shift and best practices of integrative STEM. There can also be improvements in the social and physical learning environments to support the hands-on small group work. Schools and districts should be supported by their communities and business partners in provisioning these collaborative spaces for students to learn and apply diverse knowledge and skills.

Higher education must support preservice leaders and teacher preparation programs to address the critical skill sets and competencies of integrative STEM. For example, students in higher education need experiences in building and maintaining community partnerships and developing curriculum maps with vertical and horizontal alignment in STEM areas. Professional associations and organizations can also devote time and resources (e.g., conferences, publications, online webinars, social media) to disseminate integrative STEM best practices.

There is a need for policy making by governing boards, legislators, and congressional bodies to support integrative STEM education. With support from policymakers, there should be provisions for organizational learning and decision-making by educational leaders that are collaborative in building and sustaining integrative STEM programming that is equitable for all students. Lastly, integrative STEM education itself can continue to improve as more research is conducted, more educational stakeholders commit to pilot and implement programming, and local and global challenges continue to emerge that need the collective actions of STEM-literate citizens to address.

Index

Page references for tables and figures are italicized.

A Nation at Risk: The Imperative for Educational Reform, 10
Abts, Leigh R., *187*
achievement gaps, 52
  See also equity
Advance CTE, 100
Advanced Placement, 73, 197, 200
Afterschool Alliance, 66
afterschool programs. *See* extended learning
Agency by Design, 125
Akron Public Schools, 58
  See also National Inventors Hall of Fame STEM Middle & High Schools
Al Salami, Mubarak, 162
American Association for the Advancement of Science, 10
American School Counselor Association, 210;
  Mindsets & Behaviors for Student Success, 210
Anderson-Butcher, Dawn, 98
Andriessen, Jerry, 115
assessment, 20;
  actionable feedback, 175, 180–181, *199;*
  characteristics of, 175, 188;
  data analysis, 189–190;
  diagnostic, *179*, 180;
  for collective decisions, 190–191;
  formative, *179*, 180–181;
  interim, *179,* 181;
  needs, 133–134;
  of STEM priorities, 106, 176–177;
  performance, 182, *183,* 184–185;
  planning, 176, *177,* 178;
  purpose of, 175, *179,* 180–183;
  rubric, 185, *186, 187*;
  summative, *179,* 181–182.
Association for Career and Technical Education, 100
Avery, Zanj K., 162, *163*, 165, 167

Balka, Don, 93
Bandy, Joe, 134

Basis Chandler, *57*
Battelle for Kids, 96
Baye, Ariane, 52
Behrend, Tara, *57*
Bell, Lee Ann, 51
Bernhardt, Victoria L., *177*
Bertolini, Katherine, 60
Blank, Martin J., 136
Bloom's Taxonomy for Teaching and Learning Assessment, 206
Boston Museum of Science, 102
Boulder Valley School District, *33*
Boy, Guy André, 112
Bressler, Denise M., 115, 121
Bridwell-Mitchell, Ebony, 38, 40
Britton, Lauren, 117
Brown, Benjamin D., 167
Brown, Josh, 71
Brown, Ryan, 92, 157
Brown, Sue, 71
Brownsburg High School, 190–191
Brusic, Sharon A., 71
Buck Institute for Education, 169
Burke, Mary Ann, *41*
Burns, Rebecca C., 5, 7
Burris Laboratory School, 81, *82,* 83
Bush, Sarah B., *83*
Bybee, Rodger W., 165

Calabrese Barton, Angela, 121
Canning, Elizabeth A., 52–53, 60
career and college readiness, *6;*
  exploration, 146–147, 200–201;
  goals and outcomes, *94*, 200–201.
career and technical education, 100–101
Career and Technical Education Consortium of States, 106
Carlsen, William S., 157
Casey, Katherine, 45
Charting a Course for Success: America's Strategy for STEM Education, 3, *94*
Chicago High School for Agricultural Science, *57*
Chicago STEM Ecosystem, *198*
Chicago STEM Pathways Cooperative, *198*
Chua, Flossie SG, 1
Churchill, Winston, 72
Clapp, Edward P., 125, 127
coaching:
  for professional learning, 164, *166*;
  instructional, *8*, *114*, 120, 209;
  team-building, 120, 123.
Code Nation, *136*
collaboration:
  challenges to, 121–122;
  community engagement, *9,* 27, *41,* 105, 125, 134–139, 149;
  community partnership, 40, 151;
  definition, 12, 113;
  evaluate, 144, 150–151;
  leadership approach, 122;
  need for, 28, 112;
  scheduling for, 84–86;
  student, 125.
  See also co-teaching;
  See also professional learning communities (PLCs)
College and Career Transition Initiative, 101
Combs, Elizabeth, 165, 167
Committee on STEM Education of the National Science and Technology Council, 3, 71
Common Core State Standards Initiative, 120

community:
engagement, *See* collaboration, community engagement;
needs, 34, 36, *37*, 103, 134.
Cook, Kristin L., *83*
Cook, Lynne, 118, *119*
Costa, Arthur L., 177
co-teaching:
considerations for, 120–123;
models of, 118, *119,* 120–121.
CSTEM Challenge, *136*
Cuddihy, Cheryl, 116, 118
Cunningham, Christine M., 157
curriculum, 19, 92–93;
academic, 11;
assessment, *See* assessment;
career and technical, 11, 100–101;
career pathways, 96, 100, *101;*
culturally relevant and responsive, 104;
definition of integrative STEM, *6,* 38, 92;
development of, 45, 93, 98–101, 104–105;
engineering-themed, 96;
equity and inclusiveness, *54,* 104;
evaluation, *See* evaluation, of curriculum
goals, *94,* 99;
horizontal and vertical integration, 96;
interdisciplinary, 5, *6,* 15;
intradisciplinary, 5, *6*;
learning outcomes, 93, *94*, 96;
locally developed, 103–104;
map and mapping, 105–106, 201–202;
multidisciplinary, 5;
standards, 21, *97;*
transdisciplinary, *6,* 7, 124–125;
turn-key, 102–103.
See also career and college readiness;
See also career and technical education;
See also curriculum models
curriculum models:
school-wide interdisciplinary educator planning, 123–124;
student-led, maker-centered, 125
whole class transdisciplinary STEAM projects, 124–125;

Dare, Emily A., 157
Darling-Hammond, Linda, 156, 165–167, 170
Data:
data-driven decision making, 30–31, 122;
Equity Walk, 55–56;
intersectional data analysis, 55;
student demographics, 31, 52, 55;
student use of, *12;*
Walk, 4.
See also assessment, analysis
Daughtery, Jenny, 134, 141
Deck, Anita, *83*, 87
Desimone, Laura M., 166
Dewey, John, 1
Diezmann, Carmel, 134, 144
diversity, *See* inclusion
Donna, Joel D., 169
Downey, Carolyn J., 205–206
Drake, Susan M, 5, 7
DREAM: Achievement Through Membership, *136*
DuFour, Richard, 40
Dweck, Carol S., 60

The Early College at Guilford, *57*

The Education Trust, 55–56
educational ecosystems, 3, 7, 15–16, 18
Education Development Center, *136*
Edutopia, 183
Ejiwale, James A., 141
Ekici, Celil, 104
El Paso Independent School District, *33*
engineering:
definition of, 14;
design, 44, *163*, 168;
education, *97, 101;*
for professional learning, 167–170.
See also habits of mind;
See also assessment, rubric;
See also technology and engineering
Engineering is Elementary, 102
entrepreneurialism, 87
equity, *18* ,52, *54;*
audit, 56.
See also inclusion
Esteban-Guitart, Moisés, 59
evaluation, 20;
analysis, *12,* 201;
clinical observation, 207–209;
college and career readiness models, 200–201;
educator, 203–205;
feedback, *199*, 209;
formative, 196;
goals of, 15, 195, 197, *198;*
of curriculum, 102–103, 106, 201–203;
of educators, 203, 205;
of leaders, 210;
of STEM readiness, *99*, 122;
plan and planning, 196;
questions, 195, *196;*
rubric, *199*;
self-assessment, 199;
self-evaluation, 203–204;
self-reflections, 195, 203–205;
state level, 31, 197, *198*, 199;
summative, 196;
support staff, 209–210;
systems thinking, 211;
T-chart, 203, *204;*
walk-throughs, 203, 205–207
extended learning, 20;
afterschool programs, 147–149;
assessing needs, 133;
definition of, 131–132;
family, 66;
leader actions, *9*, 133, 136, 139, 140, 142–143;
mentors, 142–143, 147;
program example, *See* Rhode Island SMILE;
rationale for, 132;
sustainability of, 150.
See *also* collaboration, community engagement;
See also collaboration, evaluate

Family Engineering, *136*
Farmer, Paul C., 34
Ferrandino, Vincent L., 133
field trip, 138, 146–148;
FIRST Robotics, *136*
Fogarty, Robin, 103
Ford, Michael, *57*
Friday Institute for Educational Innovation, 180, 201
Friend, Marilyn, 118, *119*
Frost Elementary School, *33*
Fullan, Michael, 27
funding, 86–87
funds of knowledge, 59

Funk, Cary, 53

Gabriel, John G., 34
Gao, Xiaoyi, 175
Gary and Jerri-Ann Jacob High Tech High, *57*
Gayfield, Asiah, 52–53
Geesa, Rachel Louise, 10, 18, *22*, 23, 39, 53, 73, *83*, 93, 126, 141, 161, 188, 203
gifted education, 63
Ginsburg, Lynda, 121
Girls, Inc.: Girls in STEM, *137*
Girls Who Code, *137*
Glancy, Aran W., *97*
Glickman, Carl, D., 204, 208
Global Family Research Project, 66
Glover, Todd, 120, 122
Goldberg, Gail Lynn, *187*
Gotwals, Amelia Wenk, 183
Great Schools Partnership, 27, 32, 34
Greca, Ileana M., 1
Greenberg, James B., 59
Grillo, Kelly J., 85, 119
Groves, James F., *187*
Grubbs, Michael E., *83*
Gulamhussein, Allison, 166
Gunn, Jennifer, 138
Guthrie, James W., 10

habits of mind, 12–13, 32, 177;
  See also mindset
Haden, Carol M., 144
Han, Edmund, *57*
Handal, Boris, 157
Havice, William, 168
Hawaii State Department of Education, 44
Herman, Joan L., 181
Herro, Danielle, 124, 127, 187
Hipp, Kristine Kiefer, 162
Hmelo-Silver, Cindy E., 115
Hogg, Linda, 59
Honey, Margaret, 51, *94*, 112, 132, 142–143, 175
House, Ann, *57*
Hsu, Ming-Chien, 157
Huffman, Jane Bumpers, 162
Hui Hoʻoleimaluō, 45–47
Hurley-Chamberlain, DeAnna, *119*

inclusion, 18, 22, 51, *54*;
  accommodations for, 18, *54*;
  barriers, 52–53;
  identities, 31, 51, 57, 88, 182, 189, 207;
  inclusive practices, *54*, 55–56;
  underrepresented, 52–53;
  underserved, 52–53.
  See mindset, asset-based
inclusive STEM schools, 28, 56, *57*, 58, 197
Indiana Department of Education, 31, 100, 102, *199*
information technology, 74–75;
  cybersecurity, 75
infrastructure, 19;
  definition, 71;
  educational technology, 75;
  equipment, 77–79, *80, 83*, 84;
  for active learning, 73–74, 76;
  for collaboration, 76, 81–83;
  furnishings, 75–76;
  laboratory, 81–83;
  materials, 79–80, *83,* 84;
  plan, 92–93, 96, 104–106;
  safety, 87–88.
  See also information technology;
  See also makerspace
innovation:
  culture of, *8*, 18, 27, 37;
  lab, 81, *82;*

need for innovative capacity, 3, 51.
instruction, 19;
barriers, 53;
design-based, 73–74, *114,* 116–117;
differentiated, 184;
inquiry-based, *114,* 115;
investigation, *13, 97,* 159;
problem-based, *114,* 115–116;
project-based, *114,* 117–118.
See also infrastructure, for active learning
integrative STEM:
challenges of implementation, 21, 23, 112;
culture, 9, 18–21, 27, 31–32, *37, 41, 199;*
definition of, 2–3, *4*, 5, *6*, 11;
design, 7;
goals, 10, 34;
implementation, 7;
practices, *8;*
rationale for, 1, 112;
types of schools, 71.
See also curriculum, horizontal integration
International Technology and Engineering Educators Association, 14, 84, *97,* 169, 183
internship, *9*, 20, 201
Institute of Medicine, 11
Ireland, Danyelle T., 52–53, 55

Johnson, Angela B., 59
Johnson, Carla C., 112
Johnson, Eric J., 59
Johnson, Kathryn M. S., 55
John W. Gardner Center for Youth and their Communities, 200

Kallick, Bena, 177
Karcher, Michael J., 142
Katehi, Linda, 13, 32
Katherine Johnson STEM Academy, *35*
Kaui, Toni Marie Mapuana, 45–46
Kekelis, Linda, 65
Kelley, Todd R., 74, 132, 159
Kersten, Jennifer A., *97*
Kettler, Todd, 157, *163*, 164
Kier, Meredith W., 99
kits:
Makedo, 120;
Makey Makey, 120
Kladifko, Robert E., 133, 140–141
Knowles, J. Geoff, 74, 132, 159
Kostourou, Fani, 72
Kraft, Matthew A., 120
Kupersmidt, Janis, 142
Kurz, Alexander, 120

LaForce, Melanie, 28, 56
Langford, Barbara Hanson, 136
language learners, 63–64, 184
leadership:
best practices, *8–9;*
characteristics and competencies, 16, *17*, 18;
collaborative, *See* collaboration;
team, *29*, 30–31.
See also extended learning, leadership actions;
See also mentor
League for Innovation, *101*
learning:
activities, *83, 178;*
assessing, *See* assessment;
culture, 98;
environments, *See* infrastructure;
qualities of, 2, 32, 36, *37*, 78–79, 115, 159, 182;
outcomes, 93, *94,* 96, 99, 106;
theory, *See* social constructivism.

See also instruction;
See also professional learning, communities (PLCs)
Leonard, Jacqueline, 104
Li, Yeping, 157
Llopart, Mariona, 59
Louis, Karen Seashore, 169–170
Lynch, Sharon J., 56, *57,* 58

Maconaquah Middle School, 104
Maker Faires, *137*
makerspace, 76–77, 116–117
making, 87, *97*, 121;
spaces for, 71, 74, 76
Mansilla, Veronica Boix, 1
Margot, Kelly C., 157, *163*, 164
Marsh, Colin J., 92
Martínez, Anthony, 52–53
Marzano, Robert J., 209
Massachusetts Department of Elementary and Secondary Education, 181
mathematics, 14;
computational thinking, 75, *94, 178;*
predictions, *12, 13, 183;*
practices, *97;*
standards, *See* Standards for Mathematical Practice.
See also Principles and Standards for School Mathematics;
See also Rhode Island SMILE
Matray, Shari, *57*
McFadden, Justin R., 103
McTighe, Jay, 176
Means, Barbara, 56, *57,* 63
The Meeder Consulting Group, 9
Meeder, Hans, 132
mentor:
community, *9*, 120–121;
qualities of, 142–143.
See also Dream—Achievement Through Mentorship;
See also extended learning, mentors;
See also Million Women Mentors
Merrill, Chris, 134, 141
Meyer, Anne, 64
Microsoft Corporation, 185, *186*
The Millennium Project, 1
Million Women Mentors, *137*
mindset:
asset-based, 60–61;
asset perspective, 63;
deficit-based, 60–61;
deficit perspective, 63;
fixed mindset, 60;
growth mindset, 60–61.
mission, 18, 27, 32, *33*, 34, 44
Mizell, Staci, 71
Modoono, Jane, 190
Mohr-Schroeder, Margaret J., 2
Moll, Luis C., 59
Monseur, Christian, 52
Monta Vista High School, *57*
Moore, Tamara J., *97*
Moorehead, Tanya, 119
Mullis, Ina V. S., 182

Nadelson, Louis S., 159, 161
Nā Hunaahi, 43–47
National Academy of Engineering, 1, 11, 13, 160
National Academy of Sciences, 11
National Assessment of Educational Progress, 106, 182, 184
National Association of Family, School, and Community Services, 66
National Career Clusters Framework, 100

National Center for Engineering and Technology Education, 162, 164
National Center on Safe Supportive Learning Environments, 27
National Commission on Excellence in Education, 10
National Council of Teachers of Mathematics, *97*
National Education Association, 131
National Girls Collaborative Project, *137*
National Inventors Hall of Fame, *137*
National Inventors Hall of Fame STEM (NIHF-STEM) High School, 58
National Inventors Hall of Fame STEM (NIHF-STEM) Middle School, 58
National Policy Board for Educational Administration, 21, *22,* 93, 176, 195, 210
National Research Council, 1, 14, 59, 65, *97,* 160
National Science & Technology Council, 71, *94*
National Science Board, 10, 52
National Science Foundation, 10
National Science Teachers Association, 133
National Science Teaching Association, 87
National Service Learning Clearinghouse, 134
National Student Clearinghouse, 146, 150
The Nation's Report Card, 184
NCTEF, *101*
New York Hall of Science, 65
Next Generation Science Standards, 14, *97*, 115
non-STEM disciplines, 15–16

Oakes, Jeannie, 156, 167
Olympics of the Mind, *137*
Oregon Museum of Science and Industry, 65
Oregon State University SMILE Program, 145
Orzech, Miriam, 145
Owens Jr., Emiel W., 132, 134, 138

Palmyra Area School District, 168
Parker, Kim, 53
Partnership for 21st Century Learning, 96
Pawlowski, Brett, 132
Pearson, Greg, *94*
pedagogy, 113–118;
  community-based, 120–121;
  culturally relevant, 207;
  pedagogical content knowledge, 159–160;
  signature, 73–74, 114.
  See also instruction;
  See also professional learning, gaps in
Pete, Brian M., 103
Peters-Burton, Erin E., *57,* 58, 107, 197
Pew Research Center, 53
Pitsco, 102
Planche, Beate M., 189
Powell, Arthur, 64
practices:
  community of, 61, 74;
  culturally-responsive, 104;
  gender-responsive, 18, 64–65;
  inclusive, 18, 54–56, *57*, 58, 63;
  in national STEM standards, *97.*
  See also inclusive, practices;

See also leadership, best practices
Prepare and Inspire: K–12 Education in Science, Technology, Engineering, and Math (STEM) for America's Future, 11
President's Council of Advisors on Science and Technology, 11
Principles and Standards for School Mathematics, *97*
problem-solving:
authentic problems, 2, 204, 206;
skills, *12, 97*
processes for learning:
designing, *12;*
investigating, *97,* 114–115;
modeling, 14, 74, 79, *94*, 183
professional learning:
benefits of, *163*;
challenges of, *163;*
characteristics of, 165, *166*, 167–169;
collaboration in, 162, 167;
communities (PLCs), *8,* 86, 127, 167, 176, 190–191;
considerations for, 61, 164–165;
for extended learning, 140–143;
for inclusion, 60–63;
gaps in, 157–158;
goals of, 167–169;
leadership role in, 20, 61, 161;
programs, 123–124, 160, 168;
providers of, 169–170.
Professional Standards for Educational Leaders, 21, *22,* 210
Project Lead The Way, 81, 102, 168–169

Quigley, Cassie F., 124–125, 127

R.B. Hudson STEAM Academy, *33*
Reeve, Edward M., 162, *163*, 165, 167
Reid, Jackie, 106
Renkly, Shannon, 60
Resilient Educator, *137*
Rhode Island Department of Education, Office of Data and Technology Services, 146, 150
Rhode Island SMILE, *137,* 145–152
Rhode Island SMILE Database, 146
Rider-Bertrand, Joey, 188
Rising Above the Gathering Storm, 11
risk-taking, *12*
Roehrig, Gillian H., 103
Rose, Hilary A., 60
Rose, Mary Annette, 18, *22,* 23, 39, 53, 73, 98, 105, 126, 141, 161, 182, 203
Rosenberg, David, 85
Roth, Wolff-Michael, 119
Rwanda, 118

Sammet, Kara, 65
Sanders, Mark E., 10, 44
Scanlan, Martin, 61
scheduling, 83–86, 107
Schoenfeld, Alan H., 157
The School and Society, 1
school counselors, 180, 201, 209–210;
Schultz, Dawna, 151
Schweingruber, Heidi, *94*
Science and Engineering Indicators, 52
Science and Math Investigative Learning Experiences, *See* Rhode Island SMILE
science education:
interest in, 59;
practices and skills, *13*, 14, *97;*
Science and Mathematics Pathway, *101;*

standards, *See* Next Generation Science Standards.
See also National Science Teaching Association;
See also Rhode Island SMILE;
See also Science and Engineering Indicators
Science for All Americans, 10
Science Olympiad, *137*
Seifert, Anne, 159, 161
Shafer, Leah, 38, 40
Shamberger, Cynthia, *119*
Sharratt, Lyn D., 189
Sheridan, Kimberly, M., 116
Shernoff, David J., 115, 121, 123, 141, 157
Shively, Kathryn L., 77, 165
Shulman, Lee S., 73, 159
Silverman, Sarah, 165, 167
Sinha, Suparna, 115, 121
Skrla, Linda, 56, 61
SMILE, *See* Rhode Island SMILE
Smith, Felicia, 29–30
Smith, Karl A., *97*
social constructivism, 10
social justice, 51
social responsibility, 51, 53, *54*
Songer, Nancy Butler, 183
special needs, 63–64
Spillane, Nancy, *57*
stakeholders, *29,* 30–31, 65;
advisory council, 84, 87;
STEM coordinator, 84;
teachers and leaders, *4,* 7–8, *9,* 18–21.
See also community, engagement
Standards for Mathematical Practice, *97*, 120
Standards for Technological and Engineering Literacy, 14, *97*
States Career Cluster, 101
STEAM, 43–47, 123–127, 160, 187
Stefanski, Amanda, 136
STEM:
careers, *See* career and college readiness;
certification, *199*, 200;
certified schools, 31;
citizenry, 8, 37, 175, 196;
culture, *See* integrative STEM, culture;
employment barriers, 53;
integration; *See* integrative STEM;
knowledge and skills, *8*, 12, *13,* 14, 32, 71, *97,* 177, *198*;
literacy, 2–3, *6,* 12, 93, *94;*
mission, 18, 21, *22*, 27–29, 32, *33*, 34–35;
nights, 65;
skills, *12, 13, 97.*
STEM Career Interest Survey, 99
STEM Expeditions, 102
STEM Next, 65
The STEM Schools Project, 9
Stith, Krista Marie, *22*, *83*
Stohlmann, Micah S., *97*
Stone Mountain Middle School, 99, *198*
Strengthening Career and Technical Education for the 21st Century Act, 100
Student Attitudes Toward STEM survey (S-STEM), 180, 201
Sturgis, Chris, 45

Tai, Robert H., 102
Tan, Edna, 121
Tank, Kristina M., *97*
Teacher Efficacy and Attitudes Toward STEM survey (T-STEM), 201

TeachThought Professional Development, 170
Teague, Ginger Mink, 170
technology and engineering education:
assessment, *See* Technology and Engineering Literacy Assessment;
practices and skills, *13*, 14, *97*;
standards, *See* Standards for Technology and Engineering Literacy.
See also International Technology and Engineering Educators Association
Technology and Engineering Literacy Assessment, 106
Technology Student Association, *138*
Technovation, *137*
Tennessee Department of Education and Tennessee STEM Innovation Network, 200
Theoharis, George, 61
Thibaut, Lieve, 10
Thomas, Ian, 113
Thomas, John W., 117
Timar, Thomas B., 10
Toma, Radu Bogdan, 1
Toray Plastics, 148
transdisciplinary, 7;
See curriculum.
See also curriculum models
Trends in Mathematics and Science Survey, 182
Tytler, Russell, 144

United Nations Educational, Scientific and Cultural Organization, 1, 64
United States Department of Education, 139
United States Department of Education, Office of Educational Technology, 74–75, 139
United States Environmental Protection Agency, 88
Universal Design for Learning, 63–64
University of Rhode Island Office of Institutional Research, 146–150
U.S. News & World Report, 56, *57*

Valencia, Richard R., 60
Vélez-Ibáñez, Carlos G., 59
Verizon Innovative Learning, *138*
Vex Robotics, 131, *138*
Vision, 27, 32, *33* ,34
Vygotsky, Lev S., 10

Ward, Randolph E., *41*
Watters, James J., 134, 144
Wayne Community College, 96
Wayne County School District, 96
Wayne School of Engineering, *57*, 107
Wiggins, Grant, 176
Wilkerson, Stephanie B., 144
Wilkes, Janelle, 106
Willis, George, 92
Wisconsin Department of Public Instruction, *198*
Wood, Terry, 10

Yorktown Community Schools, 160

Zemelman, Steven, 207
Zollman, Alan, 2

About the Contributors

Rachel Louise Geesa, EdD, is a faculty member in the Department of Educational Leadership at Ball State University. In addition to preparing school and district leaders, Geesa has taught visual arts education courses at The George Washington University and Indiana University. Prior to her positions in higher education, she taught PK–12 art in Indiana and served as a visual arts educator, gifted resource specialist, and assistant principal in United States Department of Defense Education Activity schools in South Korea, Japan, and Virginia. Her research interests include exploring academic, professional, and personal development and support structures for educational leaders. Current research topics are related to doctoral student mentorship, school counselor-principal collaboration, and leadership in integrative STEM/STEAM education. Geesa received the 2020 Emerging Scholar Award from the Eastern Educational Research Association based on her published research and grants record. She also received the 2020-2021 Graduate Faculty for Inclusive Excellence Award at Ball State University.

Mary Annette Rose, EdD, is an Associate Professor of Educational Studies at Ball State University. She is an advocate for integrative teaching and learning approaches, especially those that focus on the application of science and mathematics to enhance energy literacy and advance environmental sustainability goals. As a technology educator, she has collaborated with science and mathematics educators to implement and evaluate interdisciplinary learning experiences for middle and high school students. As a teacher educator and researcher, she continues to examine the conditions that support collaborative, interdisciplinary learning experiences of professional educators when operating in distributed computer-mediated environments. As a sustainability educator, she has mentored teams of undergraduate students to assess and report the performance, policies, and practices of Ball State University relative to the GRI (Global Reporting Initiative) standards.

Krista Marie Stith, PhD, is the Director of the Center for Gifted Studies and Talent Development and teaches STEM Content and Pedagogy at Ball State University. With her doctorate in Curriculum and Instruction with a focus of Integrative STEM Education from Virginia Tech, she works extensively in STEM/STEAM education and high ability programming. She is the coordinator for the Teacher's College-Project Lead The Way partnership to facilitate the PLTW Launch Teacher Preparation Programs and co-runs a K–5 STEAM Club. Her research interests are in design thinking and integrative STEM pedagogy for high ability students. Prior to her position at Ball State, she was a high school science teacher in southwest Virginia.

Joanne Caniglia, PhD, is a Professor at Kent State University and teaches mathematics education courses. She was a secondary mathematics teacher and department chair in Niles and Akron, Ohio for twelve years and spent time as a graduate researcher at Kent State University where she received her doctorate in Curriculum and Instruction with an emphasis in Mathematics Education. She taught for fourteen years at Eastern Michigan University where she was a Professor of Mathematics Education. Her research activities include creating meaningful, mathematical tasks to assist secondary and special education students.

Cheryl Cuddihy, EdD, is a K–8 Mathematics Instructional Coach in the Red Bank Borough Public Schools, New Jersey. She also works as a part-time lecturer at the Graduate School of Education, Rutgers University and as an adjunct faculty member at the College of Education and Human Services, Rider University. Prior to these positions, Chuddihy worked in a variety of school administration positions including school principal, vice-principal, curriculum supervisor, director of an early childhood center, and supervisor of English-language learners and world languages. Her research interests include student engagement and agency in the elementary makerspace setting.

Jim Egenrieder, EdD, is a longtime teacher of agriculture, engineering, science, career and technical, and STEM education, and a Career and Technical Education (CTE) specialist for schools and community colleges. He is currently a Research Professor in Engineering and Education, and the Director of Virginia Tech's K–20 STEM Education and Workforce Development Programs in the Washington, DC, metropolitan area. Egenrieder also develops international STEM education, workforce programs, and teacher training programs emphasizing project-based learning, innovation, and entrepreneurial thinking.

Carol Marcus Englander, MS, is the Executive Director of the Science and Math Investigative Learning Experiences (SMILE) Program for the past twenty-seven years. She taught middle school biology, chemistry, physics, and earth science in Rhode Island for thirty-five years and served as department chair. She has directed Rhode Island SMILE, a STEM program, affiliated with the University of Rhode Island, since its inception in 1994 which began with twenty students and one school district and now includes more than five hundred students and forty teachers in seven school districts at the elementary, middle, and high school levels. In 2015, she received the Staff/Administrator Diversity award from the University of Rhode Island Multicultural Center.

Fenwick W. English, PhD, is a Professor and Chairperson of Educational Leadership in Teachers College, Ball State University in Muncie, Indiana. He is a former Superintendent of Schools in New York and served as Dean of a school of education and Vice-Chancellor of Academic Affairs in Fort Wayne, Indiana, for Purdue University. He is the former President of UCEA in 2006–2007 and NCPEA 2011–2012. He is the author or coauthor of more than forty books, numerous book chapters, and research papers. His last book was published by Routledge in 2016, *Leading Beautifully: Educational Leadership as Connoisseurship* with coauthor Lisa Catherine Ehrich of Queensland University of Technology in Brisbane,

Australia. He was named a *Living Legend* of the profession by International Council of Professors of Educational Leadership (ICPEL) in 2013.

Michael E. Grubbs, PhD, is the Coordinator of Career and Technical Education (CTE) for Baltimore County Public Schools and oversees nearly forty different CTE programs of study; manages local, state, and federal budgets; and manages CTE curriculum development, professional development, and instructional supervision. Prior to his current position, he was the Supervisor of Manufacturing, Technology, and Engineering Education for Baltimore County Public Schools and a middle school engineering and technology education teacher, graduate research assistant for Virginia Tech, and adjunct instructor. He is the author of *Foundations of Engineering & Technology* (7th ed.) and publications related to STEM, design, and engineering education. Grubbs is also the Director of Strategic Initiatives and Partnerships for the Advancing Excellence in P12 Engineering Education (AE3). Grubbs' current focus is on P–12 engineering education and improving students' design cognition.

Toni Marie Mapuana Kaui, PhD, NBCT, is the Head of School at Nā Hunaahi, a Native Hawaiian language and culture perpetuating, design-focused, integrative STEAM, competency based high school in East Hawai'i. She is also an Adjunct Professor at Chaminade University Education Division, the American Public University System School of Education, and Grand Canyon University School of Education. Her research interests include Native and Indigenous education, cultivating creative and innovative thinking, and student agency.

Kendra Lowery, PhD, is an Associate Professor of Educational Leadership and Associate Dean for Equity and Engagement in Teachers College at Ball State University. She was a teacher and administrator in traditional public schools before entering higher education. Her research interests include social justice leadership practices, racial equity, cross-racial dialogues, and educational experiences of Black women and girls through a variety of approaches including oral history, arts-based, and community-engaged research.

Marilynn Marks Quick, EdD, is an Associate Professor of Educational Leadership at Ball State University. During her career she accepted positions in Indiana and Arizona as a school superintendent, other central office roles, principal, reading specialist, and teacher. Her degrees were earned at Indiana University and the University of Arizona. The major themes in her consulting work and research agenda center on personnel evaluation, school improvement processes, and raising student achievement. Quick has been recognized for her achievements with such awards as Ball State University's Outstanding Faculty Advisor Award, Teachers College Outstanding Teacher Award, Teachers College Outstanding Service Award, Outstanding Leadership in Education award for Indiana University, and the Edgar L. Morphet Dissertation Award from National Council of Professors of Educational Administration.

David J. Shernoff, PhD, is the Director of the Center for Mathematics, Science, and Computer Education (CMSCE) and Associate Professor in the Department of School Psychology at the Graduate School of Applied and Professional Psychology at Rutgers University. Prior to these positions, Shernoff was an Associate Professor at Northern Illinois University, where he taught courses in educational psychology, adolescent development, and motivation in the classroom. His research interests include student engagement and models of effective teacher professional development, especially in integrated STEM/STEAM and technology-supported learning environments. Research in this area informs the Rutgers CMSCE's building of new programs in integrated STEM/STEM and Makerspace education at Rutgers University.

Kate Shively, PhD, is an Assistant Professor in the Department of Elementary Education at Ball State University. Prior to her career in higher education, Shively taught first through fourth grades in Indiana, as well as served as a Gifted and Talented and Special Education instructor. Her research interests include exploring professional development and learning, design of learning environments, and STEM/STEAM teacher preparation. Current research topics are related to design thinking in professional learning, digital literacy in teacher preparation, and teaching in online learning environments.

Suparna Sinha, PhD, is the Director of Teacher Professional Development at the Rutgers Center for Mathematics, Science, and Computer Education (CMSCE). In recent years, she has conducted multiple teacher professional development workshops on Maker Education, Next Generation Science Standards, computer literacy, and many other transdisciplinary topics in STEM and STEAM. She earned her PhD degree at the Rutgers Graduate School of Education. Her research focuses on understanding how students' engagement with technological tools influences their thinking and learning. Sinha was also codirector of a Math-Science Partnership grant on the professional development of high school teachers for alignment with the next-generation science standards.

Ginger Mink Teague, PhD, is a Senior Director of Instruction with Project Lead The Way (PLTW). PLTW is a nonprofit organization that provides transformative learning experiences in STEM education for PK–12 students and teachers across the United States. In her role, she leads a team that develops curricular and professional development resources for a PK–5 program—PLTW Launch. Prior to working with PLTW, she taught elementary and middle school students in Tennessee. She served on a team that developed and implemented a STEM program in a school district in East Tennessee. Her research interests include exploring evidence-based practices in STEM education, professional development, problem-based learning, and professional learning communities.

Made in the USA
Coppell, TX
02 January 2023